England Since 1867:
Continuity and Change

THE HARBRACE HISTORY OF ENGLAND

I   Ancient and Medieval England: Beginnings to 1509
    J. R. Lander
    University of Western Ontario

II   Renaissance and Reformation England: 1509–1714
    Charles M. Gray
    University of Chicago

III   The Birth and Growth of Industrial England: 1714–1867
    John F. C. Harrison
    University of Sussex

IV   England Since 1867: Continuity and Change
    Peter Stansky
    Stanford University

PART IV

THE HARBRACE HISTORY OF ENGLAND

Peter Stansky

Stanford University

England Since 1867:
Continuity and Change

Under the General Editorship of John Morton Blum

Yale University

Harcourt Brace Jovanovich, Inc.

New York/Chicago/San Francisco/Atlanta

ISBN: 0-15-535110-9

Library of Congress Catalog Card Number: 72-97671

Printed in the United States of America

Preface

In the pages that follow I have tried to provide an overview of the history of England from 1867 to the present. My intention has been to give the reader some feeling for the nature and texture of English society as it adapted and reshaped itself in an era of continuing change. For these years a political emphasis seemed to provide the most readily accessible reflection of the changing nature of that society; politics was also a major shaping force in its development. I have tried to reveal the special relationship between change and continuity that exists in England—the tendency to hide change behind traditionalism and to maintain old habits while seeming to change, a peculiar combination of flexibility and a clinging to old ways.

In the year 1867—when this book begins—the Second Reform Act was passed, enlarging the electorate as urban working-class men acquired the vote. Political traditions as well as innovations were represented by the leaders of the two great political parties at that date, William Gladstone of the Liberals and Benjamin Disraeli of the Tories. Their ideas, careers, personalities, and political principles tell much about the shape of English history in the Victorian age, suggesting both its considerable accomplishments and the unresolved problems that would continue to face England thereafter. Many of the aspects of English society that found expression in each of these remarkable men are still present, if in vastly modified form, in contemporary England. Gladstone and Disraeli serve, therefore, as extremely suitable figures to introduce a study that begins in 1867 and concludes in 1973.

I should like to thank those who have been kind enough to bear with the various versions of the text: Thomas A. Williamson, Dorothy E. Mott, Sally Wingate-Saul, Jacqueline Lenaker, Mindy Johnson, and William Abrahams. I should also mention gratefully the patience and stimulation of students and colleagues with whom I have discussed aspects of modern England.

Peter Stansky

Contents

Illustrations

Maps

THE UNITED KINGDOM TODAY

England Since 1867:
Continuity and Change

CHAPTER ONE

William Gladstone

William Ewart Gladstone was the most important political figure in the latter half of the nineteenth century. He was the son of a Liverpool family of Scottish origins which had made its money from sugar plantations, using slave labor, and from other commercial activity. Gladstone started his political life, in Macaulay's famous phrase, as "the rising hope of those stern and unbending Tories." But as he grew older he moved steadily leftward. The Tory of the 1830s became the Liberal of the 1850s and after, led to the position largely by the dictates of intellect and character. There was in Gladstone an extraordinary consistency. He allowed no difference between the way one lived one's life as a private person and the way one conducted affairs of state as prime minister, an office he was to hold four times. To recognize the exalted religious level which Gladstone made the basis of his daily life is to arrive at some idea of his concept of politics. Which is not to say that he was not a clever, practical politician; but always in his own mind was a conviction that he was serving some "higher purpose." The saintly attitude can be trying, and one recalls the famous remark of a contemporary politician that he had no objection to Gladstone's having the ace of trumps up his sleeve, but he did object to his

Liberals
and Conservatives:
Men and Traditions

contention that God had placed it there. This conviction of "higher purpose," this refusal to differentiate between personal ethics and national ethics, was very much in the spirit of the age—it would find poetic expression in Tennyson—and endowed Gladstone with tremendous popular appeal during most of his long life. Even in the 1890s, when the glamor of imperialism robbed his "moral" approach of much of its appeal to the electorate, he continued to be revered. Until his death in 1898, he was one of the dominant and exemplary figures of the Victorian age.

Gladstone exemplifies some of the primary Victorian concerns; first, as has already been suggested, religious belief. Religion permeated the texture of English life, especially in education, where one might say that the principal goal was to present the child with a suitable God. For many —particularly those who regarded themselves as closest to the center of the state—it would be the God of the established Church: an Anglican, an Episcopalian deity. For many others—Baptists, Congregationalists, Methodists, et al—it would be a nonconformist God; for a smaller number still, a Roman Catholic God. Obviously, particular religious dogma could have its effect upon political activity. But also, in nonpolitical ways, religion made an important contribution to the style of English life. It helped determine the spirit and mode in which things were done. It accounts

William Ewart Gladstone and his wife, Catherine Gladstone, *c.* 1880. (Radio Times Hulton Picture Library.)

for that blend of altruism and self-righteousness noticeable in so many Victorian leaders. They wanted to do good for others, and were seldom plagued by self-doubt about what doing good entailed. This was especially true of Liberal leaders, who were more deeply imbued with Nonconformist values and were more likely to belong to the middle class than the Tory leaders, many of whom belonged to the aristocracy. Members of the aristocracy tended to a high degree of self-assurance and were less likely to fear being taken for eccentrics. If they wished, they could afford to be self-indulgent and indifferent to the state of their souls. But by the end of the nineteenth century, even in the houses of the aristocracy, morning prayers, which had hardly existed at the beginning of the century, had become part of the daily ritual.

Gladstone, in his paradoxical way, held two seemingly irreconcilable religious positions. On the one hand, he was a practicing Anglo-Catholic

—that is, a member of the established Anglican Church—who happened to have few objections to Catholicism. But among those few was the decisive one: a refusal to acknowledge the sovereignty of the Bishop of Rome. At the same time, he was in many ways evangelical, that is, Low Church, for his was a literal, proselytizing, fundamentalist belief. He believed in an individual relation to God and in the need of continual testimony to one's faith. He managed to encompass both these attitudes—the high and the low—without too much difficulty. It is yet another example of his ability to reconcile the inconsistencies of his time.

But the deepest quality in Gladstone's makeup, and in this he was representative of so many eminent Victorians, was his concept of service. Although it could lapse into an attitude of patronage and condescension, the notion of service was one of the most admirable Victorian characteristics. It was based upon the belief that a great position in the world or notable talent or great wealth was not meant to be enjoyed for its own sake, nor for the cultivation of one's private life and satisfactions. Rather, these privileges conferred a profound obligation upon the individual to serve, which meant that he was to improve the world in which he lived. Although often allied with the intensely individualistic religion of the evangelicals, the idea of service did not necessarily have a religious base. Among the Tories there was less a feeling of the need to serve than of social obligation: the obligation of the lady of the manor to bring soup to the poor, and of the lord of the manor to look after his tenants. But as the century advanced, even the more traditional Tory concept of this sort tended to be infused with a religious sense. Gladstone himself had planned to go into the Church, but, yielding to his father's objections, had instead entered politics. Discerning a spreading enlightenment, an increasing religious dedication among the people of England, their growing altruism, he came to believe that more and more of them were entitled to come within "the pale of the Constitution" to be responsible and participating members of society. They might even be allowed to vote.

The tendency among the English is for an elitist state verging toward a democracy. This was true before the franchise reforms. It continues to be true even now, when meritocracy has replaced aristocracy, although perhaps not quite to the degree one might expect. In England there has been an evolutionary process. The ruling group, by admitting brilliant men from below at strategic moments, in a real sense neutralizes those who might otherwise prove dangerous to the existing order. The English system assumes, and its assumptions are still extremely active, that those who have power are responsible to those "under their care," sometimes even to the public as a whole. But more often in the past the responsibility has been to some *ideal* of how a man at the top *ought* to behave. The result, at its best, has been an elite inspired by altruism and a firm adherence to certain standards of behavior and obligation. But what happens when the people who join the peerage or a latter-day ruling group are not driven, as Gladstone was, by an inner light, be it religious motivation or a secular idealism? Or when those who inherit positions of power fail to recognize their obligations?

The Second Reform Bill, 1867

Gladstone did not like change, yet he was the instrument of it. He was even willing, in the latter part of his career, to act on behalf of social change. In this respect, as in so many others, he was a symbolic figure. If in his personality he is peculiarly a product, as well as a creator, of the Victorian age, in his acceptance of change he foreshadows the modern age: change at one end of the spectrum and at the other end permanence and continuity. Presently we will be dealing with permanence in its most tangible form: the land. But first we must establish a point in time where it might be said that modern political change had its beginning, a point from which modern democracy has continued to evolve: the Second Reform Bill in the year 1867.

Let us follow the example of G. M. Young, the author of *Portrait of an Age,* and ask what would we hear if we could listen to a typical conversation of that year?

If it was a literary conversation, it might have been centered on the publication of *The Early Years of His Royal Highness, the Prince Consort,* Victoria's beloved husband, who had died in 1861. Albert had tried to modernize the monarchy, as well as to keep its power, and after his death Victoria was much more susceptible to being led by her politicians, although she could be slightly hysterical about her prerogatives. She believed Albert had died from a cold caught on a trip to Cambridge to see the Prince of Wales to reprimand him over an affair with an actress. In fact, Albert had already caught the typhoid which killed him. But this unfortunate juxtaposition of events meant that Victoria never forgave her son, and in contrast treated everything connected with Albert with utmost reverence. In court circles and for those who revered the monarchy, the publication of the late prince's biography would have been an important event.

Two other major publications of 1867, in their own fashion also marked a passing world. There was Anthony Trollope's *Last Chronicle of Barset,* the last novel of his concerned with provincial life in a cathedral town, in contrast to his political novels, beginning with *Phineas Finn* in 1869, that take place in London. Perhaps most significant, it was the same year that saw the publication of Walter Bagehot's *English Constitution.* Bagehot had been editor of the *Economist* since 1860, and an influential man of letters. This, his most famous work, celebrated the great virtue of the unwritten constitution—which allowed for all sorts of muddle, yet survived, and indeed proved very workable. Bagehot pointed to the political usefulness of stupidity and deference in helping to preserve some aspects of the status quo and in making sure that political change, when it came, would be gradual. (Eighteen sixty-seven also marked the London publication, in German, of the first volume of Karl Marx's *Das Kapital.*)

Let us suppose we overheard a politically alert conversation in that year. Almost certainly it would have included the question of the Reform Bill, with both its friends and enemies in agreement that it would be fateful in its consequences for England.

Before discussing the bill itself, it might be useful to have some idea in rough statistical terms about the country at the end of the 1860s. The population of England, Wales, and Scotland was approximately 26,000,000. Of these, 203,000 men and 1,678,000 women were in domestic service. (By 1960, the total United Kingdom population was 52,500,000. But domestic service was no longer even a census category for men, and for women it had changed to the ambiguous category of personal service and the figure was 60,000 less than 1867.) Figures can be made to mean virtually anything one wishes, and one inclines to agree with the early nineteenth-century leader George Canning, who said, "Nothing is so fallacious as facts, except figures." But the contrast here seems highly informative about the style of English life. (True, there are now, even in England, many labor-saving devices, but it makes a profound difference if it is the housewife or the servant who puts the laundry in the washing machine.) England in 1867, then, was a country with a large proportion of its people in domestic service. To cite a few further figures: 1,634,000 men and 135,000 women were in agriculture; approximately 2,500,000 men in manufacturing; 750,000 women in textiles. (For contrast: in 1951, the number of men in agriculture had dropped to approximately 1,000,000; and of women to a little more than 100,000. But in manufacturing there were 5,000,000 men, a gain of 100 percent, although the number of women in textiles had dropped to 474,000.)

The obvious point of these figures is that England became less agricultural and more industrial as the century advanced. Also, more to the moment here, there was a fairly even balance in 1867 between rural and urban interests. The significance of the 1867 figures, in terms of political development, is that none of the 4,337,000 men in domestic service, agriculture, and manufacturing had the vote, and neither did any women, whether a duchess or a scullery maid.

In 1867 a great many urban workers, under the guise of household suffrage, were introduced into the franchise. A peculiar combination of circumstances, financial, physical, personal and political, made the reform possible in that year. The country was suffering a mild financial depression. One notable aspect of it was the failure to the extent of £19 million of one of the great banking houses, Gurney and Overend. Then, to the financial sense of strain a physical fear was added. An epidemic of cholera, which spread through the country, had originated in the slums of London. The new Alexandra wing of the London hospital was jammed with the dying. The wing had been named for the Princess of Wales, who had married Edward three years before, and she was to dedicate it. There wasn't time, however. As the chaplain remarked, "The wing was to have been opened by a member of the royal family, and instead was opened by King Cholera." There were just under 18,000 deaths in the United Kingdom as a whole and 6,000 deaths in London alone. The epidemic was attributed to unfiltered water supplied by the East London Water Company, a privately owned company with little sense of obligation to the public. The result was a private scandal with decidedly public consequences. The handling of the epidemic can be taken to stand for the at times uneasy, at times effective, frequently very inefficient, relationship between private and public efforts in coping with civic problems. Often, as with the cholera epidemic, the problems were of such magnitude that efforts were needed beyond what an individual or a private group might do, although it was part of the code of upper- and middle-class responsibility that private and individual effort had the greater virtue and was the more to be desired. Yet, as the episode of the plague made clear, only the city, county, or state had any hope of dealing on a large scale with the modern difficulties of living.

One further consequence of the plague was a heightened sense of the insecurity of life. The collapse of the seemingly impregnable bank of Gurney and Overend had also contributed to this sense of impermanence. These events helped create an emotional climate favorable to reform. There was an element of uncanny coincidence; 1832, the year of the first Reform Bill, had also been marked by an epidemic of cholera.

Then there were the political circumstances of 1867. The Whig-Liberals were in power. They were believed to be in favor of extending the privileges of the franchise downward to more and more Englishmen, gradually, of course, from careful precedent to precedent. This is the conventional view of Whiggism, born in the mid-century among Victorian historians who postulated inevitable progress from the 1832 Reform Bill. In 1864, as though to certify the generalization, Gladstone, the chancellor of the Exchequer, put forth the concept that those who had shown themselves morally worthy should come within "the pale of the Constitution." In less florid words, they should be entitled to the vote. Gladstone meant no more than a select group of the working class, but his leader Palmerston was furious at the more sweeping interpretation which was inevitably put upon the phrase. Nevertheless, the vote was still considered a privilege to be earned, not a right. In 1865 Palmerston died at the age of eighty-one. As the great Whig leader, believing in liberalism in foreign affairs and conservatism at home, he had dominated politics for the past twenty years, and he had been opposed to reform. His dramatization of foreign adventures had staved off a demand for domestic political change by the simple device of keeping people interested in something else. Now with his death a potent obstacle to reform within the Whig party had been removed.

The sudden depression of 1866–67 had helped to increase popular agitation for change, most particularly on the part of the Reform League and the Reform Union. Radicalism was coming to the fore again. The Reform League grew out of the London Working Men's Garibaldi Committee, which had been angry when the authorities broke up demonstrations during that great man's visit to London in 1864. In its leadership the Reform League consisted of old Chartists and middle-class sympathizers. The Reform Union was more provincial and more middle class than the league; but both organizations, although there were tensions between them, were dedicated to achieving reform through respectable methods. Their emphasis was certainly on responsible working men and responsible agitation. But did this agitation have any significant influence? Or were the politicians who brought the bill into being comparatively unaffected by outside pressures, agitations, and demonstrations?

It is amazing, considering the many radical changes that had resulted from the growth of industrialization, how similar the political structure of England was in 1867 to what it had been in 1767. Victoria was less important than George III, and at this particular moment, after the death of Albert in 1861, she had withdrawn somewhat. It was a period of comparative moratorium for the monarchy during which its new ceremonial concept, so to speak, was being concocted: a combination of Victoria's earnestness with the ceremonial style of the prince regent, George IV. The middle classes were still not very powerful in the House of Commons, although they had many more members than they had had before 1832. About half of the members of the House of Commons were divided in proportions similar to those before 1832: 116 were members of peers' families; 109, members of the baronetage, with titles inherited, most likely, from old county families, but nevertheless commoners who could sit in the House of Commons if elected; and 100 were commoners related by marriage or descent to peers. Among these "traditional" M.P.s who took party labels, neither party was dramatically favored: 175 were Tories and 150 were Liberals. The old style was even more evident in the cabinet. Of the fifteen members of the 1865 Liberal cabinet, ten were members of great families. The South of England was still heavily overrepresented; in fact, only one-fifth of the electorate chose about one-half of the M.P.s. Not surprisingly, the concern for reform of the franchise was matched by a concern for redistribution, a means to strike a better balance in terms of population and M.P.'s. The pressure for a redistribution bill came from both parties. The Liberals were interested in securing fairer representation for the North of England; the Tories were concerned that perhaps through redistribution arrangements the country would keep its primacy over the city by extending the voting areas of the boroughs, so that those who lived in the country could balance or perhaps even overwhelm those who lived in a particular small city. There has always been a continual if low-key tension and rivalry between city and country in all the values of English society, whether these values were political, literary, or moral.

A certain dullness and sobriety characterized the election of 1865. The electorate—and the nonvoting populace, who participated actively in the "fun and games" of local elections which were still very corrupt—enjoyed themselves in typical fashion. Not to have the vote did not necessarily mean that one was completely without political power. Riots and demonstrations in constituencies were important in shaping the outcome, and the atmosphere formed by the nonvoters in a constituency, as well as their opinions, influenced those who voted. English elections were modified by the Secret Ballot Act of 1872, but the riotous aspect of general elections was not severely curbed until the Corrupt Practices Act of 1883. It is a mistake to subscribe to the cliché of the orderliness or stodginess of the English and to forget their persistent "Hogarthian" strain. The election of 1865 may have been relatively peaceful compared to earlier elections. Still, in one constituency a man was belted with dead rats and cats because he advocated stricter laws against poachers, and in Nottingham there was a two-day battle in the market square involving 30,000 people, which did not end until the Fifteenth Hussars restored order. Eventually, *both* candidates in Nottingham were disqualified because of bribery.

Many new men were elected to Parliament in 1865, including John Stuart Mill, the great utilitarian philosopher; Thomas Hughes, a Christian socialist and author of a classic of the period, *Tom Brown's School Days* (1857); and Charles Trevelyan, the eminent civil servant. Gladstone, cut loose from representing Oxford because of his increasingly Liberal ideas, now felt that as an M.P. for South Lancashire he was "unmuzzled," as Palmerston had feared. In Liverpool for the first time in his career he asked for *public* support for a measure before Parliament, an unconventional gesture in that it was still thought vulgar and inappropriate to ask for such support from one's constituents.

The first phase of the great reform agitation, both within the House of Commons and in the country at large, culminated in the early summer of 1866, when one of the great political debates of the century went on in the House of Commons. Lord John Russell, now Earl Russell in the House of Lords, was prime minister of a Liberal government. He introduced a moderate Reform Bill which would have enfranchised only about 400,000 men, raising the percentage of voters from one-fifth of the adult males to one-fourth. In the thirty-odd years that the middle class had had the vote, there had been no radical change in the practice of politics. To increase the size of the electorate would appear to have represented little danger to the social fabric. John Bright, the veteran of the Anti-Corn Law League and a radical manufacturer, regarded this limited increase as a "moral enterprise," a reward for both the self-sacrifice and perceptiveness demonstrated during the American Civil War by the Lancashire "artisans." ("Artisan" itself as a word has the connotation of independence and probity. Although in 1862 approximately half a million workers were out of work because of the cotton famine caused by the American Civil War, many working men had continued to favor the North's cause. This was in contrast to much of influential and upper-class opinion in England, which tended to support the South.) Moderate though it was, the Liberal Reform Bill was defeated, in large part as a result of the defection of thirty Liberals.

Robert Lowe, one of the most brilliant men ever to sit in the House of Commons, led this dissident group. Lowe argued that the vote was not a right but a privilege, which had not yet been earned by the group to be enfranchised. Wise counsel in the English government would be defeated, he felt, and the ignorant would take over and destroy English institutions. Very few nineteenth-century gentlemen automatically assumed that democracy was a good thing. Lowe feared that enfranchisement even on such a limited scale would lead to the lack of political discrimination he had found when he had lived in Australia and had toured America. (But Lowe was a practical man. After the Reform Act had passed in 1867, he dedicated himself to the education of those he felt were quite wrongly the new "masters.") Lowe's great opponent—in speeches outside of Parliament, which Lowe did not condescend to make, as well as in speeches delivered in the House—was John Bright. He spoke eloquently against the assumption that those who happen to have great positions and considerable wealth have the right to decide what is best for the entire country:

> The rich find everything just as they like. The country needs no reform. There is no country in the world so pleasant for rich people as this country. But I deny altogether that the rich alone are qualified to legislate for the poor, any more than that the poor alone would be qualified to legislate for the rich. . . . The class which has hitherto ruled in this country has failed miserably. It revels in power and wealth, whilst at its feet, a terrible peril for the future, lies the multitude which it has neglected. If a class has failed let us try the nation. That is our faith, that is our purpose, that is our cry, let us try the nation.

In fact, it is clear that John Bright did not really mean the *total* nation. He went on to say:

> There is no greater fallacy than this—that the middle class are in the possession of power. The real state of the case, if it were put in simple language, would be this: that the workingmen are almost universally excluded roughly and insolently from political power, and that the middle class, while they have the semblance of it, are defrauded of the reality.

What Bright really wanted, behind his language, was to make the middle class truly powerful; he felt that one way to do that was to enfranchise some of the working class, as in 1832 the lower echelons of the upper class became more powerful through enfranchising members of the middle class.

If the chief political events that led up to reform occurred on the parliamentary stage, there were other events, political in character and outside Parliament, that, it can be argued, also acted as a spur. England's leaders generally claim that they prefer to make changes when the times are calm and not in response to or as a surrender to pressure. The year 1866 was thought to be one of calm, despite the activities organized by the Reform League and the Reform Union. But the climax of agitation came with the Hyde Park Riots of July 19, 1866, after the Liberals' Reform Bill had been defeated and the Tories, under Derby and Disraeli, were in power. There was a massive protest demonstration, and the railings around the park went down when the crowds surged against them as they turned, peacefully, to leave the area, having made through their leaders a symbolic request to be admitted to the park. The aristocratic Emily Eden felt this to prove that the class war had arrived, and hers was not an isolated reaction. She wrote to a friend, "I attempted to drive around the Park, and am so indignant at the sight [she was outraged to see where the grass had been trampled and many flowers destroyed] that I felt boiling and bloodthirsty." On the other hand, Karl Marx, who had witnessed the event, was disappointed that the English had been so peaceable. "If the railing—and it was touch and go—had been used offensively and defensively against the police," he complained, "and about twenty of the latter had been knocked out, the military would have had to 'intervene' instead of only parading. And there would have been some fun. One thing is certain, these thick-headed John Bulls, whose brainpans seem to have been specially manufactured for the constable's bludgeons, will never get anywhere without a really bloody encounter with the ruling powers."

Benjamin Disraeli was in 1867 chancellor of the Exchequer and leader of the Tory party in the House of Commons; he would become prime minister in February, 1868, replacing the Earl of Derby. He was determined to stay in power and to outshine Gladstone, particularly if it meant appealing to the public by supporting a reform bill that ultimately would enfranchise far more people than the Liberals' bill. The Liberals would have expanded the electorate in the spirit of 1832; the less principled Tory bill, aimed chiefly at increasing the popularity of Disraeli, expanded the size of the electorate from approximately 1.5 million to 2.5 million, in total about one-half of the adult males who headed households. It was a move away from the idea that the voters would be a propertied elite, which might include worthy artisans. It was an act which was shaped by chance (or the determination of Disraeli to outdo his rival, Gladstone), but, nevertheless, it meant that England was to move further toward a democracy than any important political leader, even Bright, had really envisioned or wished. It was a characteristically pragmatic accomplishment. In the words of the Reform Act's recent historian, F. B. Smith, "It is the crucial act in that process by which Britain, alone among large European nations, peacefully adjusted her institutions to meet the emergence of a powerful working class." Disraeli would appear to have operated without any principles at all, and introduced democracy to England in, so to speak, a fit of absentmindedness. Practically the only thing left in the bill he had originally introduced was a "whereas." As a leader of a minority government, Disraeli accepted a series of radical amendments which greatly expanded the electorate. The Tories were likely to think, with some justification, that "deference" would endure among masters and servants, no matter what the political system, particularly as reforms were being granted from above with relatively little pressure from below. Certainly there was far less agitation than in 1832, when there had been reform, or in 1848, when there had been no concession whatsoever.

Disraeli was now determined to keep the initiative and to proceed toward reform, as was said, with all deliberate confusion. He remarked, "We do not, however, live—and I trust that it will never be the fate of this country to live—under a democracy." He attempted to prevent this by the so-called fancy franchises that would give extra votes to those with university degrees and to those with extra property. Although some of these conditions survived until 1945, most went under. Disraeli accepted the simplifications of his plans with an excessive rapidity, as long as nothing he accepted came from Gladstone. He ended by inaugurating what could be called the beginning of democracy—that the vote was more a right than a privilege—through his anxiety to demonstrate that he was really the alternative politician to Gladstone. And for some he proved the point, although at the price of producing a reform bill that was a patchwork of illogical provisions. It was said, "Why is Mr. Gladstone like a telescope? Because Dizzy draws him out, sees through him and shuts him up." That was more than enough for Dizzy, and it was a fair price to inaugurate a sort of government different in quality, more dependent upon the powerful leader and the party machine than had ever existed in England before. Disraeli's own bill had begun "as a limited addition to the borough franchise, hedged with careful safeguards, and it ended in simple household suffrage." And yet although Disraeli allowed himself to be blown along by every amendment, he gave his followers a sense that there was a real Conservative party. It would, in fact, hold office for the greater proportion of the next 100 years, despite the fact that it had just held office fleetingly and briefly during the previous 20 years. After the bill was passed, Disraeli was toasted in the great Tory Club, the Carlton, in appropriately horsey terms: "Here's to the man who rode the race, who took the time, who kept the time, and who did the trick." Disraeli felt, with more justification than the intellectual critics of the bill, that paternalism and the deference of the lower orders would keep England going along on its English course.

A more popular element was introduced into English politics, now that 47 percent of the adult males had the vote. The quality of English life was changing and the next 100 years would be devoted to adaptation to this change. Many of the politicians, writers, and intellectuals thereafter were reacting in their own ways to the need for a private life against what they regarded as the intrusion of the multitude through this act and the further Act of 1884. The sensitive and perceptive souls who had bemoaned the intolerant attitude of the few toward the many were now concerned with the potentially brutal and insensitive attitudes of the many toward the few.

This concern was particularly evident in the specific reactions of three towering Victorian intellects: Thomas Carlyle, the essayist and historian; George Eliot, the novelist; and Matthew Arnold, the poet and critic. A kind of shudder of apprehension passed over them. For the first time, they began to worry seriously about the intrusion of "demos," the populace, now that it could more closely determine the direction of British life. Before 1867, the criticism of intellectuals had been directed chiefly at the philistine nature of the middle class and the crass desire of businessmen to get ahead. They feared the triumph of middle-class values implicit in the Reform Act of 1832. Now they saw in the second Reform Act a still more devastating force. In their own fashion, intellectuals tend to be snobs, not in the vulgar sense of the word but simply in their ingrained conviction that they know best. Humility is only rarely a characteristic of superior minds, and such figures have a healthy if irritating tendency to go around telling people what is wrong with them—for their own good, of course. The fact that they are often right does not make them any the more loved. In 1867 the leaders of thought looked about them and were dismayed. Certainly, the high intellectual values that tended to be elitist, even if expressed in the seemingly open-ended language of utilitarianism, were to be challenged.

Carlyle by this time was a despairing sage. In August 1867, the month that saw the passage of the act, he published his famous pamphlet, *Shooting Niagara*. The title refers to the bill, shooting Niagara over the falls and into "American" democracy. For Carlyle the Reform Act was a distressing display of politicians attempting to please the multitude and prostituting themselves for the vote. The bill had been accomplished, he claimed, amid universal self-congratulation. He feared democracy, which would make the mere counting of heads, with no concern whatever for quality, the final court of appeal. In his famous phrase, it represented the triumph of "CHEAP and NASTY."

George Eliot's distress was less violent, but she too felt, on more modified terms, that the working men, even the slightly less than one million urban working men, were not ready for the vote. They did not have sufficient education; their culture, their intellectual development, were not yet at a high enough level. The argument is familiar and not without a certain weight. But at the same time, these are the sort of reasons that can always be found for denying power to others. During the Reform Bill crisis, George Eliot published her novel *Felix Holt, the Radical*. But Felix was not a radical who would cause any fears among the defenders of the status quo. In January 1868 she published in *Blackwood's* "An Address to

Left: George Eliot in 1865; *right:* Matthew Arnold in 1886. (*Both:* Radio Times Hulton Picture Library.)

the Workingmen," as if written by Felix Holt. Her attitude there was cautionary. She felt that working men must be very careful now that they had the vote and must try to prove themselves worthy of it. "Our getting the franchise will greatly hasten that good end, knowledge in place of ignorance, fellow feeling in place of selfishness, in proportion only as everyone of us has the knowledge, the foresight, the conscience that will make him well judging and scrupulous in the use of it."

George Eliot was extremely concerned about precipitousness on the part of the newly enfranchised voters and feared that they might choose the platform swaggerer. In this address by Felix Holt, she concluded with the reminder that the working classes received the vote not because they were wise but because they needed wisdom. It would not do for them to scorn what she called the "endowed" classes.

The nature of English politics did change from the essentially elitist idea George Eliot had favored, but the violence which she and others of the critics feared did not arise. Toward the end of the century, however, as these critics had also predicted, there was a new vulgarity of tone, particularly in the popular press. The so-called Golden Age of the private member of Parliament, the intelligent member who could be active on his own without particular regard to party, did pass. But the quasi-independence of M.P.s arose more from the fragmented nature of political parties, their inability to enforce discipline, than from any high intellectual tone maintained by a limited franchise. The change in the franchise also meant the eventual development of mass parties and a whole new relationship between party mechanics and members of Parliament.

Yet it is striking how widespread was the fear of decline in values.

As noted earlier, Matthew Arnold, in his *Culture and Anarchy* based on lectures given during the period and published as a book in January 1869, also shared a sense of distress, if not despair, about the turn of events. Perhaps more than George Eliot and certainly more than Carlyle, he had a firm sense of the need to cope with the advent of democracy. He had some hope that on the part of the multitude there would be a change of heart. His was the recurring ideal of English intellectuals that men will transform themselves and solve the problems of their society. Arnold set a tone of reaction to political and social problems which is heard again and again in England: a gently hectoring note, a plea for authority and culture. Arnold had a sense that his world of culture was collapsing, and undoubtedly the Victorian equilibrium, whatever it might have been, was nearing an end.

Although, by the coincidences of politics, it had been Disraeli and the Tories who had actually passed the Reform Act, Gladstone and Liberalism were nevertheless inclined to the principle of "progress." Trying not to be too conscious of what he was doing in this regard, Gladstone was the agent who supervised the Liberal spirit in its commitment to change, even if of a distinctly nonviolent sort. The Liberals, at least in the abstract, hold that man is a strong entity, waiting for fulfillment. All that is necessary is to remove the various obstacles that stand in his way, and he will then be able to do everything for himself. The Conservative theory of human nature tends to hold, again in the abstract, that most men are poor things, and will not be worth anything unless they accept the help of those who are wiser and more powerful than they, as well as guidance from the past. Men must respect, and never attempt to change drastically, the institutions that represent, or are *thought* to represent, the wisdom of the ages. The intelligent conservative is not dogmatically against change—this can be seen clearly in Burke—but his aim is to *preserve*, to modify, rather than to discard and substitute something new.

Despite his exotic and "un-English" character, Disraeli managed to persuade many of his countrymen that he stood for continuity. Gladstone and Disraeli really rather hated one another—Gladstone seeing Disraeli as evil, and Disraeli seeing Gladstone as hypocritical and priggish. One peculiar contrast between the two was that Disraeli, although he conceived his role to be one dedicated to the preservation of institutions, was really much readier than Gladstone to improvise and to experiment. He could always excuse himself with the thought that he was acting on behalf of great institutions—as when he somewhat impulsively bought 44 percent of the Suez Canal shares from the khedive in 1875 on behalf of the empire, or made Victoria Empress of India in 1877 on behalf of the monarchy. Gladstone, lacking the sense of operating from the *strength* of institutions and always believing that they could be *improved*, moved much more cautiously and reluctantly. This sort of paradox characterizes much of nineteenth- and twentieth-century English political and social history: the man who by definition is more conservative and theoretically more entrenched in the Establishment can do the more daring, and even revolutionary, thing. There will be little protest when he does, because the assumption is that he is taking seemingly progressive steps on behalf of ancient institutions.

Benjamin Disraeli

Disraeli was a very unlikely person to become the leader of the "gentlemen of England," that is, of the Tory party. There is a story, perhaps apocryphal, that at one point in his career he set out to prove his *solidity* to the back-benchers of the Tory party, who were likely to be country squires of the sort who justify the characterization of the Tories as the "Stupid Party." He

Benjamin Disraeli, Earl of Beaconsfield: A replica of the painting by von Angeli done for Queen Victoria in 1877. This version hangs in Disraeli's house, Hugh-enden Manor, Bucking-hamshire. (The National Trust.)

had suitable interviews with them, very much in *their* style, and his object was achieved when each interviewee emerged saying that Disraeli was far less clever than he was cracked up to be. It is always a profound disadvantage in England to be thought to be "too clever by half," which can be taken to stand for "unsound and untrustworthy." Disraeli was determined to shimmy up to "the top of the greasy pole," and it was a remarkable demonstration of the extraordinary flexibility of English society, in spite of its rigid context, that he was able to do it. On the face of it, he must have been everything that Englishmen, the Tories in particular, would have detested. Disraeli, with the disadvantage of being too clever, was also regarded as foreign, although he was born and bred in England. Worse yet, he was called "the Jew." In fact, Disraeli had been baptized when he was twelve. If he had not, he could not have had a political career, as Jews were not allowed, because of the mandatory oath, to be M.P.s until the 1850s. Disraeli was proud of his Jewish heritage, although he believed that Christianity was the logical development from it. It pleased him to know that, theoretically, at least, his ancestors were studying the law, while the ancestors of most Englishmen were, presumably, skulking about in caves. One important point that Disraeli demonstrates is that it is possible to get ahead in England even if one is an exotic, a dandy, and a novelist—everything that, in theory, should mean disaster. But Disraeli was a master of strategy and played his cards with great skill. Nevertheless, he had to be prepared for disappointments. There were many setbacks, and it was some years before he began to succeed in politics. He had to keep casting about for a constituency and a set of principles; he did not enter Parliament until he was older than most who had political careers—he was thirty-three. The indisputably respectable Gladstone was a friend and contemporary with Lord Lincoln, whose father, the Duke of Newcastle, put him into Parliament when he was twenty-three. For all their differences, Disraeli and Gladstone also demonstrate how necessary it is to have a combination of idealism and opportunism in one's makeup to ensure success. With Disraeli, it is impossible to tell where the one stops and the other begins. Even with the upright Gladstone, each characteristic has a peculiar way of merging into the other. Disraeli did make himself stand for the great Conservative principles of the institutions of England, ranging all the way from the monarchy to the manor, from the empire to the parish. If there was any consistent principle in his career, it was to try and revivify those institutions through imperial gestures and social legislation.

The Sense of Property

But the foundation stone of the Conservative attitude, quite apart from imperial gestures, is the sense of property, the sense of land. The assumption is that those who have a stake in the land will naturally be conservative. Disraeli's ability to appeal to those landed interests gave him a considerable part of his strength. Obviously, the most immediate symbol of the Conservative approach would be the land itself. Owning land was the most tangible way to have a stake in things and was more "real" than business or investments. Disraeli aimed to represent the gentlemen of England. A gentleman was thought to be someone who did not have to work for a living, and who had property. Conservative principles for most of the nineteenth century go back to the land.

The idea of land and the permanent values of the countryside are still important components of the emotional appeal of the Tories. This, of course, was not as widespread in the eighteenth century and the first part of the nineteenth century, when many of the great landowners were Whigs, the immediate ancestors of the Liberal party. But the feeling about land is an abiding principle for those who believe in continuity, while those on the side of change tend to be less attached and sentimental about it. There is a nice contrast on the matter of land between Gladstone and Disraeli. Disraeli, of course, was landless. His father, Isaac Disraeli, was a literary figure well known and successful in his time, a recluse, who couldn't have cared less about having a large estate. All that he wanted was a small comfortable house in the country where he could work. He had no conception, nor means, of giving an estate to his elder son. But Disraeli's political associate Lord George Bentinck and his two brothers, sons of the Duke of Portland, felt that it was most inappropriate for a leader of the gentlemen of England to be without land, so they advanced Disraeli money for an estate at High Wycombe, a squire's estate of a thousand acres, producing £1,500 annual rent. It is there that Disraeli lived and there he is buried. Disraeli assumed that the money was a gift, but the eldest brother, when duke, demanded repayment, and Disraeli was saved from embarrassment by a rich Yorkshire friend. On the whole, Disraeli was an exotic plant for the wholesome countryside, although that particular part of Buckinghamshire, on the high road between London and Oxford, is congenial to eccentricity. It is the same area where Sir Francis Dashwood had his Hell Fire Club at Mendenham Abbey in the eighteenth century, and in the twentieth century where Lady Astor would entertain at Cliveden, most notably those who became known in the 1930s at "appeasers."

For Disraeli, some sort of continuity in the land had had to be created. Gladstone had a different problem as his family had traveled "light." They came down from Scotland to Liverpool, where they made their fortune. Gladstone married into a family grander than his own, the Glynns, related to the great Whig cousinhood. Disraeli married well, too, but in a more rakish manner: he married the wealthy widow of the man who had helped him start out in politics, Mrs. Wyndham Lewis. She said later, "Dizzy married me for my money, but he would have married me again for love." Gladstone as a married man demonstrated the Liberal virtues of efficiency, honesty, and stick-to-itiveness. His brother-in-law, the owner of a considerable estate, had through foolish business speculations crippled the estate with debt. Gladstone, gleaming with probity, set himself the task, in the midst of a very busy life, of clearing from debt an estate he did not own and making it an efficient enterprise. Having accomplished this, it was characteristic of him that he did not follow the standard Victorian practice of tying—through strict settlement—the estate in his own family, his brother-in-law having remained a bachelor. Instead, in 1875 Gladstone made the land over in "fee simple," that is, without any limiting restrictions, to his son, so that his son could have *full* responsibility and freedom—a Liberal concept. The idea of the son being able to do exactly what he wishes contrasts with the Tory idea that restriction must be placed through entail, a practice that lasted in almost full power as a strong legal concept until 1922. The point was to prevent the man in possession at the moment, or his heir, from breaking up an estate. The individual man was not to be trusted, but the race or the family was thought to be wise. In fact, many ways were found of breaking settlements, and the land market was a very lively affair long before the 1920s.

The idea of land is still basic to Conservative feeling in England. A place in the country and a title remain the traditional objects of veneration for many Englishmen. Throughout the nineteenth century and until about 1920, to be an aristocrat or a squire represented power. Together, aristocracy and squirearchy were probably the single most powerful group in England. Today, aristocratic landowners are more powerful and far richer than one might expect in a democratic society, but their position is rather a symbol of social status than the true locus of power. The squirearchy, ancient families who have lived in the same place for years, are not completely without power, but their power is a mere shadow, the barest remnant, of what it was. The old title stands for the principles of order and continuity, the Tory principles, without actually providing them. The gradual way in which institutions are changed in England can be shown in the story of how the landed classes lost their power.

The landed classes still had considerable economic power into the 1920s despite the great agricultural depression at the end of the nineteenth century. Yet they had already been replaced in a financial sense in the mid-nineteenth century by the industrialists and businessmen. The curious fact is that such men as well as professional men continued, and to considerable extent still continue, to imitate the landed classes, to emulate the style of the gentleman—a man without visible occupation who derives an income from land. A gentleman in this sense feels that he can follow his own bent, be neither hypocrite nor conformist, and practice the virtues of honor, dignity, integrity, considerateness, courtesy, and chivalry. That, of course, is very much an ideal. It is true that such an ideal will be somewhat easier to realize for a landed magnate or a squire, a little monarch in his own landed kingdom who can pursue his own ideals. In one sense, the land dream is crusty and conservative, and, in another, it represents the generalized wish to go one's own way, to have the independence to pursue one's own goals. But that was never really true for the landed man, although he might be nearer to that ideal than most people. He was caught by the traditions of his position, the necessity to be a good lord or a good squire, to help and protect his tenants, to perform the rituals of his class. The head of a family also faced an obligation to revivify the family fortunes through a wealthy marriage, most frequently to the daughters of bankers and industrialists at the beginning of the nineteenth century, and to the daughters of wealthy Americans at the end of the century. (It was only as the Edwardian era approached that the peerage became more frivolous and seemed more concerned with having a permanent good time, rather than an occasional fling combined with a solid marriage. This statement can be very loosely based on the fact that nineteen peers married actresses between 1884 and 1914, while only ten such marriages had occurred in the 100 years before 1884!)

During most of the nineteenth century, what constituted a magnate? A man who had approximately 10,000 acres and an income of about a pound an acre. A squire had about 1,000 acres and proportionately the same income from it. That sort of income conferred a considerable freedom in the era before income tax amounted to any serious sum. The spirit of the landed classes was very much what the Conservative party aimed at on a national scale and what one still hears occasionally echoed in today's party. The head of the family was an autocratic leader. With his position went various responsibilities to his dependents. The extent of the landed power in England is indicated by the so-called new, informal Doomsday Survey, made in 1876, which stated that 202 individuals owned 24 percent of the land. These were the great magnates such as the Duke of Marlborough and the Duke of Bedford with great country seats such as Blenheim or Woburn Abbey. But in a way it is more impressive to learn that at the same time four-fifths of the land of England was owned by only 7,000 individuals. What did these estates mean? The fundamental difference between a lord and a squire was that for the lord everything from the house on down was on a greater scale. The lord, therefore, could not give the same close attention to a local parish as a squire. A lord might have many parishes under his supervision, while a squire would have just one. In fact, since his estate might be scattered about several counties, a lord's attention was much more likely to be given to national than to local problems. But the basic necessity for continuity was to have a seat, an estate, then an advowson, the right to appoint a local clergyman so that whatever the particular religious sensibilities of the patron within the Church of England they would not be offended on Sundays. A lord or a squire might also have the right to determine the local member of Parliament. He would have various manorial rights, including game rights, and enough land to allow him to keep up an appropriate social position. By design or chance—owning urban or coal property—he might also have income from commerce and industry. The agricultural depression of the later nineteenth century made this life a little more difficult to maintain, but it still went on, despite the comment of Lady Bracknell in Oscar Wilde's play *The Importance of Being Earnest*: "What between the duties expected of one during one's lifetime and the duties exacted from one after one's death, land has ceased to be either a profit or a pleasure. It gives one position and prevents one from keeping it up. That is all that can be said about land."

This sort of grand land life went on until the break-up of the great estates in the period from 1910 to 1919. The First World War did not cause, although it hastened, the break-up, and these changes in landholding fitted into the pattern of violence and unrest of the period before the war. The landowning classes at last became convinced of what, in fact, had been true for sixty or seventy years: more money was to be made outside of the land. It took that long for the intangible advantages of landowning to be overbalanced by the questions of cold cash. The aristocracy and squirearchy in England are realistic and hardheaded, but to a certain degree sentimental about their landed position. In the latter half of the nineteenth century, this grand style continued through the creation of new peers who had the wealth to acquire and maintain such large estates. In fact, the style of living became even grander, assisted by the tradition attached to it, the habit of respect and deference from the so-called lower orders—"there is something about a lord"—and sheer snobbery. The idea that a peer should have an estate to support his title did not die out until after the First World War.

In the history of many nineteenth-century titled families the first generation would have made the money, even the second was likely to be born at the older, simpler house, close by the source of the family's money, although shortly thereafter he might be removed to the purer country air. But the third generation might be blissfully free of any such memories and could devote itself completely to country interests, develop a sense of cohesion with the estate, and pass it on to the eldest son, through the rule of primogeniture. Other sons might go into the Church, the army, the navy, even the professions, and conceivably into business and start the process all over again. That was the traditional procedure for new peers. Of course, managing land itself was a business. If there were minerals on the estate, most particularly coal, a peer would be directly involved in business, unless the rights were leased to a combine. But there was a style and feeling about the conduct of landed interests that made it easier to identify them with the Conservative principle of continuity than with the go-ahead spirit that one more readily associates with business. (Of course, it is possible that the trouble with much business in Great Britain in recent years is that it, too, is treated as if it were a rather sleepy estate.) Public schools attempt to confer upon all their pupils the identifying air and manner of the upper classes—one source of their power, but a style that has profoundly irritated not only foreigners but other Englishmen who are victimized by their manner. This has provoked the feeling that there were, and still are, two nations in England.

Disraeli was, of course, profoundly aware of this division, having coined the phrase, "the two nations"—of the rich and the poor. It was the "nationalization" of the mannerisms of the rich which accentuated this feeling. Previously, there had been hundreds of little societies with a lord of the manor at the head of each, rather than a class feeling throughout England. An upper-class style became more uniform at the end of the nineteenth century. But what is the upper-class attitude? Fundamentally, it was and is an assurance of being right, an authoritative manner and an air of gentility, an ability to claim privileges with an air that goes along with inherited authority, a conviction that farmers, servants, and the laboring poor all look up to one. In return, one was expected to do one's duty. The political power of this relationship had been declining ever since the middle of the nineteenth century. But the style of life continued in its most extravagant form to the years right before the First World War. The habit of deference is a difficult one to break, particularly if the yoke is not an excessively onerous one, and the benefits are real. Seeing refuge and security in the small country unit where everything and everyone was in his place— "the rich man in his castle, the poor man at his gate"—was reassuring. It was easy for the country interests, still to some extent the "many little kingdoms," to present a united front to the crass commercial and industrial world, in itself so divided and self-seeking.

This is an idealized picture; there was considerable rural poverty and oppression all along. And the little self-sufficient world became harder to maintain when the agricultural laborers acquired the vote in 1884. After the Liberal party split in 1886, the landed interests were almost inevitably Conservative, and as rural workers voted against their landlords, the myth of community lost its inspiring force. An agricultural depression, starting in 1873, and agricultural specialization, starting at the end of the century, interfered with the "golden haze" of rural life. This financial decline in real power was bound to affect the magnates and squires. They could continue to hold their positions only by an increasing number of compromises with the new forces of society.

While the Reform Acts of 1867 and 1884 dramatically increased the franchise, it was still far from universal, and, in any case, assertion of power by the electorate was too gradual to suggest violence. The political power of the landed classes declined gradually. They were allowed to keep the appearance of power and position, but it became more and more a front. In 1885, for the first time, commercial interests had a majority in the House of Commons, although the middle class had numerically dominated the electorate since 1832. It would appear to take approximately forty to fifty years for a class to elect themselves to Parliament on any considerable scale. And it would take the working classes as long as the middle class to elect on a large scale their own representatives.

Another reason that the aristocracy was losing ground was that it was being diluted. Peers were being created before they had really gone through the three-generation clarification. In part, the peerage was literally being diluted by beer, and some referred to it as the "beerage of millionaire brewers," a symbol of what was happening in general. As though to prove that it was its own defenders who could operate against the institution with greater freedom, it was Disraeli who created the first of several Guinness peerages. Between 1886 and 1914, 246 new titles were created. Of these, about a third represented new wealth. A third were professional men, and the further third were those who would have been created peers in the years before, families who had already acquired positions that justified and supported a title before it was actually granted by the monarch. But the men with new wealth received recognition much sooner than they would have in earlier days, a sort of instant recognition, rather than the slow, gradual growth dear to conservative hearts. Of course, many of those who received peerages, as professional men, might well be younger sons of the landed families. There was no longer, as there had been earlier in the nineteenth century, the worry about having enough land, not just income, to sustain a title in the style a title deserved. Since it was a bad investment, few men would go about building a considerable estate. They would content themselves with the country house in order to achieve the appearance of the country life without the roots and responsibilities which would have been expected of a peer in earlier times. As of 1911 one-eleventh of the peerage were businessmen. At the same time, the flow between the peerage and the world of business was a two-way process. As land became less profitable, it became even more incumbent upon the peerage and the squirearchy to look into commercial and industrial enterprises to support themselves in the appropriate style, or at least to lend their names as directors in order to "up-class" the world of business and, if possible, to avoid any reduction in their style of life. In 1896 a quarter of the peerage, 167 noblemen, held directorships.

Gladstone, in a way, had his revenge upon the peerage in his concept of individualism, although he himself, as Arthur Balfour, the Tory leader, said of him, was a great conservative in everything but essentials. The lords were put on the defensive by the Liberal idea that institutions had to justify themselves, prove themselves efficient and helpful. It became clear in the early years of the twentieth century that the lords and the squires were not doing their bit. The squires simply tended to disappear from Parliament and hunt foxes. The peers were, in theory, if not in fact, at their House, but the basis of their power, the land itself, was rapidly disappearing. Not that it was eroding, but what one might consider a sort of Liberal dream of individualism—a return of the yeoman farmer—was taking place, and the land was being sold to the tenants. The lords were selling because they feared that the Liberal government might confiscate their lands, particularly as this was the period when the ideas of Henry George—that the unearned income of land must be much more heavily taxed—were gaining ground. As a result, the peers in their panic lost much of the traditional basis of their power, in attempting to be "realistic" about land, in regarding it as merely one possible form of investment which did not yield as great a return as other forms. Lawyers broke entails making it possible to sell. Starting before the First World War in 1910 and continuing until 1921, it has been estimated that one-quarter of the land of England changed hands, a transfer of land "probably not . . . equalled since the Norman Conquest."[1]

The movement had started before the First World War, but the death in that war of many heirs to landed estates weakened the emotional reasons to hold onto an estate, as did death duties, rising taxes, and inflation. As in so many other areas, the war, rather than causing change, accelerated an ongoing process. *The Times*, recognizing what was happening, wrote in a rather sentimental editorial:

> England is changing hands. Will a profiteer buy the great house? Will it be turned into a school or an institution? Has the mansion house electric light and modern drainage? For the most part the sacrifices are made in silence. The sons are perhaps lying in far-away graves. The daughters secretly mourning someone dearer than a brother. The daughters have taken up some definite work away from home, thinking thus to still their aching hearts, and the old people, knowing there is no son nor near relative left to keep up the old traditions, and so crippled by necessary taxation that they know the boy will never be able to carry on when they are gone, take the irrevocable step.

A conservative way of life has largely passed. Many of the great estates were broken up. Small farms were owned, not rented. Once the financial bubble burst in 1921, many of these new owners found themselves in a difficult position, in part because they could no longer call upon the landlord to help them in their difficulty. The tiny welfare state of the landed estate, frequently despotic, and certainly not democratic, but at its best very much in keeping with the paternalistic aspect of Tory democracy, was not there to help. The grimmer side of Gladstone's world had taken over, in a free enterprise system where the small landowner was expected to look after himself. Much of the Disraelian romance of the land had faded away. Yet the remnants of continuity can be seen now in the way the English think about land, the almost involuntary respect they seem to give, even in the form of resentment—which, after all, is yet another way of paying homage—to those who are the heirs of greatly reduced, or tax encumbered, estates of the magnates and squires. The tradition of liberalism and individualism represented by Gladstone continues in England, and so does a strong conservative sense of permanence, associated with land, and somewhat incongruously represented by Disraeli.

[1] F. M. L. Thompson, *English Landed Society in the Nineteenth Century* (London, 1963), p. 33. Much of the material, and the quotations, used here about land come from this superb study.

CHAPTER TWO

The Liberals in Power

The Liberal party came to power in the General Election of 1868, having won a majority of 112 seats in the House of Commons; it continued in power, with Gladstone as prime minister, until 1874. This was the last period of unrivaled prosperity and preeminence for England. In the 1870s, she was entering upon a period of comparative decline—gradual and, for many years, almost imperceptible—measured against such rising countries as Germany and the United States. It was also a time of social change. Gladstone and his colleagues embarked on a conscious attempt to create what they considered a more equal society. Gladstone, something of a utilitarian in his thinking, believed in making the institutions of England work more efficiently. He also believed in fairness. These two beliefs propelled him forward as the Liberals, under his leadership, set out to make the great institutions of the state—Church, schools, army and navy—more accessible to the great body of Englishmen, not merely to the aristocracy as in the past but to the middle classes and even, to a limited extent, to the working class. Privilege, which could be held accountable for much that was inefficient and that made unfairness all the more glaring, was at last to be curtailed.

For example, the Church of England had long held a position of

The Swing
of the Pendulum:
The Triumph
of the Two-Party System

primacy in the state, and it would continue to be the Church by law established. But in the early years of Gladstone's ministry, Church rates—the local tax paid by every resident of a parish, no matter what his religious belief or affiliation—were abolished.

Education, deeply involved with questions of religion, was the most important domestic area in which Gladstone's ministry made progress. The ancient universities, Oxford and Cambridge, were barred until 1871 to non-Anglicans. Consistent with their histories, Oxford and Cambridge differed, Oxford being the more conservative. At Oxford a student could not matriculate, that is, register, unless he first subscribed to the Thirty-Nine Articles of the Church of England. At Cambridge, where there were stronger Low Church traditions, a student could matriculate but could not take his degree until he so subscribed. The Act of Parliament that changed this in 1871 was consistent with a general liberalization of rules that was taking place within the universities, although they probably would not have reformed themselves, at the speed at which they did, without some outside pressure.

But the most basic progress—at the primary school level—came a year earlier through the Education Act of 1870, sponsored by W. E. Forster. In effect, this act established a network of schools in England, opening the way for more English children to receive an education than ever before. (Even so, the Act was imperfect and lacked uniformity. Not until 1891 was it finally made possible for all children to receive a free primary education.) The curious combination of private and public endeavors in the development of education was indicative of how institutions shape themselves in England: the state does not intervene until the problem is extremely pressing and after private enterprises have shown the way.

For a number of years, the government had been giving financial aid to schools; in return, there had been some right of inspection. But, in general, the central authority had very little direct supervision over education. The 1870 act provided that if a particular school in a designated area was found to be offering a good education to its students, it would be encouraged in its activities and would receive state aid. However, if the civil servants who made the inspection decided that the school was inadequate, or if no school existed in the area, then a new school would be established which would receive state support and support from local rates, with control remaining in the hands of the local council. In many areas, an adequate school was already in existence, and was almost inevitably controlled by the Church of England. While control of such a school might be slightly modified by the 1870 act, it was left fundamentally unhampered—a continual source of irritation to nonconformist interests and parents. The intense sectarian disputes that marked English educational life from the legislation of 1870 to 1902 did not really diminish until the intensity of religious belief itself, so characteristic of Victorian England, began to wane toward the end of the century. But, in order to cope with these various sectarian interests, successive governments, whose leaders were often men of intense religious conviction, would almost intentionally fudge or muddle the issues. And so schools that were entrenched and operating well were allowed to go on without interference, even if they were being run by a particular religious denomination. As a counterweight, the so-called Cowper-Temple Clause, part of the 1870 act, provided that a parent could remove his child during the period of official religious instruction.

Whatever its deficiencies, the 1870 act was an extremely important step toward achieving public education in England, in this instance in the primary schools. Such an act fitted into the Liberal creed of creating opportunities for all. Yet it was a response that any government, Liberal or Conservative, might have had to make to a growing population with its widening aspirations.

Beyond the schools, other institutions of the state were opened up, indeed almost pried open, by Gladstone's government. The army, which traditionally was to a considerable extent under the control of the upper classes and the aristocracy, had demonstrated in the Crimean War that it was not adequate to its tasks, but it had not changed to any notable degree since that disaster. Change, it was evident, would have to come from outside, and so the Liberal government moved to bring it about. In 1868 flogging was made illegal. In 1869 the commander-in-chief, who before had been responsible solely to the monarch, was put under the authority of the secretary for war, a first step toward bringing the military under civilian control or supervision. But the most important reforms were devised by Edward Cardwell, a close associate of Gladstone's, who had moved over the years, like Gladstone himself, from the Tory to the Liberal party. Cardwell had a firm commitment to the idea of efficiency, of making institutions work. The structure of the British army was basically changed by his reforms.

Military service continued to be voluntary—there was to be no draft until 1916—but recruitment of the armed force was an unattractive business even without a draft: press gangs for the navy and recruiting sergeants who took advantage of tipsy young men in pubs and lured them into accepting "the Queen's shilling," that is, enlisting. Cardwell tried to make a career in the army for an enlisted man more attractive, reducing a potential lifetime enlistment to a period of twelve years, six years on active service and six years in the reserves. The organization of the army itself was similarly balanced, with the creation of "twin" battalions, one "twin" in the field, generally fulfilling either garrison duties or "police" actions, which were the continual responsibility of an empire, and the second "twin" in England. At appropriate intervals, the two would be rotated.

In effect, Cardwell was attempting to "rationalize" a structure that over the several decades had become totally inadequate to the needs of Britain and its empire in the latter part of the nineteenth century. The most serious blow he delivered to the social pretensions of the army that had defeated Napoleon was to abolish the purchase of commissions, which had acted to keep the "wrong type" out of the officer class. Purchase meant that officers were restricted to members of the upper class who could afford to pay for promotion and purchase commissions. The bill to change this system was passed by the House of Commons. Not surprisingly, it was defeated by the House of Lords. Thereupon it was imposed through administrative (and reluctant royal) fiat: an order in council in 1871.

Another considerable area of reform during Gladstone's first and greatest ministry was the civil service. Change had been called for some years before, in the famous Trevelyan-Northcote Report of 1853. In response, open competition for places in the civil service had then been initiated in India, but not at home. Again, administrative fiat seemed the best way to implement reforms, as it was felt it would be extremely difficult to persuade the House of Commons and the House of Lords to rule against the tradition of recruiting into the civil service largely through patronage. Vested interests could more easily be curbed and custom modified by the queen in her council. Like the army, the aristocracy had its power checked, but it was replaced—and to a considerable degree this was also true in government itself—by the upper middle class. Although rigorous examinations were set up for entrance into the civil service, it was the well-trained amateur who was encouraged, and the study of the classics became the best road to high position in the civil service, including the treasury, the most powerful bureaucratic arm of the government. The prevailing view was that it was far better to have a well-trained mind which could then turn in any direction than to have a specialized prior knowledge of one area to which one would devote oneself. The value of a training in Latin and Greek was accepted on faith. Benjamin Jowett, the master of Balliol College, Oxford, and the translator of Plato, grasped this fact and made his college a training ground from which emerged a large number of important civil servants.

Still another great reform, put into effect by the Liberal government in 1873, was of the legal system, again with the purpose to simplify, to make justice fairer and more accessible.

But although these extremely important reforms were the most characteristic achievement of the Liberal ministry, and most accurately reflected its philosophy, the overriding problem for the ministry, as it would continue to be for English government well into the twentieth century, was the problem of Ireland. Ireland increasingly dominated Liberal politics, so much so that it transformed the Liberal party in 1886. Gladstone had been intensely aware of the problem all his life, although at first, in keeping with his other conservative ideas, he had not been sympathetic to the Irish cause. Most particularly he had been against the English state support of the training of Catholic priests at Maynooth in Ireland. As early as 1845, a year after leaving Peel's government over the Maynooth issue, Gladstone had written, "Ireland, Ireland, that cloud in the West, that coming storm, the minister of God's retribution upon cruel and inveterate but half-atoned injustice."

In his early career, Gladstone had been primarily concerned over the welfare of the Anglican Church in Ireland—the established Church there. As he grew older and altered his conception of how God could best be served, he changed his mind on many topics, but always with the same aim: to shape the state so that it could better serve God's glory. Initially, Gladstone had believed that an assertion of the power of the Church in Ireland was essential, as he had demonstrated when he had precipitously resigned from the government over Maynooth. But early in 1868 he persuaded Parliament to pass a bill which disestablished the Anglican Church in Ireland. He had no wish to disestablish the Church of England in England; indeed, at the very end of his life, in the 1890s, he would oppose the disestablishment of the Church of England in Wales, although the majority of the Welsh were Methodists. He was not against an established Church as such. He had become convinced, however, that it was outrageous and unfair that a minority Church, a Church of the Ascendency, as the Protestants were called in Ireland, a Church of the conquerors, should be financially supported by the entire population in Ireland. Gladstone's concentration on this issue reflected the religious concerns of his age; the issue had immense emotional and symbolic significance to many, yet it might have yielded its place as *the* issue to other more pressing problems of economics and politics.

After the spirit, the earth; and Gladstone was intensely aware of the need to improve the relation between the Irish peasant and his tenure of his land and to work against the many evictions which had so embittered earlier Irish history. He attempted to move toward what was referred to as the "three F's": *free sale*, that the peasant should be allowed to sell his land if he wanted; *fixity of tenure*, that so long as the peasant paid his rent he could remain on the land; and *fair rent*, that the rent charged should be a legitimate sum. The year 1870 was marked by the passing of a Land Act for Ireland—to improve the position of tenant farmers—which fell a good deal short of what the Irish themselves wished and was not particularly effective. The Land Act was viewed as a concession and was accompanied by the Peace Preservation Act, designed to maintain order and to make its enforcement stricter. The Irish gratitude for the former was lessened by an act such as the latter. At the same time, the Protestant landowners, while welcoming the strengthening of the forces of order, were not pleased at the concessions that were granted in the Land Act. It was a fine, troublesome example of concession coupled with coercion.

The period from 1868 to the end of the nineteenth century is thought of as the Golden Age of the two-party system, although only from 1868 to 1885 was there an ordered alternation between the two parties. It might, in fact, be said that with Disraeli's death in 1881 this Golden Age was over. Perhaps many have tended to overemphasize the symmetry of the political history of the time and to exaggerate the addiction to a two-party system because this was—despite the beginnings of economic problems in the 1870s—the last epoch of Britain's unquestioned preeminence. In fact, it might be argued that a functioning two-party system was more the exception than the rule. It is true that voting patterns in constituencies—and the physical layout of the House of Commons—favored the two-party system. A sense of a regular alternation—the so-called swing of the pendulum—is evident as the first great Gladstone ministry was succeeded in 1874 by the first great Disraeli ministry when Disraeli was unencumbered by the leadership of the Earl of Derby. In the early 1870s Gladstone's immense popularity began to ebb. He had come to power on a great wave of gratitude, despite the fact that it was Disraeli and the Conservatives who had actually passed the Reform Act of 1867. But presently he began to alienate certain special-interest groups, some of whom had fervently supported him before, most notably the Nonconformists. The latter were upset by the Education Act of 1870 because it further strengthened through state aid those Church of England schools that were already flourishing. Yet there were groups within the Church itself who were offended by the state intervention, however benevolent, in Church-sponsored schools. Other vested interests—in the army, the civil service, the legal system—were ruffled by the changes that had been made in their institutions. And Gladstone had also attempted to move against the powerful brewers, distillers, and publicans by limiting the number of pubs. Although he failed to put through any legislation to that effect in Parliament, he ensured that the support of the "drink" interest would henceforth go to the Tories and that many pubs would virtually serve as Tory recruiting offices.

The Liberal leaders had used up their considerable energies in putting through an extensive and important program. Disraeli characterized them, as they sat opposite him on the front bench, as a row of exhausted volcanoes. The volcanoes collapsed, so to speak, into the Irish Sea, for it was the Irish University Bill, potentially not an important piece of legislation, that provided the occasion for the fall of the Liberals. The Irish were dissatisfied and regarded the bill as a good issue on which to make a stand. Opposition within the party summarized the dilemma in which the Liberals found themselves. Gladstone was simply proposing a new Irish university, but his proposals did not go far enough for the Catholics and went too far for the Protestants. The bill was defeated by 287 votes to 284, with 43 Liberals (among them 35 Irish) voting against the government. The pattern of by-elections, those seriously regarded barometers, had already been going against the Liberals. Gladstone wished to resign and have Disraeli form a government before another General Election, but Disraeli was too shrewd to accept the gambit. He insisted on Gladstone's staying in power, no doubt hoping he would be discredited further while he himself could continue to attack. It was not until January 1874 that Gladstone finally asked the queen to dissolve Parliament. At the General Election in February, the Conservatives came into power.

Disraeli had technically been prime minister before in 1868, and with the Earl of Derby he had been leader of the Tory party during its brief ministries in 1852 and 1858–59. But it was not until 1874 that he came into his glory. Lacking so many political advantages, he had started his career, as we have seen, comparatively late; now he was almost too old to enjoy his great triumph. In order to lessen his task, he accepted a peerage, as Earl of Beaconsfield, in 1876 and thus avoided the taxing excitement of leading his party in the House of Commons. And he only survived this ministry by a year, dying in 1881. But it must have been with a certain reluctance that he abandoned the face-to-face rivalry with his old enemy, Gladstone.

Disraeli did manage to reunite his party. Lord Cranborne, who had resigned from the cabinet in 1867 because he disapproved so strongly of Disraeli's plans for the Reform Bill, now returned to the cabinet as secretary of state for India, having meanwhile inherited the title under which he would become the great Conservative prime minister later in the century: the Marquess of Salisbury.

What sort of appeal did Disraeli make to the voter, to public opinion, to his followers? Too much weight has been put upon the speech that he gave in the Crystal Palace in 1872, which was probably not meant as the trumpet call to imperialism it is sometimes thought to be. Disraeli was shaped too early in the century to care passionately about the empire, although he recognized its appeal to the electorate and to the queen. His own conception of imperialism was emotional and flamboyant, with little consideration for its effectiveness in keeping the economy at a level impossible with dependence solely on domestic sources. Disraeli, consciously and unconsciously, played on the theme of imperialism to create a mass appeal for his party. He was not, certainly, a politician in the modern style concerned about his popularity with the voters. He was in no sense a demagogue. He would have disapproved of the innovation had he lived long enough to see Gladstone stump the country for his beliefs. Yet, in his way, he was aware of the need to appeal to the voters. He was trying, in the Crystal Palace speech with its suggestion that the interests of Englishmen were of necessity imperial, and in speeches in Parliament which inevitably were reported widely, to appeal to the urban working classes which had been enfranchised in 1867—to capture their imagination with the idea of England's imperial destiny. In contrast, Gladstone had attempted to make what might be called a middle-class appeal to efficiency and fairness.

Disraeli's greatest triumph in foreign and imperial affairs was at the Congress of Berlin in 1878, where Russia was prevented from overwhelming Turkey. The congress was dedicated to the Western European powers— more specifically, the "Anglo-Saxon" powers of Germany and England— asserting their control over the fate of the world. Disraeli, who had always had a soft spot in his heart for Turkey, returned to England in triumph and coined his phrase for what had been achieved at the congress: "peace with honour." England traditionally had been the arbiter of Europe through much of the nineteenth century; at the congress she held the position again. Yet, increasingly, through the rest of the century, England would be isolated; rather than being an arbiter of European affairs, she would be forced to extend herself within her own empire and have little choice but to attempt to be more self-sufficient in terms of policy. In this sense Disraeli, in his ministry, practiced the older form of diplomacy while laying the emotional groundwork for England's new stance.

In domestic affairs, too, Disraeli set the style and provided the leadership for the important social reforms of 1875, the second year of his ministry, although much of the actual work was done by his home secretary, Richard Cross. Disraeli was attempting to live up to the promises, however vague they had been, of Young England, and the vague idealism of his political manifesto novel, *Coningsby* (1844). *Coningsby* had been mostly spirit, and very little substance, but it did support, as Disraeli was now supporting, a Tory theory of responsibility, a form of noblesse oblige: that the great men of the state, indeed, possibly the state itself, did have an obligation to be concerned with the plight of the ordinary man. The great acts of the year 1875 were the Public Health Act, which committed the state to a concern for sanitary arrangements, and the Food and Drug Act, which introduced some conception of government supervision in those areas. The potentially exploitive and casual arrangements which characterized laissez-faire economics, although never as free as the economists might argue they should be, were proving too dangerous for an increasingly crowded and complex society. The Trade Union Act of the same year was, in fact, an extension of Gladstone's act favorable to the trade unions, which had been passed in 1871, but it went further and eliminated aspects of the original act that were unfavorable to the unions. The 1875 act reflected the Tory tradition of favoring corporate bodies over individuals, and it protected the unions from the sort of legal prosecution to which an individual was liable, particularly in the case of strikes. Not until "Liberal" ideas had permeated the Tory party toward the end of the century, and early in the twentieth century, did this sort of thinking about unions, on the Tory side, reverse itself. Gladstone's attitude had been to treat the trade union as an individual and give it both privileges and responsibilities. Disraeli was more realistic and recognized that a worker had disadvantages not shared by his employer. Therefore, in his legislation of 1875, he eliminated the possibility of legal prosecution because of breach of contract or conspiracy. Such an act gave a considerable impetus to the ability of unions to operate and to strike.

Another extremely important bill which was passed in this extraordinary year of 1875 was the Artisan Dwellings Act, which stated for the first time that the government could subsidize the building of housing for the poor. Not surprisingly, this bill horrified laissez-faire thinkers, even though the subsidy was extremely limited. But as is so frequent in England, an important principle had been enunciated, and would not be abandoned. In the twentieth century, government support of housing for the poor continued steadily, and was a striking accomplishment in the legislation of both the Tory and the Labour parties.

New Politics and Three New Politicians

These were considerable accomplishments of a distinguished ministry, but Disraeli's popularity, like Gladstone's, began an almost inevitable decline. And the style of politics was changing. Gladstone and Disraeli were such major figures that they were almost immune to changes of style, although in their radically different ways they had been well suited to their periods. Gladstone with his overwhelming seriousness and Disraeli with his theatrical grandness appealed mightily to the two dominant aspects of England during the century: its seriousness about its power and its position and its enjoyment of playing the role of top dog. Certainly, both men were masters at exploiting the moods of their times. But, inevitably, other politicians were looking with envy at their preeminent positions.

Three men—Joseph Chamberlain, Lord Randolph Churchill, and Charles Stewart Parnell—marked the growing ascendency of a new style and content of politics. Joseph Chamberlain had greeted the Tories' Artisan Dwelling Act with considerable enthusiasm, and he used it in Birmingham, the city whose politics he dominated, to help the workers. Such an act was a coming together of some aspects of left-wing and right-wing traditions and was congenial to Chamberlain's sort of radicalism.

In England a man's background—what part of society he comes from —is extremely important in telling the sort of opinions a particular politician, or indeed any member of that society, may hold. Of course, such societal factors can be no more than possible indications of a direction that a man's thoughts and actions may take, but they would appear to be especially identifiable, and powerful, in England. Joseph Chamberlain had been born in London in 1836 into a middle-class family: his father was a cordwainer, a manufacturer of shoes. This social group was on the way up, and in the early nineteenth century tending to radicalism. The family was Unitarian in religion: not only was Chamberlain not a member of the Church of England, but he was in a Nonconformist group who had not achieved quite the general respectability of the Presbyterians and Methodists, although Unitarians had a distinguished intellectual, commercial, and social tradition of their own. His religion put him on the perimeter of English society, far from the established center. Chamberlain was educated in a day school in London, not in one of the boarding schools to which the upper classes were more and more frequently sending their children, and to which Chamberlain would send his own sons. His two famous sons, Austen and Neville, went as a matter of course to Public Schools. As we have noted earlier, these are actually the most private of schools, charging considerable fees. They are called "public" because, unlike medieval centers of education, they are not by charter limited to a certain group of students, such as the sons of clergymen, and may admit whomever they wish who meet a particular school's social, financial, and even intellectual standards. Austen, the elder child, would go on to university; Neville was sent directly into business: even within a successful family, there were social discriminations based on age and sex.

Joseph Chamberlain's education had stopped when he was sixteen. He worked for his father for two years and then was sent to Birmingham, where his uncle, a screw manufacturer, was in a somewhat beleaguered state because, ominously, his firm Nettlefolds was threatened by American competition. Chamberlain's father invested some money in the firm—which was used to buy American machinery—and the son went to work there.

Eventually, Joseph Chamberlain became extremely wealthy, a fact he made manifest by wearing a fresh orchid in his buttonhole every day. He was so financially successful that he could retire from an active role in the business in 1874, while still in his thirties. He was now able to enter politics, but he was entering late, some ten or more years behind the sons born into wealthy families, who, if interested, would have started an active political career at the age of twenty-one. Chamberlain began his career as a radical, and on the local level, although his experience rapidly was useful on the larger scene and made him a prominent figure in the nation.

At the age of thirty-two, in 1868, while he was still an active business-man, he had founded the National Education League of Birmingham, which was devoted to protecting the interests of the Nonconformists in whatever educational reforms might take place. In 1870, the year in which the Liberal government passed an Education Act not really pleasing to the party's Nonconformist supporters, the league became national in scope. Chamber-lain, almost inadvertently, had devised a new and important form of politi-cal organization which was transformed in 1877 into the National Liberal Federation: countrywide and permanent—not like the Anti-Corn League, a pressure group organized around a particular issue and then disbanding once the issue was settled. Even Chamberlain, however, did not believe that the popular organization should direct the politicians, but rather that it could be useful to particular politicians, such as himself, and also provide an accurate impression of what those who supported the Liberals on a national level wanted. Both the league and the federation marked the fact that, through communications, politics was becoming more national in scope, despite the continued importance of the constituency. Now, under Chamberlain, there was for the first time a national political organization to work on behalf of a national political party. Before there had been a party structure consisting of whips and central agents: Liberals, who oper-ated out of the Reform Club, and Tories, who operated out of the Carlton Club. There was a party agent in the constituency and a constituency organization, but they were not linked as they would be in the national federation. Chamberlain also introduced what was known as the caucus in order to control more tightly the disposition of votes in the constituency and tactics in general. He was accused of "Americanizing" English politics. Chamberlain's brilliant strategy was to arrange things, with the able assist-ance of Francis Schnadhorst and Jesse Collins, so that a maximum of his supporters could be elected to office. Instructions would be given to voters; they would be organized and told to vote in certain ways. This strategy paid handsomely: the Chamberlains would dominate Birmingham politics well into the twentieth century.

Chamberlain did much for Birmingham in return. He was its lord mayor from 1873 to 1875; and there, in what had been the most back-ward of the great industrial cities, he introduced reforms, which became known as "municipal" or "gas and water" socialism. He paved and lighted the streets, provided various other services which we now take for granted as an ordinary part of city life, and introduced modern methods of business so that the city was not run at a loss. He did not worry about what was the gentlemanly thing to do, but rather about what was the efficient thing to do; not worrying about niceties, he managed to accomplish a great deal for his adopted city.

Both on the local level and through the National Liberal Federation, Chamberlain was appealing to a new sort of voter, or a voter who now had much more power than he had had previously: the man of the lower middle class. At the same time, the federation itself made only a pretense of being democratic. Soon the Tory party constructed a similar organization, but it gave even fewer indications of being controlled by its membership. As A. Lawrence Lowell remarked in the early twentieth century, both popular party organizations, as democratic organizations, were shams; the Liberals an opaque sham and the Tories a clear one. The latter-day political scientist Robert McKenzie says much the same thing about the present Labour and Tory party organizations. These were new sorts of mass organizations, but although the purpose of forming them had been to ensure support for the party leaders, within less than thirty years they were making demands which the leaders did not always find congenial.

Another leading Liberal radical was Sir Charles Dilke. Many thought that Dilke was likely to go further than Chamberlain, that he had a better chance to end up as prime minister. He was a radical M.P. who had scored a great success in 1868 with the publication of *Greater Britain*, a book which managed to be both radical and imperialist. Chamberlain and Dilke would appear to have been the logical successors to Gladstone; they were trying to infuse some firmer and more far-reaching concept of social concern into the Liberal party.

When the Liberal cabinet was formed, after Disraeli's defeat in 1880, Gladstone had to choose between Chamberlain and Dilke. He chose Chamberlain then, but admitted Dilke to that level two years later. One reason that Gladstone hesitated to bring Dilke into the cabinet was that, as a one-time republican, Dilke was personally abhorrent to the queen, and a minister had to "kiss hands" of the monarch on appointment. There were a few absolute republicans in England, but the greater part of that movement reflected chiefly an unhappiness or irritation at the vast expense of maintaining the monarchy. As noted earlier, after Albert's death in 1861 the queen attempted to withdraw from public life as much as possible. Many felt that the period of mourning was excessive: it represented that deep strain of melancholy and indeed morbidity which was the other side of Victorian optimism.

A number of pamphlets had appeared in the 1870s attacking the queen, the most famous being called "What Does She Do With It?" Victoria was an extremely wealthy woman in her own right—as are her descendants—but she also received, as does the present monarch, a considerable sum on the so-called Civil List voted by Parliament to assist in the performances of the functions of monarchy, particularly the ceremonial functions. It was the Civil List that Dilke had wished to reduce in 1872. Despite Disraeli's blandishments and his making her Empress of India in 1876, Victoria did not reemerge to play her full public role until the Jubilee in 1887.

After the Jubilee Victoria was extremely popular, republicanism was an absolutely dead issue: the style had been set for the contemporary monarchy. In her long reign she made the transition from a monarch who had considerable political power, and for whom the ceremonial and emotional role was secondary, to a monarch who, although not without some political power, serves primarily as a symbol of unity and provides a continual national show, presented generally in scrupulously good taste.

In any event, Dilke's own political career was blighted by the conventions of Victorian morality. As recent investigations have amply demonstrated, although attitudes toward sexual practices were quite different in the nineteenth century from what they are today, the practices themselves were not. But the social punishments for being publicly involved in scandal were more severe, and Dilke's attempt to clear his name, when he was cited as a correspondent in a divorce case, was proof enough to the public, whether true or not, that he was guilty of sexual misconduct. The scandal was unforgivable, and any hope he may have had of greater political prominence abruptly ended in 1886. Six years later he did return to Parliament, but he was no longer a significant political leader. Both Chamberlain and Dilke represented the possibilities of some sort of left-wing imperialism which came to nothing in the collapse of Dilke's career and the switches in Chamberlain's. Anti-imperialism became the more usual position on the left.

The Tory who held a position parallel to Chamberlain's, who attempted to infuse a new concept of politics into his party, was Lord Randolph Churchill, a younger son of the Duke of Marlborough and the father of Winston Churchill. He was certainly the most important rising politician on the Tory side and, like Chamberlain, was a thorn in the side of the official leadership. (The most interesting men in politics are usually troublemakers when they are not at the top themselves.) Lord Randolph, born in 1849, came to prominence in the late 1870s as leader of the so-called Fourth party, consisting of himself, Sir Henry Drummond Wolff, Sir John Gorst, and Arthur Balfour, the nephew of the Marquess of Salisbury. They comprised a distinguished group of irreverent, comparatively young men who would enjoy themselves in harassing not only the leaders of the Liberal party but the leaders of their own party as well. In large part they were moved by high spirits, but they also attempted to push the Tory party toward a greater concern with social problems. Churchill, like Chamberlain,

Queen Victoria as Empress of India. (Radio Times Hulton Picture Library.)

was aware of the need to create a popular organization and to win the support of the new working-class voters. Churchill was active in the 1880s in the founding (in 1884) and in the workings of the Primrose League (named after what was reputed to be Disraeli's favorite flower, at least according to the queen). The league was set up with all sorts of hierarchies, consciously to cater to snobbish instincts. Before he founded the Primrose League, Churchill exploited a more down-to-earth group, the National Union of Conservatives Association, established in 1867. While he attempted to develop, in a not particularly sophisticated way, a snobbery of aspiration on the part of the "lower orders"—as though to be Tory was somehow to better oneself—he also wanted to develop a concept of Tory democracy. The traditional Tory concept, more a sense of obligation to the "ranks below" than the individualism of the Liberal creed, was now combined with the idea of participation from the lower ranks, particularly as they had won the right to vote. Churchill, like Chamberlain, would appear to have been on the wave of the future. He had managed to rise with extraordinary speed. He overestimated his strength, however, and gambled for more and more power.

When he was chancellor of the Exchequer in 1886 and the war minister, W. H. Smith, would not give up part of his budget in order to lower taxes on tea and tobacco and to increase grants to local government, Churchill tried to get his way by threatening to resign. He chose to interpret the reply of Salisbury, the prime minister, as an acceptance of his resignation rather than as it was meant to be, a request to continue negotiations. Salisbury was relieved to lose such a disturbing element in his cabinet, but the departure robbed the Conservative party of one of its most imaginative politicians. Churchill had thought he was irreplaceable, but, of course—as anybody else—he was not. He rapidly faded from the political scene. He was likely to have done so in any case, as he was suffering from tertiary syphilis and died less than ten years later, in 1895, in his mid-forties. He is remembered as one of the most interesting and imaginative of late nineteenth-century politicians, a politician in a new style.

The third great new figure, also with some suggestion of late nineteenth-century Wagnerian gloom about his career, was Charles Stewart Parnell, a Protestant Irish landlord, who adopted the Irish Catholic cause as his own and in the process changed the tone and manner of debate in English politics. Parnell, who was born in 1846, had been elected to the House of Commons in 1875. Even more than Gladstone and Chamberlain, he set the political style of the 1880s, in the sense that he was the man to whom the political system had to react, and the Irish problem as he focused attention on it became the compelling issue of the decade. In 1879 Michael Davitt had formed the Land League, to further the principle that land in Ireland should be owned by the peasants and to maintain political pressure in the countryside. Such a claim went well beyond the gestures made previously by Gladstone toward improving the Irish situation. It was this movement that Parnell now took over, becoming president of the league, strengthening it, and making political progress on its behalf by becoming an obstructionist in the House of Commons. John Stuart Mill, the great utilitarian philosopher, had envisioned a House that would serve as a kind of debating society or forum in which ideas and positions would be discussed fully and rationally and a sensible decision then be reached. Such a hope presupposed a wide range of prior agreement and considerable agreement on procedure. Parnell was willing to exploit the procedures and to bring the progress of the nation's business to a halt, if necessary, for the cause of Ireland.

The ideal of full and rational discussion probably had never truly existed, but from 1832 to 1867 fewer party pressures were brought to bear on and more independence was allowed to members of the Commons than after 1867. Very likely this was the result of a limited electorate, fragmented party structure, and the country's prosperity, rather than any instinctive capacity of Englishmen for rational discussion. If one political leader does not accept the conventions of a parliamentary body or wishes to use the conventions for his own purposes, it is easy to upset such a delicate organization based as it is on a certain shared assumption that no one will be too difficult. Parnell was not willing to accept the convention, so he prolonged debate and made use of other techniques that were technically permissible but that ran counter to the spirit of Parliament. In retaliation, so that business could be done, closure was introduced, so that debate, contrary to Mill's dream, could be cut short. At first, it was called by its French name, *clôture*, as though to emphasize that it was an "un-English" way of proceeding. Parnell had his base of power in the sixty to seventy Irish M.P.s, a considerable voting block, who were "home rulers," in favor of greater independence for Ireland. The Secret Ballot Act of 1872, a measure introduced by the Liberals, made it easier for the Irish tenantry to express their opinions without their landlords' coercion. As Catholics already had the vote, they now could vote secretly for supporters of Parnell. The famine of the 1840s had driven many an Irishman to America, and eventually this emigration led to a source of considerable funds for the Irish party.

Before considering the dark future of the Irish problem, we should look at those factors that were making politics more a popular concern rather than, as in the past, discussions among those who "really counted." Thanks to new political participation, the sharp division of Disraeli's two nations, although still in so many ways apparent, was lessened through the idea that politics could be shared by the bulk of the male population. Chamberlain, Churchill, and Parnell were all interested in exploiting the new voters, as they recognized that such groups would increasingly determine the course of politics, but, ironically, it was the "grand old man," Gladstone, who was still able, without seemingly caring about it, to use such opinion in the most effective way.

The issue that dominated the later period of Disraeli's great ministry at the end of the 1870s was the fight between Gladstone and Disraeli over the Eastern Question: the relations between Russia and Turkey, and what should be the role of the Western nations, particularly England, in this dispute. Would more voters favor English interests and thus wish to support Turkey to keep Russia out of the Mediterranean, or would they wish to attack Turkey because of her cruel actions toward Balkan Christians? The high point of Disraeli's career had been the Congress of Berlin in 1878, which he and Bismarck had dominated. There, Disraeli had achieved a triumph for British foreign policy and for his conception of what it should be: a strengthening of Turkey in order to keep Russia at bay. But this contention, which served English interests, most particularly in India and in the Mediterranean, conflicted with another tradition, more cited than followed: English idealism in foreign affairs and her alleged belief in fairness. Frequently, of course, it could also be called hypocrisy when it so happened that idealism and English interest coincided, but in the Eastern Question it would appear that England could gain little through espousing the cause of the Christians persecuted by the Turks, and it was to that cause that Gladstone eventually subscribed. The English, in taking up causes, frequently are able to exude an attitude that they know what is best for all! Gladstone was a paragon of such an attitude, so that, putting the moral good of the nation first, he was also serving the cause of his party. The memorable exchange in *Alice Through the Looking-Glass* applies. " 'What curious attitudes he goes into,' said Alice. 'Not at all,' said the King. 'He's an Anglo-Saxon messenger and these are Anglo-Saxon attitudes.' " Gladstone had Anglo-Saxon attitudes—that is, stern and moralistic, but not without a certain semihidden practicality—toward foreign policy, while Disraeli had more romantic and yet, paradoxically, perhaps also more realistic ideas of what foreign policy should do.

In April 1876 the Bashi-Bazouks, an irregular part of the Turkish army, massacred 12,000 Bulgarian Christians. Gladstone's response was a compound of idealism and shrewd politics. He was appalled by the massacre, but he also prided himself on his sense of timing and was concerned to choose the most effective moment to launch a campaign against the Turks (and against Disraeli), if indeed a campaign should be launched at all. As he wrote to his colleague Earl Granville, "One must have the right time for the virtuous passion." It took him some time to react to events in the Balkans, and—as he waited for the right moment—the more extreme members of his party had to apply pressure to get him to act. Then, in September 1876, he issued his famous pamphlet "The Bulgarian Horrors and the Question of the East." Two hundred thousand copies were sold in the first month of its publication. In the pamphlet Gladstone argued that the Turks must leave the Balkans "bag and baggage." It was a significant and important stand. The idea of the self-determination of nations was not common in the nineteenth century, and clearly it had had little to do with the disposition of nations made at the Congress of Vienna in 1815. Gladstone's attitude toward the Balkans was an important part of a change in attitude, the belief in self-determination that would have so much to do with the disposition of nations made at Versailles in 1918. And he used this sort of appeal to "fair play" for all, which characterized his politics from 1867 to 1880, to make those politics attractive to the new voter. His concern was with a moral commitment to an issue—paradoxically, an issue that did not directly involve Englishmen—not with overtly political considerations, such as preoccupied Chamberlain and Churchill. Even the issues those two men discussed were more concerned with the texture of life at home than England's role abroad.

Gladstone made the Eastern Question his central concern in his two great tours of speeches, which became known as the Midlothian campaigns of 1879 and 1880. Midlothian was a constituency outside of Edinburgh that had been held by a Tory. Gladstone was asked to contest it, with a safe seat reserved for him at Leeds, where his son was running and could resign in his favor should he be defeated in Midlothian. He was "adopted" by the constituency, and in 1879, in anticipation of a General Election which was bound to come soon, he made a series of speeches there and then in 1880, the year of the General Election, a second series of speeches. For a candidate to "nurse" a constituency, touring it and "speechifying," was not unusual, and obviously Gladstone would receive special attention for any speeches he might choose to make. These were the days when the game of politics was increasingly becoming a central interest for the English public. Not only were more of them eligible to vote, but considerably more than ever before could read. They read with great fascination, in minuscule print, the complete reports of major politicians' speeches in the press. But even such attention was not enough for Gladstone in his anxiety to inform the English world of Disraeli's bad policies. An M.P. conventionally did not make speeches outside his constituency, although it was becoming more common for leaders to speak in behalf of candidates in trouble. Gestures of national leadership might take place in London, but rarely in the provinces. But now that was changing, and Gladstone, as he took a train up to Scotland, made what was almost a royal progress. In the two campaigns he used the "whistle-stop" technique, pausing along the way to give short speeches. Such actions were considered by other politicians somewhat "vulgar" and demagogic. Before these campaigns party leaders had issued, as Disraeli did, a statement of principles in the form of a letter to their constituents. Perhaps major political leaders might make a few significant speeches in great cities. But for this sort of "whistle-stopping" Gladstone was largely responsible, making politics more "popular" and responsive. The approach had already been apparent in the activities of Chamberlain and Churchill, but Gladstone put the stamp of approval *and* success upon it when he won his great electoral victory in 1880.

Gladstone's Second Ministry

That election was also a great victory for the Liberal party, with 347 Liberals and 240 Conservatives in the House of Commons. In the course of his campaigns, Gladstone had become a reluctant democrat. He now felt that the response to the Eastern Question by the Disraeli government was an example of how the ruling class, those whom he regarded as the "top 10,000," had failed and that the "people" were needed to redeem the balance. He had called upon the "people" over a matter of conscience and idealism and had been surprisingly successful. He was adored as "the people's William." The irony was that, once given this mandate, he failed to accomplish much, either in the Balkans or in other areas of concern. The pressures that could be applied to Turkey to treat its Christian subjects with less brutality were not noticeably increased by Gladstone's coming to power. The two parties had differing views of foreign policy—the notion of a continuity in foreign policy was not introduced until the 1890s. But frequently English interests, and the pressures of other countries, meant that the number of choices for English foreign policy was limited, as Gladstone was to discover.

Disraeli compared Gladstone to Napoleon and likened his return to power to Napoleon's return from Elba. Gladstone had resigned the leadership of the Liberal party in 1874, in order to turn his attention, as a man in his seventies, to eternal matters. The Bulgarian atrocities had brought him back, but he had not resumed the official leadership. Earl Granville, an old-style Whig, led the party in the House of Lords and the Marquess of Hartington, the courtesy title of the eldest son of the Duke of Devonshire until his father died and he became a peer, was the leader in the House of Commons. Both men belonged to the more traditional part of the Liberal party, the great Whig families gently on the left, a tradition stemming from their leadership against established authority in 1688.

Officially, Gladstone was nothing more than a private member of Parliament, and the queen would have been pleased if he had remained so. Originally, when he was a follower of Sir Robert Peel's, she had liked Gladstone, but as he moved leftward she came to dislike and fear him. The contrast to Disraeli also worked to his disfavor. For Disraeli was extraordinarily attentive to the queen; he flattered her outrageously, which she adored, and in 1876 he had passed through Parliament the Royal Titles Bill, which made her Empress of India. In contrast to this personal relationship, she complained that Gladstone addressed her as if she were a public meeting, and she felt that his aim was to destroy her state. (In fact, Gladstone was, if anything, excessively loyal and considerate despite great provocation.) She most decidedly did not want Gladstone to be prime minister. She tried to persuade Granville to form a ministry, and she tried to persuade Hartington. But they both realized that after the Midlothian campaigns Gladstone was the only man who should form a government, and the queen had to yield.

Balfour said that Gladstone was a determined conservative in everything but essentials; his old-fashioned aspect was reflected in the cabinet he formed in 1880. He had a deep sense of precedence, and of the need to earn one's way up the cabinet. Reluctantly including Chamberlain, he balanced him by creating one of the most aristocratic cabinets of the century. He appointed a considerable number of Whig grandees: Earl Spencer, the Duke of Marlborough, Earl Granville, the Marquess of Hartington. The few other radicals included were past their prime, or respectable Quakers, such as John Bright, who had been so deeply involved with the Anti-Corn Law League in the 1840s and the fight for an extended franchise in 1867, or former Quakers, such as W. E. Forster, who had moved up-Church when he married the daughter of Thomas Arnold, the headmaster of Rugby, and who had earned the enmity of many radicals through his tenderness toward the Church of England in his Education Act of 1870. Sir William Harcourt, who became home secretary, had a certain radical reputation, only superficially deserved. The cabinet was given a very slight bias toward the left when Sir Charles Dilke joined it in 1882.

This administration, which lasted from 1880 to 1885, was a sad one for Gladstone, for his vision of the role that England should play, and the course of its empire, would not be realized. In society and the economy as a whole, it was a time of retrenchment and even of depression in certain areas. The period of expansion was ending. At the same time, other countries were surging on, most notably Germany, which had been unified in 1870 after a surprising and complete victory in its war with France, and the United States, which continued her bumptious economic expansion as the wounds of her civil war began to heal. In England there was growing intellectual questioning: whether the country was pursuing the right values, whether its success was worth the price being paid for it. Gladstone's administration, in its way, was an epitome of these problems, for he found that he was critical of the position England had made for itself in the world and yet the commitments were such that it was next to impossible to withdraw.

In domestic affairs Gladstone was able to take some strides similar to those he had made in his first administration and consistent with his hope of creating a fairer world. He put through Parliament in 1881 the Employers' Liability Act which stipulated that injured workmen would receive some compensation, but it was a limited bill still overly concerned with the problem of fault and responsibility. The last great Reform Act, that of 1884, was also passed. It added the rural proletariat to the voters' list, an increase of two million voters. Theoretically, all males over twenty-one now had the vote; that principle was firmly established; no further changes would be made until the twentieth century when women were given the vote. But in 1884 there were many technical limitations on a complete male franchise: because of various complicated requirements about length and type of residence there were still many men who did not have the vote, and it was not until 1918, when women over thirty were added to the ballot, that the regulations were sufficiently simplified so that virtually all men could vote. Gladstone's administration itself began the liberation of women, for in 1881 it passed the Women's Property Act, which lifted married women out of the degrading position of being virtually their husbands' chattels and gave them some control over their own property. The English are hardheaded about money and recognize the responsibility and freedom that it confers, so it was appropriate that the moves toward female emancipation began with questions of property. The 1884 Reform Act was also concerned with property in another sense— eliminating the historic boroughs and attempting to introduce a more rational system of equal electoral areas.

The most serious concerns for this ministry, other than Ireland, were imperial problems, notably in South Africa and Egypt. In South Africa, where the English were confronted by a revolt in the Transvaal, the crucial event was the battle of Majuba in 1881. It led in some degree to a withdrawal from empire, for the battle had been won by the Boers, the Dutch settlers in Africa, and the situation was temporarily resolved through the Treaty of Pretoria. This arrangement gave the Transvaal and, ultimately, the Orange Free State a considerable degree of independence; the whites from Holland, who had been in South Africa before the British had taken it over at the time of the Napoleonic Wars, protected their rights for which they had "trekked" away from their earlier settlements in the 1830s. Their rights involved not only comparative independence for themselves but a harsher treatment of the natives than the English practiced. However, the English maintained residual rights of supervision, particularly of foreign relations. It was from these remaining rights that further problems, and ultimately war, would arise at the end of the century. An economic balance had been temporarily achieved; it had been in flux since the discovery of diamonds in the area and the establishment in 1867 of two diamond companies, one belonging to Barney Barnato and the other, with the Dutch name of De Beers, run by Cecil Rhodes and Alfred Beit. With the discovery of gold in 1886, problems would again intensify and play their part in leading to another war. But for the moment, with the Treaty of Pretoria, Gladstone's wish not to commit himself to any extension of empire was granted.

The situation was quite different in Egypt. There, as elsewhere in the imperial area, Gladstone was trapped by English obligations which, ironically, became more rather than less pressing during his administration. The situation in the 1880s was unusually difficult. The Suez Canal, built in 1869 by a French company, was extremely important to English interests in trade and strategy as the route to India. Disraeli, in a romantic and practical gesture when Parliament was out of session in 1875, had bought a controlling number of shares in the canal company for England through a loan from the Rothschilds' bank. Inevitably, such a step enmeshed England even more deeply in questions of international finance. The actual company which ran the Suez Canal was still operating from Paris. But by the 1880s the financial situation of the canal had become quite unstable, and certain English interests attempted to exploit it to their advantage. They succeeded to the extent that England completed her domination of Egypt, but not so completely that other European nations were prevented from fishing, so to speak, in her troubled waters. A technique of imperialism, practiced by the English in Egypt, China, and elsewhere, was to lend money—in some cases strong-arm tactics had to be used to force people to borrow. The English were very anxious to lend to foreign governments. Being a creditor gave England a certain degree of control over a borrowing government's policy, advantageous in an informal empire of trade and finance. In 1881 and 1882 Egypt was unable to pay her debts to France and to England, the two countries most closely involved in Egyptian affairs: France through the canal and strong cultural ties, and England through her web of financial activities there and her compelling interest in the canal. France was unwilling to take over further control of Egypt. England, half willingly and half not, felt herself forced to participate even more in Egyptian affairs. Increasing financial difficulties of the country were compounded by intense nationalist activities. It became necessary for the English to assert their power. In July of 1882 the English bombarded Alexandria and landed troops. The French refused to participate, and England, through the Organic Law of 1883, in effect took control. Their consul-general, officially nothing more than the adviser to the khedive, was in fact the virtual ruler of the country, particularly since from this date until 1907 the man in the post was the formidable Sir Evelyn Baring, Lord Cromer. This commitment in Egypt was one of the most considerable that England made during the century, and it would continue, in some degree, until the Suez disaster of 1956. Thus a far-reaching and pervasive obligation had been undertaken by a government that had earnestly wished to reduce its obligations abroad.

Determined to limit such expansion, the government in London ordered the withdrawal of English troops from the Sudan, the vast area to the southwest of Egypt. General Gordon, who had earlier distinguished himself in China, was sent to effect the evacuation, but he exceeded his orders, hoping to maintain British interests there. On his own responsibility, he attempted to deal with the Mahdi, who was leading a religious and political revolt against the English, but the Mahdi was opposed to any sort of compromise, and Gordon was presently besieged at Khartoum. The Liberal government, which had ordered Gordon to the Sudan expressly to effect a withdrawal, was reluctant to expand its military efforts. Finally, however, recognizing its responsibility to Gordon and aware of what would happen to its reputation if nothing were done, the government sent a relief mission, led by General Wolseley. It arrived just too late; Khartoum fell and Gordon was killed in January 1885. His death was a considerable blow to English prestige, and Gladstone's popularity dropped precipitously. He had been referred to admiringly as the "GOM," Grand Old Man, and this was now reversed to read "MOG," Murderer of Gordon. The queen sent him a public telegram of distress, expressing her grief at Gordon's death, which was tantamount to an open and unprecedented reprimand. Thus the Liberal government had been forced into imperial adventures, for which they had no taste and which were not successful.

Ireland

During Gladstone's second ministry, the Irish issue intensified, in part because of that country's continuing and deepening depression, in part because Parnell, now coming into his period of greatest prominence, asserted the importance of Ireland in Parliament by using every possible parliamentary technique and creating some new ones. Gladstone attempted to improve the situation: in 1881 he passed his most important Irish Land Act, which came close to fulfilling the ideas of fair rent, free sale, and fixity of tenure initially approached a decade earlier. Still, it was far short of what Parnell or his supporters wanted; they continued their agitations both inside and outside Parliament. The government regarded Irish provocations as so extreme that in October 1881 Parnell and some of his lieutenants were jailed for fomenting trouble and encouraging boycotts in Ireland. (The term "boycott" was invented at this time after Captain Boycott, a land agent in County Mayo who was isolated for evicting a tenant.) Parnell was also held responsible for the increasing number of "rural out-rages" in Ireland, most frequently the mutilation and killing of cattle. Such actions not only offended the Englishman's sense of property but also his sentimentality about animals. Yet Parnell had a firmer sense than his followers of how much violence English leaders would tolerate before becoming adamant. Some thought that Parnell was intimidating the Irish tenants and preventing them from taking advantages of the Land Act because it was too limited in its provisions. Inadequate reform or threatened revolution became the choice of policies. Should Parnell have accepted the act in order to improve the situation in Ireland for tenants? Or did he follow better tactics in forbidding cooperation until greater satisfaction was given?

Parnell led his party from the Kilmainham jail from October 1881 to May 1882. By the spring of 1882 he had decided that he should cooperate with Gladstone. An informal arrangement was made between them, known as the Kilmainham Treaty. It stipulated that Parnell would urge his followers to cooperate with the Liberals. In return, the government promised an Arrears Bill to provide funds for Irish tenants to pay their rent, to prevent their eviction, and to allow them to take advantage of the Land Act. Parnell's more extreme followers, however, disapproved of the treaty, feeling that their leader had betrayed them. Some Liberal moderates, most particularly the Irish chief secretary W. E. Forster, resigned. The "treaty" was arranged late in April, and Parnell was released from jail on May 2.

It seemed that conditions must improve, but then assassination intervened. Gladstone had appointed Lord Frederick Cavendish, his nephew-in-law and a younger brother of the Marquess of Hartington, as the successor to Forster. On May 6, 1882, Thomas Burke, the most important English civil servant in Ireland, and Lord Frederick were assassinated while walking together in Phoenix Park in Dublin. These violent deaths seriously weakened the Kilmainham arrangement, although it went forward. Parnell offered to resign as head of the Home Rule party, but his followers would not allow him to do so. Gladstone was considerably distressed; Lord Frederick was a young man of whom he was extremely fond, and he had had to persuade him to take the post. There was considerable suspicion that Parnell himself was involved in the assassination, and many of those "who counted" now argued that only coercion would work in Ireland.

The impression grew that the Gladstone administration was weak, most particularly in its handling of the Irish situation. Parnell, who had attempted to cooperate with Gladstone, now felt that he could get more from the Tories. (The Liberals had passed a stiffer Crime Bill to cope with the increased number of murders.) The Tories were less sympathetic to the Irish cause, but they were also less sentimental about power and were willing to make promises to Parnell in order to unseat the Liberals. Parnell felt no ideological commitment to the Liberals; rather, he would treat with anyone whom he believed would help the Irish cause. Approximately seventy members of Parliament were his followers, so he had something substantial to offer. Over the budget of 1885 the Irish voted against the Liberals, and helped bring down Gladstone's government.

The Events of 1886

Gladstone's followers themselves were distressed with the direction of Gladstone's policies, particularly in Ireland, where they felt he was doing too much, and on the same budget vote seventy-six Liberals had abstained. Salisbury was summoned by the queen to be prime minister for the first time. He would hold the post for thirteen and a half years out of the next seventeen.

Parnell had clearly become the arbiter of English politics. He had supported Gladstone; Gladstone had stayed in power. He switched his support to Salisbury; Gladstone fell. Parnell's standing was strengthened by the General Election of 1885 which found the Liberal party in a state of crisis. Joseph Chamberlain put forward the so-called unauthorized program—his unofficial claim for the reversion of the leadership of the party, an assertion that he was the man of the future, the natural successor to Gladstone. That program frightened the Tories as well as the more conservative Liberals. Chamberlain was regarded by some as a wild revolutionary through a phrase in the program that "property must pay ransom for its security." This was probably far more a rhetorical device than a serious statement, although, in a sense, it was a precursor of the violent days ahead. The program, with its emphasis on social services, did differ from Gladstone's letter to his constituents, his official program, and it demanded the disestablishment of the Church of England in England itself. Chamberlain believed in land and local government reforms and tried to attract the rural voters, enfranchised in 1884, by putting forth a goal for them of "three acres and a cow." More dramatic in its language than in its intent, the program was far removed from any socialist scheme to remake the state and was essentially an appeal to the self-interest of the lower middle class.

Chamberlain's unauthorized program made the Liberals more popular as had the Act of 1884, which enfranchised rural workers. The Liberals were hurt, however, by Parnell's directions to his Irish supporters in England to vote for the Tories. Hence, the Liberal vote in their traditional places of support, London, Liverpool, and Manchester, was considerably lowered. The death of General Gordon also hurt. The votes balanced out so that the Liberals emerged with a majority of eighty-six over the Tories in the House of Commons. Considering the blows to their popularity and the expected swing from one party to another, the Liberals might well have been defeated. And their victory was tentative: the number of Home Rule M.P.s elected was also eighty-six, and hence gave Parnell a decisive grip on the House of Commons. Even before the election, however, Gladstone had become convinced that some form of Home Rule for Ireland was essential for both political and moral reasons. He felt that the Tories themselves were moving in that direction when Salisbury appointed Lord Carnarvon, known to be somewhat sympathetic to the Irish cause, as lord lieutenant in Ireland. Assuming the Tories might favor some form of semi-independence for Ireland, Parnell accordingly supported them at the election.

The Tories were also popular with the Irish because Salisbury during his brief government—from June 1885 until January 1886—had passed a strong Land Act in favor of the Irish tenant. Land acts came to represent the total Tory solution to the Irish problem—to kill with kindness—which they would follow in subsequent years. But they combined the land acts with increasingly stringent coercion acts to keep order. The two techniques helped keep Ireland comparatively quiet, if deeply discontented, until the Easter Rebellion of 1916.

In December 1885 Gladstone's son Herbert, a Liberal leader of some prominence in his own right, made a calculated political gaffe which misfired disastrously. This was the "Hawarden Kite," Hawarden being Gladstone's country house near Liverpool. The "kite" itself was flown in Leeds, which Herbert represented in Parliament. It was there that Herbert said to some editors, allegedly in confidence, that his father was now completely committed to Home Rule, a revelation which he thought would maintain his father's political initiative. The General Election had already taken place; it was too late for Parnell to order his followers to vote Liberal. The result of the "kite" was exactly the reverse of Herbert's intention. It locked Gladstone into a position that gave him little room to maneuver.

Gladstone had wished that the Tories would pass some form of Home Rule to cope with the situation in Ireland, but after the "kite" Salisbury quickly dropped the Irish issue back into Gladstone's lap. Like Gladstone, he recognized that the issue was explosive and would hurt whichever politician had to deal with it. To be the alternative government was the strong position at the moment. But when Parnell switched his support to Gladstone, Salisbury resigned, leaving Gladstone no choice but to form a government that would introduce some form of Home Rule designed to make Ireland semi-independent.

Gladstone introduced his bill in his great Home Rule Speech of April 8, 1886. It was one of the last of his great speeches and a noble and grand failure. He was in his late seventies, at the summit of his career, elevated and most alone. He had twelve years to live, and would lead one more ministry. The party that he had joined in 1859 and had led since 1867 was disintegrating about him, and many have held that despite its great victory in 1906 it was mortally wounded in 1886. Gladstone was a practical politician. What he proposed, he wished to pass. He thought that the moment was opportune. But also he felt a personal compulsion to do what he thought was right. This made him grating to lesser spirits, led him needlessly to alienate possible followers, to be stubborn and irritable, but at the same time it gave him moral grandeur and greatness. Both these characteristics can be sensed in the accounts of the immediate preliminaries —there had also been months of preparation over the details—leading up to the speech. His daughter Mary gave a fine picture of the occasion, the day of the Home Rule Speech, in her diary:

> *Punch* came and brought a great lump in my throat with its noble and pathetic cartoon and poem, *Sink or Swim.* . . . Excitement ran at its highest pitch as we threaded [through] the waiting crowds, and I found Helen, Agnes [her sisters], Mama all more or less quaking. . . . The rain came down in torrents, but above the storm and above the roar of London thrilled the cheers, all the way fr. D.[owning] St. we heard them. We stared and stared as if we'd never seen him before. . . . The starting to their feet of

the M.P.'s, the wonderful cheers. . . . The air tingled with excitement and emotion. . . . The most quiet, earnest pleading, explaining, analyzing, showing a mastery of detail and a grip and grasp such has never been surpassed. Not a sound was heard, not a cough even, only cheers breaking out here and there—a tremendous feat at his age. His voice never failed.

Gladstone has left his own account of the day in his diary:

The message came to me this morning: "Hold thou up thy goings in thy path, that my footsteps slip not." . . . Reflected much. Took a short drive. H. of C. 4 1/2–8 1/4. Extraordinary scenes outside the house and in. My speech, which I sometimes thought could never end, lasted nearly three and a half hours. Voice and strength and freedom were granted to me in a degree beyond what I could have hoped. But many a prayer had gone up for me, and not I believe in vain.

Gladstone felt his proposal of Home Rule was a necessary redress of grievances. It also marked a change in the political atmosphere in London and in the comparatively easygoing nature of those who ruled in their associations with one another. The veneer cracked for a while; but there was a realization that over an issue such as Ireland, politics really mattered. As John Morley, one of Gladstone's chief lieutenants on the Irish issue, remarked in his rich prose in a biography of his hero: "Great ladies purified their lists of the names of old intimates. Amiable magnates excluded from their dinner tables and their country houses once familiar friends who had fallen into the guilty heresy, and even harmless portraits of the heresiarch were sternly removed from the walls."

As for the speech itself, the immediate cause of all this excitement and the summation of Gladstone's commitment to Home Rule, it was, considering the expectation and fervor built up, extremely practical. This was an appropriate tactic, for Gladstone's aim was to demonstrate that Home Rule would work and would save England money. The speech united two of Gladstone's characteristics: the moral man and the careful spender. He did not concern himself with those problems of Ireland, land and order, that had in the past taken up so much of Parliament's time. They were subsumed within the great problem of giving Ireland self-government. He announced the double objective of his proposals. Characteristically, one was practical, for it would "liberate Parliament from the restraints under which of late years it has ineffectually struggled to perform the business of the country." And throughout the speech he played upon the fact that Irish business had taken so much time that it prevented much valuable domestic legislation from even coming to the fore. But his primary aim was idealistic: "The question [is] whether it is or is not possible to establish good and harmonious relations between Great Britain and Ireland on the footing of these free institutions to which Englishmen, Scotchmen, and Irishmen are alike unalterably attached." As he said in conclusion:

I ask the House to assist in the work which we have undertaken, and to believe that no trivial motive can have driven us to it—to assist us in this work which, we believe, will restore Parliament to its dignity and legislation to its free and unimpeded course. I ask you to stay that waste of public treasure which is involved in the present system of government and legislation in Ireland, and which is not a waste only, but which demoralizes while it exhausts. I ask you to show to Europe and to America that we, too, can face political problems which America twenty years ago faced, and which many countries in Europe have been called upon to face, and have not feared to deal with. . . . I ask that we should apply to Ireland that happy experience which we have gained in England and in Scotland, where the course of generations has now taught us, not as a dream or a theory, but as practice and as life, that the best and surest foundation we can find to build upon is the foundation afforded by the affections, by the convictions, and the will of the nation: and it is thus, by the decree of the Almighty, that we may be enabled to secure at once the social peace, the fame, the power, and the permanence of the Empire.

It was a noble bill and it was a pity that it was not put into practice. Gladstone played up its economic and efficient advantages in order to try to drain away from it the emotion that inevitably associated itself with Ireland. But the idea of Home Rule questioned too many firmly held beliefs: of religion, of the nature of the Parliament located in Westminster, of the empire, of the menaces of Catholicism, of the dangers to Ulster—Northern Irish—Protestantism. It also hurt too many vested interests, particularly of English landlords of Irish land. Gladstone had wanted to put into effect what he considered the most practical plan for coping with the Irish problems. And he wished to demonstrate that England was a nation which could redress grievances on a generous scale and was capable of acting justly from a position of strength. But Parliament would not agree; Home Rule was delayed until the twentieth century, when Irish independence came to birth in blood and civil war. On June 7, 1886, the bill was defeated by 343 to 313. Gladstone fell, and Salisbury became prime minister with his nephew Arthur Balfour, later called by some "Bloody Balfour," a surprisingly strong Irish secretary from 1887 to 1891. Gladstone had hoped that the scheme would pass, as much for its practical as for its idealistic nature; he was not the sort of politician who pledged himself to hopeless causes which would not work. His Home Rule Bill and the speech presenting it, with so much practicality and idealism, revealed the unity of Gladstone's character, a unity achieved by the fusing of his religious conception of the need to serve and to lead, with his sense of the capacity and obligation of the people of the United Kingdom to rule themselves.

Ninety-three Liberals had voted against the bill, thus marking the end of the historic Liberal party, which in fact had only existed in what might be called its "classic" form since 1868. Through loyalty quite a few Whig noblemen had remained in the party they saw as the inheritor of traditions of 1688, but others had steadily been moving to the right within the party, and some had already gone so far that they had crossed party lines. Another group which also had supported the Liberal party was beginning to change: the business interests. In the early nineteenth century businessmen had been, with few exceptions, radicals who were deeply opposed to the vested interests in their society, interests that were allegedly dedicated to preserving a dream of a rural England. But as the businessmen influenced their society and were able to participate more fully in its workings, they became less discontented and began to move to the right. Yet, like the Whigs, many were still loyal to the Liberals, and would not change unless they received a considerable jolt. Ireland was that jolt. The Marquess of Hartington led a great number of the Whigs out of the Liberal party; Joseph Chamberlain led a lesser number of radicals, who believed as he did in the need to maintain the union with Ireland. His defection was perhaps the most serious blow for the future of the party.

Ireland was a genuine issue, a legitimate reason to change party, but for some it also provided an excuse to take the step long implied when successful businessmen had changed their places of residence, their church, and had sent their sons to Public Schools. The great magnates had rather enjoyed being in the party of the left, over against the dull squires, but what they considered an attack on property, and their estates in Ireland, was more than they could tolerate. The two factions came together as an independent party that eventually became part of the Conservative party: the Liberal Unionists—Liberal for their past and Unionist for their belief that the union must be maintained. One might say that Gladstone maintained the Liberal spirit but killed the Liberal party, although it was in power twice again, weakly from 1892 to 1895 and in a last great spurt of strength in 1906.

Parnell's subsequent career was an example of the public role of respectability in Victorian politics. He triumphed over a public attack, but private scandal finished his career. Early in 1887 *The Times*, in its magisterial way, attacked Parnell in a series of articles entitled "Parnellism and Crime." There it was stated that he had been directly involved in the assassination of Cavendish and Burke in 1882. Parnell denied the allegation vehemently and demanded an investigation. In 1890 that investigation was completed; the letters from Parnell on which *The Times* had based its claim were proven to be forgeries. Parnell enjoyed a considerable upsurge of popularity. The English Establishment, with *The Times* in the forefront, had been determined to vilify him on what turned out to be false evidence, manufactured by a rogue.

Parnell's triumph was brief. The same year he was named co-respondent in a divorce case by Captain O'Shea, the husband of Parnell's long-time mistress. Captain O'Shea, who had made no objection when Parnell had been helpful to him, now ruined Parnell's career. Those "in the know" had been aware for some time of Mrs. O'Shea, but when the affair became

public knowledge the Irish Catholic bishops and the Nonconformist supporters were so shrill in reprimand that Gladstone felt he had no choice but
to disown Parnell. In the wake of Gladstone's action, the majority of Parnell's followers voted against him in a caucus of their party. His power
was over, and he led only a handful of followers until his death the next
year at the age of forty-five. He had dominated English politics for a
decade.

CHAPTER THREE

The Tory Triumph

The premierships of Disraeli and Gladstone mark the classic period of the alternating two-party system. At the end of the century there was a curious return to older forms of leadership—first, to two somewhat disdainful men who resented far more than Disraeli or Gladstone the pretensions of the new voters of 1867 and 1884. The Marquess of Salisbury, head of the Tory party, fitted the pattern of the great aristocrat who felt obligated, yet feigned reluctance, to participate in government. It is likely that many such persons ultimately enjoyed the wielding of power. Gladstone's successor to the leadership of the Liberal party was a man similar to Salisbury: the Earl of Rosebery, a Scottish peer of considerable wealth who added to his fortune by marrying a Rothschild. He appeared to take more interest in horse racing and literature than in politics.

The style of this sort of aristocrat was to regard doing one's "duty," fulfilling one's obligation to society, as a great bore. Certainly, both Rosebery and Salisbury had somewhat phlegmatic ways. Rosebery's immediate successor, Sir Henry Campbell-Bannerman, did not repress his natural good spirits, although he did not wish to work too hard and would not give up his annual visit to Marienbad. Asquith, the next Liberal leader, dedicated

England in Trouble

himself to appearing.unflappable. But no political leader could more obviously give the impression of being langorous than Salisbury's successor, another member of the so-called Hotel Cecil, Arthur Balfour, Salisbury's nephew. He hid within his bored and lengthy looks, so frequently to be caricatured by Max Beerbohm, a hard, relentless will, most vividly demonstrated when he was secretary for Ireland after 1886.

A certain sense of England's coming to the end of her period of greatness was evident in Salisbury's relish in dealing with China: he regarded both empires as great nations in a state of decline and both as approaching senility. It was a style that a great power such as England felt it could afford. But Salisbury could not have been such a successful politician if he had been completely taken in by his own pose.

Perhaps it would be helpful in understanding how English politics works to look briefly at the background of Robert Gascoyne-Cecil, the Marquess of Salisbury. The name itself is indicative. The "Cecil" suggests accurately that the Marquess is a descendant of the second son of William Cecil, Lord Burghley, Elizabeth I's chief minister. This family had been prominent for a long time, although between the sons of the great Burghley who flourished in the early seventeenth century and the Tory prime minister it had been comparatively quiescent, politically. Salisbury's family name was hyphenated: Gascoyne-Cecil. This suggests that an ancestor had married into a wealthy family called Gascoyne, who insisted on a preservation of the family name as a price for the further riches they brought to a noble house. And, in fact, the Gascoynes were an extremely rich family, who had made their money from brewing and medicine and whose heiress married Salisbury's grandfather. Salisbury himself was on a minimal allowance, for his father disapproved of his marriage to the daughter of a judge; it was a perfectly respectable marriage, but it was neither a grand nor a rich one. However, once his father died, Salisbury came into his inheritance and was a man of considerable wealth.

Education also informs about class position. Salisbury, as did Rosebery, went to the private school with the greatest social reputation, one of the so-called Public Schools: Eton. As education at home became less common for the aristocracy they went increasingly to such boarding schools. Parents in the upper middle class would also try to send their sons to these schools so that they might receive the patina, and sometimes the substance, of a classical education and could associate with such men as Salisbury. Boarding school education from the ages of approximately thirteen to eighteen was more important, socially, than university education, but attending the university as well had some social and educational significance. There were few universities in England: Oxford and Cambridge were the most famous, and the University of London, started in protest against the exclusiveness of the ancient universities, was growing in reputation. But even within Oxford and Cambridge, both divided into colleges, there were social gradations. The college at Oxford grandest socially was Christ Church; both Salisbury and Rosebery went there. Salisbury was not initially intended for a political career: he was the third son in the family. If a great family, such as the Cecils, were political, the assumption was that the eldest son would have a political career, the second son might go into the army or navy, a third into the Church, a fourth into the professions. The eldest son was expected to carry most of the honor and responsibility of a family, as he would receive, eventually, most of its property. Salisbury's children were heavily politicized, and his sons all went into politics. But Salisbury himself went into politics almost by coincidence; he took up the responsibility of the eldest son when his two elder brothers died, and he became his father's heir, which also meant that he used a "courtesy" title, Lord Cranborne. Even the constituency for which an M.P. sits can tell something about his career: Salisbury first sat in Parliament as a member of the borough of Stamford, a town dominated by the senior branch of the Cecil family, the Marquess of Exeter.

His family background and education helped to shape his career. At the same time, the special form of a man's career obviously owes much more to his own individual character. Salisbury was a somewhat strange man to be prime minister for thirteen and a half years at a time when it was becoming increasingly evident that a politician should play the political game in a way that would at least seem to appeal to a number of voters. Salisbury affected to be very disdainful of his job: one of his most famous remarks was about bishops, whose successors he had to recommend to the queen. He claimed that they died simply to vex him. The contrast between Salisbury, the political leader of his country, and those whom he allegedly led was made more dramatic with the increase of voters. The public became, in certain ways, more vociferous as it became more literate, assisted by the Education Act of 1870. Newspapers, which were now entering their great period of growth, had to expand their appeal. It has been claimed that in mid-century the public was more selective, but the high level of literary efforts then has been exaggerated. At mid-nineteenth century, as today, a small number of extremely influential publications, read by comparatively few, played a sometimes important role in the making of policy.

The rise in literacy affected politics and was one factor in the development of the Labour movement. But the level of discussion did not reach anything like that which the idealists might have hoped for; many newspaper readers were primarily concerned with amusement. In response, the newspapers tried to supply what was wanted and gradually began to stop printing the complete versions of speeches given by major and minor political leaders. There had been "catchy" journalism in earlier periods, but as journalism became a bigger industry, the demand for short and snappy paragraphs increased greatly. Alfred Harmsworth, later Lord Northcliffe, catered to this taste with such journals as *Answers* and *Tidbits*, containing bits of stray information. Harmsworth went into the daily newspaper business in 1894 when he acquired the *Evening News*. But his greatest achievement came two years later when he founded the *Daily Mail*, a popular half-penny paper that introduced a new sort of journalism to England. From 1908 until his death in 1922 he would even own that central paper of the English Establishment—*The Times*. The imperialism which the *Daily Mail* fostered and catered to helped provide and reflect a popular support which gave Salisbury a great deal of his power. But Salisbury was properly disdainful, remarking that the *Daily Mail* was a newspaper written by office boys for office boys.

Salisbury did maintain his country's international position in an increasingly hostile world, both despite and through the policy associated with his name, "Splendid Isolation." He did not want England to be tangled with affairs on the Continent if it could be avoided. He felt that ideally she should continue her role as arbiter, stepping in to adjust the balance if one nation or another became too powerful. But ever since the Franco-Prussian War of 1870 and the consequent growth of German power, England of necessity found herself paying less attention to the Continent and more to imperial concerns.

The great vehicle of English power was the navy. In 1889 the government passed the Navy Act, which set up the "two-power" standard: the navy pledged itself to being as strong as or stronger than any other two navies in the world combined. This naval commitment, and race, particularly after 1900 against Germany, continued up until the outbreak of the First World War. And there was also a growing fear of Germany as a trade rival, so that, at a time when it was becoming increasingly difficult to do so, England was determined to maintain her sense of industrial, financial, and military superiority over every other nation in the world.

Imperial feeling, seeing England as the hub of a great empire, was intensified through the queen's Jubilees—the fiftieth in 1887 and even more markedly at the sixtieth in 1897. The latter was a great festival of empire, an exotic family affair, as imperial representatives from all over the world gathered in London. In 1897 England controlled one-quarter of the land surface of the world. She would continue to expand into the twentieth century and would control even more land, but without the same imperial spirit.

At this period the Marxist analysis of economics and imperialism seemed particularly appropriate. Economic imperialism was the style of nations, and particularly of industrialists in South Africa. The power of an economic analysis was caught most effectively in the works of J. A. Hobson: *The Evolution of Modern Capitalism* (1894) and his more famous *Imperialism* (1902). The latter served as a basis of Lenin's argument that it was possible, if only for the short run, for a working class, such as the English proletariat, to survive economically—in a sense to be bought off—through the prosperity of empire. Certainly, something of the sort happened in England at the end of the nineteenth century. Although it is unlikely that much of the profits of empire and the extensive English investments elsewhere in the world went into the pockets of the English working class, the workers' economic levels did improve. Some of the money spread downward, and raw materials from the empire helped to keep some English industries going. There was a sense of uplift and excitement from the feeling that one belonged to the most powerful nation in the world. England's financial relationship to her empire, and even more her investments in the rest of the world, became the central sources of economic strength at the end of the nineteenth century. But she was losing ground as a manufacturing power, and her entrepreneurial and industrial imagination was weakening.

She was also losing her agricultural position. Toward the end of the century wheat, for instance, was one-quarter of the price it had been in 1850, and, in general, rental income from agriculture was down to one-third of what it had been at mid-century. Droughts and wet rot at home, and cheap wheat from America, hurt her agriculture. England compensated for her weakening position in industry and agriculture through vast profits in the carrying trade—shipping—and from investments abroad. To a certain degree, she financed, particularly in America, the industrial development that competed with her own domestic enterprises. There was no direction of investment, and a merchant banker in the City of London would not worry about the effects of his investments abroad on industry in the North of England unless he happened to be an investor there as well. Money was put in the empire and also in the "informal empire," such as South America, America, Russia, and elsewhere. Money made money, and the City of London was the hub of this enterprise. London took an increasingly imperial position not only in the world but in England itself. For this and other reasons the quality and extent of provincial life and culture began to decline.

This development was even reflected in the organization of the government of London. The London County Council became increasingly important, and London lost some of its character as a collection of little villages. At the same time, through the Local Government Acts of 1888 and 1894, local government throughout the country was made somewhat more democratic.

The end of the century in England can also be seen as the last period in the century when there was some unity in community thought, and a willingness by many to take direction in politics and thought from above. There had been a coming together of what could be called the private and public voices. Such feeling was associated with the thoughts and poems of Alfred Tennyson, the poet laureate (the official muse of England, a court post involving £100 a year and "one terse of canary Spanish wyne yearely"); the ideas and politics of William Gladstone—that there is no real difference between private and public life; and Victoria's approach to politics, a merging of England's and her family's concerns. These feelings about life and society still had a hold in the 1890s. But from 1867 on, and reinforced by the Irish events of 1886, there had been a growing belief among Victorian intellectuals that a unified world of ideas and feelings was no longer possible. There was a spread of aestheticism, a distancing from society, associated with the Pre-Raphaelite brotherhood—the most famous being the painter Rossetti—finally culminating in the rich dank flower of the drawings of Aubrey Beardsley and in the life and some of the writing of Oscar Wilde, whose plays can be seen as an extraordinarily witty commentary on the amusing dead end that English society appeared to have reached. In the nineties the intellectual and artist was no longer so willing to serve society as he had been in the 1850s. There was a decreased sense of a vigorous reading public. The large public that enjoyed the *Daily Mail* was clearly of a different character from that smaller reading public, however jumbled its tastes may have been, of earlier in the century.

Salisbury was prime minister for most of the 1890s. The mood in England was marked by a bluster which, in retrospect, indicated the beginnings of some loss of confidence but, at the same time, gave evidence of remnants of an extraordinary assurance. International rivalry impinged to an increasing degree on England, and class rivalry grew within the country, as in the great dock strike of 1889. The importance of that strike as marking the development of a new mass unionism has perhaps been exaggerated, but it can be taken to stand for the workers' growing concern about their situation and the concern, in reaction, of the middle and upper classes.

Salisbury and the Tories fell from power in 1892. Gladstone had his last, his fourth, ministry from 1892 to 1894. He only had a majority of forty and could not accomplish much in the way of legislation. Again, he was committed to Home Rule; again, it was defeated. The various other measures to which he had pledged himself somewhat reluctantly through the Newcastle Program of 1891 could not get off the ground. The National Liberal Federation had devised the program, and many of the Liberal leaders, Gladstone among them, had paid lip service to it. It was a ragbag which tried to attract the ill-assorted components of the Liberal party: the Celtic fringe (Scotland, Wales, Ireland), others on the left, and Nonconformists. The measures it advocated might pass the House of Commons—and some did—but they would be reversed by the increasingly Conservative House of Lords. The Liberals did not feel they were strong enough effectively to resist this situation. Gladstone resigned in distress in 1894, in part because of the failure yet again to pass Home Rule but also because he opposed increased navy spending. He was against an increase in "militarism," which he called "mad and drunk." The Earl of Rosebery, who was very much like Salisbury, became prime minister, winning out over the more flamboyant and unreliable Sir William Harcourt. Harcourt had been chancellor of the Exchequer, while Rosebery had been foreign secretary. Now the two leaders of both parties, in a period when England was supposedly moving toward a more far-reaching democracy, were great magnates. Although not of the purest Whig variety, they were the sort of men who would have led political parties at the beginning of the century and who shared, to a considerable extent, similar feelings about their society.

Rosebery introduced the concept of continuity of foreign policy, which rather bedeviled the party of the left in the future. Did this mean that it was unpatriotic to criticize foreign policy? Certainly, this had not been true in the past, most notably in the differences between Gladstone and Disraeli. Rosebery, officially the leader of the Liberals, through introducing this concept gave credence to the idea that, somehow, the Tories, his opposition, were the more patriotic party. Ironically, it had been Rosebery, when younger, who had invited Gladstone to contest Midlothian in which the main issue was Gladstone's attack on the government's foreign policy. For Gladstone, "Beaconsfieldism"—his scornful name, coined from Disraeli's title, for the Tory support for Turkey—had not been national policy. He had more respect for Salisbury than for Disraeli, whose policy was probably a compromise between the two traditions. As a further irony

Lord Rosebery in 1896.
Cartoon by Max Beerbohm.
(Courtesy of Mrs. Eva
Reichmann.)

—and perhaps it provided the experience from which Rosebery derived his doctrine—Gladstone's second ministry had been brought down as a consequence of being enmeshed in English commitments abroad.

Rosebery, like England herself, was a triumph of wealth and position and intelligence, but he was too diffident, his party too weak, and his country somewhat too assured to make best use of the situation. The most important domestic development of his very brief Liberal government was the introduction in 1894 by Harcourt of "death duties." This new tax was to be paid on the total value of an inherited estate. Death duties severely challenged the powerful concept of maintaining and increasing the family estate. The duties which Harcourt actually introduced came to less than the assorted taxes that had existed before. Nevertheless, the previous taxes on a man's death had been incidental; they had no principle behind them. Death duties were a unified and expandable tax, a deliberate challenge to the rich! The first application may have been comparatively insignificant, but it presented a notable opportunity for expansion. (At present, death duties can claim most of a man's estate, although the rich in England have devised various ways of getting around the taxes.)

The Liberal government fell over a debate on cordite, a question of military preparedness, to which the Tories were more firmly bound. The Tory imperial stance, along with a belief in maintaining an immense naval position, seemed to suggest that old-style Liberalism—Peace, Retrenchment, and Reform—had had its day and that the Tories would rule the country almost permanently.

The Tory government, again led by Salisbury, with Chamberlain as colonial secretary the most important member of the cabinet, did not do

Map of the British Empire in 1897.

much in the way of social legislation. In 1897 Chamberlain fulfilled an earlier pledge and passed the Workmen's Compensation Act, the only significant social legislation of the government. Chamberlain's evolution fits into a pattern of concern for empire. He had been a great radical and continued to be, in some aspects, even after he left the Liberal party over the Irish question. But he became increasingly interested in the empire. When the government was formed in 1895, he surprised the political world

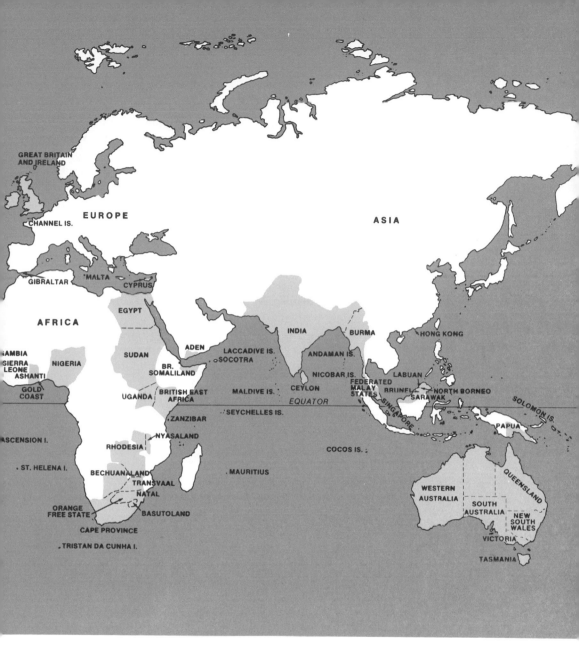

by taking the colonial secretaryship. Such a major figure, by going into that office, emphasized the importance of the colonies. He wished to work toward stronger economic ties between the colonies and the mother country, feeling that the empire should be drawn closer in terms of trade and that tariffs might be used against other nations. England, however, was still committed to free trade, which was thought to explain her continuing wealth and power. To go against that explanation was regarded as heresy, particularly by the Liberal Unionists who had left the Liberal party over Ireland but were still committed to free trade. This fight greatly weakened the Tory party early in the next century.

The empire was changing in a peaceable manner. Australia and New Zealand were moving rapidly toward self-government. In Canada a compromise was achieved between the French and the English populations. India was a special case. There was some talk of self-government but it was theoretical, and the first tentative steps would not be made in that direction until the Morley-Minto reforms of 1909.

In the 1890s the most significant imperial clash was in South Africa. According to the Treaty of Pretoria of 1881 and the Convention of London of 1884 the Boers had been granted self-government with some vague supervision by England, particularly in foreign affairs. The discovery of diamonds in 1867 and the discovery of gold in 1886 made the English covetous and anxious to participate in the Boer government. The Jameson raid in 1895 was an abortive and violent step in this direction. The raid had had the blessing of Cecil Rhodes, the prime minister of the Cape Colony and the dominant financial figure of the area, who had made millions of pounds from diamonds and gold. Captain Jameson, an English officer and Rhodes's personal physican, made an attempt with a handful of men to take over the Transvaal. The raid was supposed to be assisted by an internal rising, which did not materialize. Rhodes, fearing failure, had tried to stop it at the last moment. The raid, ending in fiasco, discredited Rhodes as a politician, but his policy was pursued, although slightly more subtly, by the colonial secretary, Chamberlain, and Alfred Milner, the great "proconsul" who went to South Africa as governor-general in 1897. The tensions between the Boers and the English continued to mount over the issues of whether London, and the governor-general, had the final say over Boer policies and over the right to vote of the so-called uitlanders, mostly English, in the Transvaal. Milner and Paul Kruger, the president of the Transvaal, attempted to iron out their differences in June of 1899, but both sides were adamant, and war broke out in October. It was a war relished by other European countries: they saw the dominant European power beleaguered and driven to distraction. The war heightened England's sense of isolation and also her feeling of internal disunity. To some, it seemed to abandon principles that England had attempted to stand for, most particularly as enunciated by Gladstone at the time of the Midlothian campaign. A considerable segment of public opinion, including a large group within the Liberal party, disapproved of a war dedicated to asserting English control without a clear issue of principle.

There were strategic worries about the Cape as well as pride and money at stake. The army's lack of preparedness prolonged the war. As was so frequently the case, the army was one war behind. It had learned from the lessons of the Crimean War, but it was not prepared for the Boers' brilliant strategy of movement, so that while the English might take town after town, they were still harassed and attacked by guerrillas. Not until 1902 did Kitchener, who had revenged the murder of Gordon and contained the expansionist hopes of the French at Fashoda in 1898, and Roberts, the hero of India, manage to subdue the Boers.

The issue of attitudes toward the blacks was another problem, but it would largely be an issue—indeed, a whirlwind—of the future. English tactics during the period of guerrilla warfare which followed the fall of Johannesburg—at which point the war should have ended—were harsh and unsparing. Kitchener built blockhouses to assist in clearing the countryside of hostile forces. The army turned families out of farmhouses and then destroyed the houses so that the guerrillas could not use them. The evicted Boers, mostly women and children, were placed into what came to be called concentration camps. Although the army considered these tactics necessary, they horrified many at home, especially as news and rumors filtered back about the camps where, through disease and neglect, approximately 20,000 of the 120,000 imprisoned women and children died. Within the Liberal party there was a profound split over attitudes toward the war. Although Lord Rosebery, Asquith, and quite a few of the younger and more

Map of South Africa at the time of the Boer War.

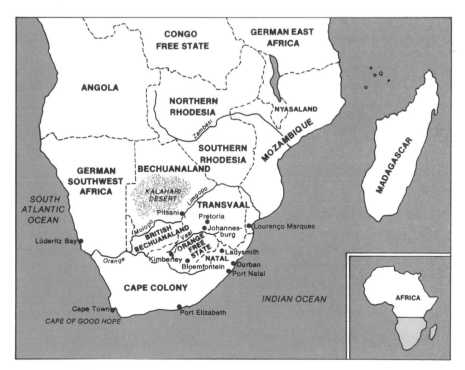

promising leaders felt that the government should be supported, others, like David Lloyd George, an up-and-coming Welshman of great dash, believed that the Boers were right in defending their country, despite their previous agreements with the English. At the same time, the Tories were not above exploiting the Boer War politically. In the General Election of 1900, the so-called Khaki election, the Tory campaign suggested that to vote for the Liberals—some of whom did have doubts about the war—was treasonous. The Tories managed to win 402 of the seats in the Commons in this election, and the Liberals only 184.

Sir Henry Campbell-Bannerman, who emerged as leader of the Liberal party in 1899, tried to straddle the fence in his own party. In a famous speech, however, he branded the use of concentration camps as "methods of barbarism." He was heavily attacked at the time; later, it was felt, with considerable justification, that such a statement expressed the true spirit of Liberalism; indeed, that it said something about the nature of English civilization. When the Liberals came to power in 1905, they negotiated a final settlement with the Boers. Traditional English principles of the right to self-government were asserted, but peace was made with the Boers through a tacit agreement that the English would not interfere with their treatment of blacks. The English, although not necessarily, might ultimately have been more liberal toward the native population than the Boers, but they did not feel the same economic pressures, reinforced by the doctrines of the Dutch Reformed Church, as the Boers did, and so were not as disposed automatically to dismiss the idea of self-government for all who lived in South Africa.

The most important immediate effect of the war was that it led England, which had come to feel increasingly isolated internationally, into a system of alliances, beginning with the Anglo-Japanese agreement of 1902. That was a limited agreement, but it marked the moment when England no longer regarded herself as the arbiter of the world, but rather as a power who had actively to seek allies. A more important step in this direction, but an informal one, took place in 1904: the Anglo-French Entente. This was an extraordinary achievement, considering that the two countries had been on the verge of war when French and English military missions met in Fashoda in 1898. In a small way the path to the agreement was smoothed through the francophile feelings of Edward VII, who had been the King of England since 1901. Far more important were the hardheaded negotiations of two governments convinced that they might have to make common cause against Germany. The heart of the entente was its settlement of outstanding colonial differences. England would allow France to have a free hand in Morocco and France would do the same for England in Egypt, where English policy had been hampered by French and German interference. The entente prevented Germany from trying to make trouble in Egypt and Morocco. It also ended a long tradition of enmity between the two countries. The further effect of the agreement was that Germany now tended to be thought of as the enemy, despite a strong tradition of "Anglo-Saxon" emotional ties with her.

The Labour Party

In the years before the First World War there was a growing feeling that neither of the two parties—the Liberal party, so racked by dissension and the Unionist party, potentially divided over free trade—really cared about the working man. And it is true that neither party did much for the workers in terms of social legislation. Except for a young group of Liberals— among them Herbert Samuel, Charles Masterman, and Charles Trevelyan —the Liberal party seemed to have abandoned, at least in theory, any particular steps it might take for the oppressed in England. Yet beyond official circles, but still largely within the upper and middle classes, various discontented intellectuals were eager to do something to improve the quality of English life—a notable example was William Morris, poet, socialist, and furniture maker. This strain of discontent and idealism contributed to the making of the Labour movement and the Labour party. Also contributing to that development was a hardheaded investigating tradition. It was most vividly represented by Beatrice Potter, the daughter of a wealthy railroad man, who was one of the prime forces in the Fabian Society, a "ginger group" that believed in planning and socialism. Beatrice Potter married Sidney Webb in 1892, and the two made a great contribution to social investigation and social reform in twentieth-century England.

Earlier, Beatrice Potter had been involved in the important survey into the condition of London launched by her cousin Charles Booth, a wealthy shipowner; the survey was published in a series of twenty-five volumes from 1891 to 1903. Booth started his investigation from an optimistic premise: he could not accept the claim that 20 to 25 percent of those in London lived in dire poverty. Booth believed in capitalism, and his survey did not make him a convert to socialism, but he did discover, on the basis of a careful scientific investigation of monumental proportions, that the original figure was an underestimate by 5 to 10 percent. This sort of information (although it might not convert a Charles Booth to a new way of political thinking) made many feel that something must be wrong with England's economic system. It was a country that could dominate the outside world but not take care of its own inhabitants. A similar investigation by B. Seebohm Rowntree of York, published at the end of the century, reached a similar conclusion. Rowntree, too, was wealthy, a member of the great Quaker cousinhood of chocolate-makers: Rowntrees, Frys, and Cadburys. These were men who had the leisure and money to make such investigations, and to concern themselves with the social world about them.

There was now a new sense, among some of the men of this class, that perhaps their profits came out of misery. The information gathered by the Booths and the Rowntrees, as well as by the government through its extensive royal commissions and select committees, provided considerable material for the Fabian Society and others in their campaigns for a change in society. Leading figures of the time joined the Fabians: George Bernard Shaw, the great playwright; Graham Wallas, an important theoretician who was trying to form a new theory of politics, most particularly in his *Human Nature in Politics* (1908); and for a while H. G. Wells, the novelist, before he turned on the Webbs and satirized them in *The New Machiavelli* (1911).

Another group who played a significant role in the making of the Labour party was comprised of the self-taught and political workers. Here the most eminent example was Keir Hardie, a poor Scot who had trained himself through preaching to speak to large crowds. He seethed with indignation at the paradox of an England so rich yet with so many of its people in dire poverty. He had little patience for the niceties of society, the conventions which practically everyone accepted. Hardie created a considerable stir in 1892 when he was elected to Parliament and, rather than wearing the ordinary frock coat and top hat, appeared in that sacred precinct in a tweed suit and cap. For some Englishmen this meant "the beginning of the end"; as Thomas Carlyle has pointed out, clothes reveal a great deal about the conventions of a civilization.

The mass support for the Labour party eventually came from the unions. There had been new developments in union history at the end of the century, hastened on by the great London dock strike of 1889, which can be taken as the beginning of mass unionism. But the unions of skilled workers continued to dominate organized labor. Laws created in the 1870s had protected unions from being sued for damages caused by strikes, a protection against the old conspiracy charges which had undone unions earlier in the century. But the courts were undercutting these laws. The older unions—specifically, the Amalgamated Society of Engineers and other rich unions—were worried about their position, particularly as some employers were being less cooperative than in the past. These unions accepted the need to turn toward political action to protect themselves.

Dissident intellectuals and working-class politicians combined to form the Independent Labour party in 1893. There was a characteristic fight at the founding conference: should the new group be called the Independent Socialist party or the Independent Labour party? The latter name won, but at the same time the party committed itself to socialism. The old Lib-Lab compromise—labor unions supporting Liberal M.P.s—was no longer satisfactory. Finally, in 1900 a meeting was called, including a goodly representation of union strength, to form the Labour Representation Committee. Now unions would cooperate in trying to elect members of Parliament committed to the labor cause. The I.L.P. belonged to this new group that would become the Labour party in 1906, but it also continued its independent existence. The political labor movement was launched.

The Beginning of the Twentieth Century

The world of the nineteenth century began to end with the death of its poet laureate, Alfred, Lord Tennyson in 1892, drew closer to its end with the death of William Gladstone in 1898, and finally, irretrievably ended with the death of Queen Victoria herself in January 1901. These deaths were symbolic of the end of that combination of the private and public world, the private and public voice, that had been evidenced in Tennyson and Gladstone and, in a less sophisticated way, in Victoria herself. Tennyson felt that his own private emotions and the emotions of the standard Victorian were more or less the same. Gladstone felt that politics was his own personal code of morality writ large. Victoria felt that the world and England were just a larger extension of her family. In many European monarchies, that was precisely true. By the time of her death most of the crowned heads of Europe were Victoria's grandchildren.

Victoria was tactful in her death. There had been a dispute in *The Times*, the home of such disputes, over the issue of when the twentieth century begins: January 1, 1900, or January 1, 1901. Victoria waited until the nineteenth century was absolutely and indubitably over, and on January 22, 1901, she died, supported in the last two and a half hours of her life by the one good arm of her grandson, Kaiser Wilhelm II. Her death was the end of the nineteenth-century version of a united monarchical family which still possessed some few remnants of its power and some European sense. To the kaiser and others in her family, and also to many an Englishman, she had been both Grandmama and V.R.I., Victoria, Queen and Empress. With Albert and Victoria, the German connection had been very strong. Edward VII, her son and successor, had a heavy German accent, but he enjoyed the high life in Paris more than visits to his nephew, the kaiser. Even the family name of the royal family was German—Saxe-Coburg-Gotha—until 1917, when the family shed all its German titles and changed the family name to Windsor, a concocted name derived from the castle.

Victoria can easily be taken to represent the period that bears her name despite the many variations which had characterized the years since 1837. She stood for the proprieties of the age—the belief in probity, in family, in morality. Salisbury, the prime minister at the time of her death, in his eulogy of Victoria in the House of Lords, pointed out that she stood for what the man in the street thought—at least the man in the street in a

Edward VII and Queen Alexandra, 1905. (Radio Times Hulton Picture Library.)

middle-class suburb. A sense of her death is captured in the remark of Sir Almeric Fitzroy, the clerk of the privy council (when a monarch dies, the privy council—officially, the "trusty" advisers of the Crown—gathers together to proclaim the new king):

> The heart that beat so true to England and to duty for eighty years is still forever. It is not only the passing of a great personality, the disappearance of a potent influence, the sudden and irreparable rupture of a relation that has bound things to a common center for so long. It is a change from era to era; it is as if the standards of comparison, the criteria of taste, the very categories of thought which have regulated the judgments and molded the desires of two generations were abruptly swept into the limbo of the past.

Edward was certainly not a worthy successor of his mother. In large part, that was her fault: because she had felt (incorrectly) that he had been a partial cause of his father's death in 1861, she had not given him any training in how to be a king. He came to the throne at the age of fifty-nine with next to no experience: his chief interest was in ceremonials—he was a stickler for the wearing of the right uniform at the right time. Temperamentally, he was sympathetic to the Tories, but he had a firm sense of how a constitutional monarch should behave.

Edward seemed to be a man who believed more in the forms of monarchy than in its substance. He tried to redesign the monarchy for the twentieth century. He redecorated his palaces. As he remarked, rolling his "r's" in the German manner, he did not know very much about "arrt" but he knew a great deal about "arrrrangement." There was much arranging to be done at Windsor Castle and at Buckingham Palace—both residences had hardly been touched since Albert's death; in fact, in both palaces Albert's rooms had been preserved as they were at the time of his death.

There was no change of government when Edward came to the throne. Salisbury continued as prime minister until he resigned in July 1902 in favor of his nephew, Arthur Balfour.

Some sense of the nature of England's rulers can be gained by considering the composition of the Tory cabinet at this time, as well as the biographies of its members. The biographical details, often trivial, taken together are curiously illuminating: they offer a profile in tradition and privilege. The Tory cabinet had twenty-one members, including Salisbury. Balfour's mother was Salisbury's sister, and Balfour's family was Scottish and extremely rich. His grandfather had made a fortune in India; when he came back to Scotland he married the daughter of a prominent Scottish peer. This situation was indicative of all of the Tory cabinet, all of whom were wealthy. Only one had made his fortune himself: Joseph Chamberlain, who had come over from the Liberal party. The grandest figures in the cabinet were those who had been Whigs, most notably the Duke of Devonshire, formerly the Marquess of Hartington. He had an income of something like £130,000 a year, at a time when income tax was practically nonexistent, and numerous estates, of which the most famous was Chatsworth in Derbyshire. When his father died, he succeeded to the appointed posts of lord lieutenant of the County of Derbyshire and chancellor of the University of Cambridge.

The other great Whig leader in the Tory party at the time was the Marquess of Lansdowne, the foreign secretary. He, too, was extremely wealthy and owned a considerable amount of land, both in the South of England in Wiltshire and in Ireland; his land in Ireland had been one of the motivating forces behind his change of party. Also, it should be noted, he went to Balliol College, Oxford, as an undergraduate. Balliol was famous for the number of its students who became prominent politicians and civil servants. Benjamin Jowett, its master, a translator of Plato and a liberal churchman, believed that aristocrats such as Lansdowne should become politicians and also that bright, if poorer, boys such as Asquith, the leader of the Liberals, should be influenced at Balliol to undertake a political career. Both Jowett and T. H. Green, the Hegelian philosopher and tutor at Balliol who believed that the state should be more concerned with social service, had an important influence on a considerable number of young men who, later in life, did "some service to the state."

Of the twenty-one members of the Tory cabinet of 1902, seventeen had gone to Public Schools. Ten of the seventeen had gone to Eton. Most of the cabinet had aristocratic and rural backgrounds. This was all in the old-fashioned style that one would expect from the Tory leadership. Seventeen members of the cabinet had also gone to university; none to provincial universities or to the University of London. Twelve had gone to Oxford—Oxford tends to be more closely allied with the powers-that-be than Cambridge—and five to Cambridge.

In contrast to the Liberals, Tories tended to enter politics at a younger age. Most of Salisbury's cabinet started their political careers in their twenties, as they were on the whole free of financial worries. (M.P.s were not paid until 1911.)

Tories tended to believe very strongly in the monarchy and the Church of England. They were almost inevitably Anglicans. They were not believers in democracy, even if they accepted it as an unfortunate necessity. They saw their role as trying to work with democracy in a way that would preserve their power to run the state as they thought best, which, because of the ideal of service and responsibility generally drilled into the English upper classes, they believed accorded with the best interests of all.

Chamberlain was the exception in the cabinet, a new style of radical businessman in the Tory party. But his radicalism was being superseded by a much less imaginative businessman's approach to politics, whose chief representative, Andrew Bonar Law, a Glasgow iron merchant, would become leader of the party in 1911. Salisbury handed over the prime ministership to Balfour, who had earlier distinguished himself as a brilliant and firm administrator in Ireland in the 1880s, but who proved to be quite unsuccessful as prime minister. He was an eminent philosopher, and his object in that discipline was to attempt to achieve a belief in God despite manifest doubts. His politics were equally insecure: his object was to rid himself of as many troublemakers as possible, particularly over the issue of free trade, and still have a government.

Free trade was a main article of faith in the Liberal creed. Many of the Liberal Unionists who had left the Liberals in 1886 still firmly believed in it, although Chamberlain himself was becoming increasingly convinced that there should be tariffs and an Imperial Customs Union. The dominions favored this for largely selfish motives, despite their considerable sentimental attachment to the mother country. They favored excluding foreign goods from England, but they were not sure that they saw their way to favoring English goods in their own countries.

The Duke of Devonshire, with Chamberlain the other great Liberal Unionist leader, firmly believed in free trade. Devonshire was in politics out of a sense of obligation—noblesse oblige. He was a poor speaker and phlegmatic in temperament, but he was a "rock" in his convictions. Balfour's idea was to push Chamberlain out of the cabinet but to keep his support through having his son Austen stay as chancellor of the Exchequer. Balfour also hoped that he could keep Devonshire unexcited. But Devonshire, who would not bother to rouse himself unless he felt that the principle of free trade was seriously endangered, finally decided that Balfour was playing fast and loose with this sacred principle, and in December 1903 he resigned from the cabinet. Chamberlain had also resigned over the issue of free trade versus, as it was called, fair trade. The issue would be the single most important cause of the great defeat of the Tory party in the General Election in January 1906.

Balfour's most notable achievements were the Education Act of 1902, the entente with France in 1904, and the establishment of the Committee of Imperial Defense in the same year.

The previous great stride forward in education had been the Act of 1870. It had moved toward a guaranteed primary education for all, although not until 1891 was that education made available to all those who could not afford to pay fees. The Act of 1902 established the basis for a free secondary education. But it was deeply offensive to Nonconformist supporters of the Liberal cause, who saw it as further strengthening the Church of England. As we have seen, in 1870 those schools run by the Church of England that were deemed to be functioning well were left comparatively free of government supervision (they were inspected) even though they received government subsidies. New schools were established in areas where they were needed, and these were under the supervision of local authorities. The 1902 act moved all schools, new and old, under the jurisdiction of local government. It did not, however, abolish the religious affiliation of the schools already established on a sectarian basis; in almost all cases, these were Anglican. Nonconformists felt, with some justification, that this favored to an excessive degree Anglican religious education. Parents could remove their child from the religion class but being run by a particular religious, sectarian group shaped the spirit of a school.

The 1902 act was firmly backed by the Fabians, who saw it as good administrative practice. They were perfectly willing to cooperate when the Tories took what the Fabians considered right actions. The act caused considerable distress: many Nonconformists resisted it by refusing to pay rates (local taxes) that might go to support a sectarian school. The bailiffs would then seize their furniture to be sold to meet the unpaid taxes. This spirit of resistance was an important factor leading to the Liberal victory of 1906. Yet the act was consistent with the practice in England of the state coming to the support of private enterprise, when such an enterprise had demonstrated its usefulness.

Another great achievement of Balfour's government was the establishment of the Committee on Imperial Defense, which came into existence because of the inefficiencies and failures of the army during the Boer War. Despite the reforms that had been made after the Crimean War, it was felt that the army was still too amateur and that staff planning was not sufficiently worked out. Much of the army establishment continued to regard its fundamental loyalty as being to the Crown and not to the civilian government. This problem had been attacked in the 1890s when Campbell-Bannerman, the secretary of state for war, had finally managed to curtail the power of the queen's cousin, the Duke of Cambridge, as commander-in-chief of the army. The committee was a further step along these lines and helped England's military preparedness, as did the pledges of friendship with Japan and France, and with Russia in 1907. On the other hand, these steps meant that England was now more likely to be involved in international difficulties.

The Tories had been in power since 1895, having easily defeated the divided Liberals in that year. They reinforced themselves in the election of 1900 and held on after 1903 in the face of internal dissension and continual defeats in by-elections. Having lost parts of both wings of the Liberal Unionists, Balfour finally resigned in December 1905. He persuaded Campbell-Bannerman to form a government before a General Election, a clever move on his part as it meant that he did not have to go to the country quite in the position of a head of government who had to defend a long and unsuccessful record. It was also felt that Campbell-Bannerman would be more moderate in forming a government if he had to do so before an electoral campaign, when his concern would be to offend the fewest number of people. He had been regarded as a weak figure and a temporary leader. True, he demonstrated more backbone than expected in taking a stand against the concentration camps in Africa, while he was trying within his own party to bridge the gap between the anti- and pro-Boers. In fact, he was a strong-minded Scotsman. He was most successful in outfoxing Lord Rosebery, the previous Liberal prime minister who now broke completely with his party over Ireland. Campbell-Bannerman was also particularly successful in coping with the three bright young men of the Liberal party—Asquith, Grey, and Haldane. They had made an informal agreement, the Regulas Pact—named after a stream of which Grey, a fanatical fisherman, was particularly fond—that none of them would go into the government unless Campbell-Bannerman was willing to take a peerage and lead from the House of Lords, in short, to be little more than a titular leader. Campbell-Bannerman refused to give in, and cleverly playing on the emotions and the ambitions of the three persuaded them all to come into the government.

It might be useful to consider in a little more detail the government Campbell-Bannerman formed at this time, particularly in contrast to the Tory government of 1902. Campbell-Bannerman himself makes a considerable contrast, not so much in wealth but in terms of social position, with the leaders of the Tories. As with Gascoyne-Cecil, his name represents the coming together of two fortunes, although in his case they were both commercial and northern, rather than noble, professional, and southern. There were twenty-one men in his cabinet as well. In both cabinets it was essential to have a certain number of leaders in the House of Lords. There were six peers in both cabinets, but there was a striking contrast between the peers who had served Salisbury and Balfour and those who were in the Liberal cabinet. Great wealth and position marked the Tory peers, such as Devonshire and Lansdowne, as well as the Marquess of Londonderry, a descendant of Castlereagh, a coal-mine owner of great wealth. In the Liberal cabinet there were peers of necessity, such as the lord chancellor, the head of the legal system in England and the equivalent of the speaker in the House of Lords. In the Tory cabinet the lord chancellor had been Lord Halsbury, an encrusted Tory who would lead the fight to preserve the powers of the House of Lords in a few years' time. In the Liberal cabinet the chancellor was Lord Loreburn, a radical, a very active pro-Boer, a Scotsman who went to the House of Lords because of the office and not out of desire. The Liberal cabinet had representatives of the Celtic fringe: Liberal support came more from Scotland, Wales, and Ireland than from the richer parts of England.

One of the most important peers in the Liberal cabinet was the Marquess of Crewe, an immensely wealthy man in his own right, whose father was the Victorian poet and gadabout Richard Monckton-Milnes, Lord Houghton. The son was a more respectable character than his father, and when he came into his inheritance he disposed of his father's famous collection of pornography. The Marquess of Ripon was another Liberal peer in the cabinet: he had been an active Liberal for decades. (He had been born in 10 Downing Street when his father, Viscount Goderich, had been briefly and ineffectually prime minister.) Ripon was an unusual peer, however, who was regarded as a traitor to his class. In his youth he had been a Christian Socialist, then a convert to Roman Catholicism. Old Catholic families, the so-called recusants, had a certain standing and respect and were regarded as having loyally "kept the faith." But to become a Catholic was frowned upon. Ripon had also been viceroy of India, and in that post he had shocked English opinion because he had made it possible in certain cases for Indian judges to sit in judgments on Europeans.

Other peers in the Liberal cabinet were, on the whole, not as rich or as well-established as their Tory equivalents. There was Lord Tweedmouth, whose money came from beer. He was married to a sister of Lord Randolph Churchill, and his mind, like that of his deceased brother-in-law, was beginning to go. Then there was Lord Elgin, a Scottish peer, whose chief claim to fame was that his ancestor had acquired (stolen) the statues from the Parthenon and brought them to England.

The most revolutionary step in cabinet-making was the appointment of John Burns as president of the Local Government Board. Burns had been the leader, with another socialist, Tom Mann, of the dock strike in 1889. He was the first working man to sit in a cabinet. Ironically, he became a prisoner of his civil servants, and in any case the board, despite its title, could not do very much toward social improvement. An upper- or middle-class radical, less worried about his social position, might well have accomplished more.

Sir Edward Grey became foreign secretary in the Liberal government. Here, too, the contrast between the Marquess of Lansdowne, the foreign secretary of the Tory government, and Grey is instructive. Both were Balliol men, although neither did particularly well there. Lansdowne received a second-class degree, a respectable performance. Grey, on the other hand, was asked to leave Balliol for "incorrigible idleness." This was not a common contrast between Liberals and Tories, and the brilliant academic careers of the other Balliol men in the cabinet, Loreburn and Asquith, made up for Grey's slackness. Both Lansdowne and Grey were imbued with a concept of service due in large part to Jowett's influence. Grey would have much preferred to spend his life fishing and bird-watching, and yet a sense of duty made him active in government; he was to be the foreign secretary who took England into the great war.

One area in which the Liberal cabinet excelled, not represented at all in the Tory cabinet, was the world of the intellect. The most famous of the intellectuals in the cabinet was John Morley, the journalist, editor, intellectual historian, and the biographer of Gladstone and others. James Bryce was another eminent intellectual and man of letters in the cabinet, a Scotsman whose most famous book was *The American Commonwealth* (1888).

The most exciting single figure in the cabinet was David Lloyd George, president of the Board of Trade. He was a radical Welshman, obstreperous and imaginative, a poor boy who had had to make his own way. He had been trained as a solicitor (a position lower in the legal profession than a barrister) and had gone on to distinguish himself in politics. Already he was a force most Englishmen could not quite understand or satisfactorily place.

Richard Burdon Haldane, the secretary of state for war, also came from the Celtic fringe; in his case, a wealthy Scottish family. Herbert Henry Asquith, the chancellor of the Exchequer, was a comparatively poor boy from Yorkshire in the North of England who had gone to Balliol. He would succeed Campbell-Bannerman as prime minister in 1908.

One of the most exciting newer politicians was an undersecretary when the cabinet formed, but he entered the cabinet itself in 1908: Winston Churchill. He was the son of Lord Randolph Churchill, who treated him rather badly; so much so that in a sense his later extraordinary career was a posthumous demonstration to his father that he was genuinely worthy of being his son. Churchill had left the Tory party over the issue of free trade

Fourth of June celebration (George III's birthday), Eton, 1911. (Radio Times Hulton Picture Library.)

and was now a convinced Liberal. Lloyd George and Churchill were the most imaginative Liberals in terms of actually coping with the problems of society, although Asquith, Haldane, and Grey, in more traditional Liberal ways, believed in some degree of social betterment. These two suspect "activists," less ideological, less conventionally intelligent than some of their colleagues, were nevertheless the chief architects of the most important accomplishments of the Liberal government.

Something of Churchill's special quality can be suggested by the first meeting he had with Violet Asquith, the daughter of the chancellor of the Exchequer, in 1906. Churchill asked her how old she was. She said she was nineteen and he replied, "And I am 32 already. Younger than anyone else who counts, though. Curse ruthless time, curse our mortality. How cruelly short is the allotted span for all we must cram into it." And then he concluded this conversation by saying: "We are all worms, but I do believe that I am a glow-worm." Churchill believed that political parties should be used for one's own benefit and, consequently, he was the sort of man whom the party regulars hated and distrusted. They felt with good reason that they were being exploited by a maverick.

The cabinet had eleven Public School old boys, in contrast to the seventeen in the Tory cabinet. Of these, only four were Etonians, in contrast to the ten among the Tories. (Harold Macmillan, after having formed a recent Tory cabinet, pointed out that he had twice as many Etonians in his cabinet as the previous Labour cabinet. As he blithely observed: "Things are twice as good under the Conservatives.")

Unlike the Tories, some of the Liberal leaders had to earn their own living. They were more likely to have urban backgrounds. They were more likely to be professional men. In general, the Liberal leaders were not quite in the social position of their counterparts, and their attitudes were quite different. Yet there is a certain basis for the contention that the groups were somewhat similar: they were groups who, on the whole, had done well in English society. The emerging Labour party did legitimately represent a part of England which had not received much attention from either of the older political parties.

The Liberal Government

It was this cabinet that led the Liberal party into the General Election of 1906, when the party won its greatest victory since 1832. There were 400 Liberal M.P.s in the House of Commons, 300 of whom had never sat in Parliament before. There were only 157 Unionists. It had taken almost three-quarters of a century for the promises of 1832 to be realized. The Reform Act of that year had suggested that one day the middle class might rule England, and now in terms of the House of Commons it had happened. The promises put forward in 1867 and 1884 were also beginning to come to fruition. The Labour Representation Committee, formed in 1900, succeeded in electing thirty M.P.s. In 1906 they joined together with some of the M.P.s who considered themselves "Lib-Lab" to form the Parliamentary Labour party, a group of fifty or so in the House of Commons. This striking achievement had come about, in part, by collusion between the political managers of the Liberal and Labour groups. Ramsay MacDonald, the secretary of the Labour Representation Committee, and Herbert Gladstone, chief whip for the Liberals, had agreed that as far as they could arrange it Liberal and Labour candidates would not oppose one another in the election. Constituency organizations were independent; but they could be strongly urged not to run a Labour man against a Liberal, and the other way round. A few people, particularly Balfour, enjoyed pointing out the possibility that despite the extraordinary victory Labour's M.P.s might well represent the end of the historic Liberal party.

Despite Balfour's prediction of trouble to come, the Liberal government was able to accomplish a great deal during its period of power. It passed the Trade Disputes Act, undercutting the Taff Vale Case of 1901. That decision by the courts had made unions liable for damages from strikes and had taken away their special legal position bestowed by the Acts of 1871 and 1875. The judges appeared to be applying class attitudes in their decisions, and, indeed, it was a time of the hardening of class attitudes, of greater psychological antagonism perhaps because there was less overt oppression than in the past. The working class was becoming more powerful and involved in the political process. The Liberals recognized that one reason for their great electoral victory was the workers' support, and the Trade Disputes Act was passed in return for that support. Earlier, the Tories had been more sympathetic to prounion legislation, as was consistent with their tendency to favor institutions over individuals. But now more and more former businessmen-Liberals were becoming Tories. Younger Liberals began to worry about social problems, and this too was reflected in the act.

The Liberal government of 1906 passed a strong Compensation Act for injuries to workmen in a tradition for which the Tories had been more notable in previous years. They failed to pass an Education Bill. As we have seen, the 1902 Education Act, a progressive law in terms of efficiency, was hated by the Nonconformists. The Liberals wished to pass a new bill that would undercut the support of the Church of England in education. The bill easily went through the House of Commons but was thrown out by the House of Lords. In effect, the House of Lords was requesting the Liberals to have a new election over the Education Bill, on the theory, probably accurate, that the public, less interested in religious matters, no longer cared much about the issue. But such a demand by the Lords was presumptuous. The unelected house was claiming that they were more the "true nation" than the House of Commons. The Nonconformists' "conscience" was in a state of decline; religious issues that had mattered so much in the nineteenth century were becoming less and less significant as a political force. It was likely that the country at large would *not* back the Liberals over the Education Bill.

The same story held true for the Plural Voting Bill. The Liberals had tried to eliminate the inequity that some voters had more than one vote, largely on the basis of property holdings. The House of Lords threw out the bill. Again, the Liberals felt that the country, in an election, would probably not support them dramatically on this issue. A Licensing Bill to cut down the number of pubs was also defeated in the House of Lords, loyal to pubs as likely Tory strongholds. Liberal policy came to be known as "plowing the sands" or "filling the cup" of inequity. Both sides were consciously moving toward some sort of confrontation. In 1907 Campbell-Bannerman had passed a resolution in the Commons stating that steps must be taken about the attitudes of the House of Lords.

Although the Liberal government could not accomplish as much as it wished, it did pass two great acts in addition to the Trade Disputes Act and a few others. These were the fruits, primarily, of the imaginations of Lloyd George and Winston Churchill, assisted by civil servants and other politicians. The Old Age Pensions Act of 1908 and the National Insurance Act of 1911 have been taken as the origins of the contemporary "welfare state." The acts were not generous, but they enunciated important principles. The Old Age Pensions Act stipulated that every individual over seventy who had an annual income below £31 could receive a pension from the government of one to five shillings a week. It was a small sum, but a great help to many. For the first time the state accepted an obligation to all of its elder citizens.

A similar principle was true of the National Insurance Act of 1911. It was limited to those who earned less than £160 a year and were not self-employed. It did cover most of the working class for sickness benefits, based on contributions from the worker, the employer, and the state. It also provided approximately 2.5 million workers with some rudimentary unemployment insurance.

The Liberals attempted to continue the old traditions of Liberalism in such areas as education and temperance. It made its most considerable gains, however, in new areas of social concern, where it extended benefits of state action without the implications of patronage which might have characterized such gestures on the part of the Tories. The Liberals also made considerable strides in an area that the Tories had given the impression of being exclusively theirs: military preparedness. The traditional Liberal slogan was "Peace, Retrenchment, and Reform." Yet they were caught in a pattern of increased military expenditure, in part initiated by the establishment of the Committee of Imperial Defense by the Tories and the implications of the informal agreement with France.

Improvement in the navy had taken place, under the Tories, through the brilliant administration of one of the more remarkable figures of recent English history: "Jackie" Fisher, who was first sea lord from 1904 to 1910. Fisher carried out many reforms. He cut through what he considered the amateur aspects of "the Senior Service," with all its outmoded customs and traditions. Engineers were despised, much as Indian army officers, who were most likely to have actual experience, were looked down upon. Fisher recognized the danger of this snobbishness for the future of the service, particularly as the age of sail was past. He upgraded the position of engineers; in fact, he improved and modernized the training that all navy officers received. He redistributed the placing of the fleets, in part made possible by the entente with France. He brought the armaments of ships up to date—scrapping obsolete ships—and was the great force behind the introduction of the dreadnought class of battleships. The building of these ships had actually started under the Tories in 1906, but it continued under the Liberals as an aspect of the naval race with Germany.

Extremely important army reforms also took place during the Liberal administration, under Haldane, the secretary of state for war. A distinguished barrister, somewhat pompous, he saw himself on the woolsack, the seat of the lord chancellor in the House of Lords, and thus the head of the legal system. Campbell-Bannerman was determined that his old friend R. T. Reid would become lord chancellor. He felt that Haldane would be very competent at the war office, and he was amused at the incongruity of a philosophical lawyer in charge of the army—a Schopenhauer in the "kailyard," a Scottish term for the kitchen garden. Haldane, initially disappointed, came to enjoy the challenge; he took the greatest strides forward in army organization since Cardwell's reforms in the 1870s. He modernized the militia into a well-organized territorial army. He was very clever in making use of traditional hierarchies. He made the lord lieutenant in the particular county, a man who was likely to be the great local landed magnate, the head of each unit of the territorial army. In 1907 he put through the Territorial and Reserve Forces Act. He created an Officer Training Corps for schools, replacing the previous informal training system. He modernized the great military training school of Sandhurst in 1909. He also created a general staff for the army as well as the framework of the expeditionary force, the B.E.F., which was essential when the First World War broke out.

The House of Lords

The Liberal government made great strides forward in many ways, but its path was also marked by considerable difficulty, most of which originated in the House of Lords. As Lloyd George remarked: "The House of Lords is supposed to be the watchdog of the constitution, instead it is Mr. Balfour's poodle." When there was a Conservative government, its bills went through the Lords without any difficulty. When there was a Liberal government, the Lords, at the command of Balfour, would throw the bills out. The unelected house was in a position to force the party with a vast majority in the Commons to go to the electorate again if there was an issue on which the Lords felt they knew better. The House of Lords believed themselves somehow more representative of the true England—born to privilege—than the elected M.P.s. They stopped some very important Liberal legislation: the Plural Voting Bill, the Education Bill, the Licensing Bill, all of which had passed with overwhelming majorities in the House of Commons. Gladstone, as long ago as 1893, had been aware that the House of Lords would be a great stumbling block for legislative progress. His last gesture for the Liberal party in 1894 was to try to persuade it to mount a campaign with him as leader against the House of Lords. His followers had been anxious to get rid of their distinguished but now rather antique leader and so were unwilling then to take such a course. In his very last speech in the House of Commons Gladstone said in his conclusion:

> Nearly the whole work of the session has been wrecked. The question is whether the work of the House of Lords is not merely to modify but to annihilate the whole work of the House of Commons. The issue which is raised is between a deliberative assembly, elected by the votes of more than 6,000,000 people, and a deliberative assembly occupied by many men of virtue, by many men of talent, of course with considerable diversities and varieties; [it] is a controversy which, when once profoundly acute, will demand a settlement from the highest authority [i.e., the electorate].

In 1906 the House of Lords consisted of 602 peers, about half of whom had been created in the nineteenth century, the period of greatest growth in the House of Lords. This expansion had begun at the end of the eighteenth century through the younger Pitt, who used titles as political rewards. At the time of the Home Rule crisis of 1886, the number of Liberal peers had decreased dramatically. In 1906, of the 602 peers, only 88 called themselves Liberals, 34 had no affiliation, and 480 declared that they were Unionists—as the party of Tories and Liberal Unionists was frequently called. The tendency of an established family was to move to the right. Even if a Liberal government recommended to the monarch one of its supporters as a peer, there was no assurance that he or his successors would remain loyal Liberals. This tendency was reinforced at the end of the century by the growing intensity of class antagonism: the line must be held against the pretensions of those below in the class structure.

The Liberal government's ultimate weapon against the Lords was to ask the king to create new peers, but with 480 opponents to be outvoted the number of peers that might have to be created could place an almost unbearable strain on the royal prerogative. The question then became, in the words of John Morley, whether to "mend 'em or end 'em." Many lords were considerable Irish landlords and were thus overready to see the threat of Home Rule behind every act which the Liberals sent to their house. The Unionist leadership seemed uncertain as to what course to follow. Balfour was weak over the question of how far the Lords should go in opposing Liberal legislation. Lansdowne, the leader in the Lords, allowed the peers to go their own way. He was in favor of some sort of compromise in the rapidly worsening situation, but he could not persuade many of his followers to be anything but adamant in their reaction to compromise with the Liberals.

The crisis started in 1909 when Lloyd George presented his first budget. He had become chancellor of the Exchequer in 1908, but the budget that year had been prepared by Asquith, his predecessor. In 1909 Lloyd George was under an obligation to raise the budget in order to pay for a larger navy and for old-age pensions. He increased death duties, taxes on unearned income, and, even more offensive to the Lords, he increased and established new taxes on land, particularly unused land, such as that which was used for hunting. The Lords felt, with some justification, that Lloyd George was out to attack them. The House of Commons for the past 200 years had never had a finance bill touched by the other house, as the tradition of the British constitution, a matter of convention, was that the House of Commons should have total control over finance.

The Lords who opposed Lloyd George contended that his budget was much more than a financial bill: it was an attack on the structure of society. Lloyd George delivered a series of inflammatory speeches in Limehouse, a poor district in the East End of London, and elsewhere, in which he attacked particularly the dukes—whom he pronounced "dooks"—claiming that they cost more to run than a dreadnought. Unfortunately, the dukes replied and threatened to fire most of their servants! A certain sense of hysteria began to affect the activities of both houses of Parliament. Those two august institutions seemed to more and more observers to be "footling talking shops" which had little real connection with the business of government, or the true structure of society.

The Commons passed the budget; the Lords rejected it by a vote of 350 to 75. In January 1910 there was a General Election in which the Unionists gained 116 seats, making a near balance between the major parties of 275 Liberals to 273 Unionists. But the Liberals still had a decent majority because they had the support of 40 Labour and 70 Irish Home Rule M.P.s. The Lords had been against the Liberal party because they feared the Liberals would put through legislation favorable to the causes of Labour and Ireland. But by forcing a General Election and cutting down the majority of the Liberals, they made the Liberals more dependent on the support of Labour and the Irish and, by necessity, more likely to take steps to please them.

A Parliament Bill was introduced in the House of Commons in 1910. It limited the time the House of Lords could hold up an act passed in the Commons to three sessions, about two years. The next step was delayed by the death of Edward VII in 1910. His son, George V, came to the throne amidst a feeling that a new king should not have to plunge immediately into a great constitutional crisis. In order to help smooth the accession, an unsuccessful series of conferences were held between the Liberal and Tory leaders. Also, Balfour was willing to form a Tory government if the king so asked him. This would have been very dubious constitutional practice: for the first time since 1835 a government supported by a majority in the Commons would have been dismissed by the king. The king had two private secretaries: Lord Knollys, whom he had inherited from his father, and Sir Arthur Bigge, his own appointment. Balfour had made his suggestion to Knollys, who decided not to tell the king about it, thus taking constitutional practice into his own hands. Balfour's offer was not revealed until Harold Nicholson wrote the official biography of George V in 1952.

In order to make the will of the electorate absolutely clear, the two major parties agreed that, as Edward VII had originally demanded, before a creation of peers there should be another General Election; it was scheduled for December 1910. Again, the House of Lords showed itself capable of causing its opponents a great deal of difficulty, forcing them to put their electoral position in jeopardy twice in one year. The voters were bored by the issue: a half-million fewer voted in December than had voted in January. The proportions in the Commons remained exactly the same.

The Parliament Bill came to the House of Lords. The question was whether they would accept the bill which decreed the end of their power or would refuse to do so, and so force the Liberals to press the king to create enough new peers to pass the bill. Asquith drew up a list of 249 men who would be created peers, if necessary. The list reveals how concerned the Liberals were to preserve the institutions of England. Most of the names on the list were the sort who might well become peers eventually. Asquith did not dream of packing the Lords with those on the left. His list included 20 sons of peers, 48 baronets, 59 knights, 23 members of the privy council, and 19 M.P.s. It was hardly a startling list; very few even belonged to the aristocracy of literature—Thomas Hardy, Sir James Barrie, Bertrand Russell (who, in any case, was a brother of Earl Russell and would eventually inherit the title), and Gilbert Murray.

The political atmosphere became extremely tense. Asquith was howled down in the House of Commons, and for the first time the speaker had to declare that there was a state of grave disorder and to suspend the seating of the house. The social fabric of England, or at least of London life, was not, however, rent by this issue, and social life went on, as it had not in 1886 nor would again in 1914 over the Irish crisis of that year. At a famous masquerade ball given by the Duchess of Devonshire, Balfour and Asquith were seen chatting together in a friendly fashion, and the somewhat pushy American, William Waldorf Astor, came to the party in a peer's robes with a number on, indicating that he was willing to help the Liberals in return for a peerage.

The fight in the House of Lords itself was between the "ditchers" and the "hedgers." Appropriately, the language of the hunting field was used—more familiar to many a lord than that of the discussion chamber at Westminster. Another phrase used at the time for the more extreme group was the "die-hards." The "die-hards" and the "ditchers" were willing to defeat the Parliament bill and accept the flooding of their chamber with new peers. The "hedgers" felt this would be a disgrace. Their opponents felt it was better to go down fighting. The "hedgers" were supported by the Tory moderates such as Lansdowne and also by that supersnob the Marquis of Curzon, who was horrified at the idea of so many "new men" coming into the House of Lords. Finally, in the sweltering heat of August 10, 1911, the bill came to the house. It was one of the few debates there in which the outcome was unknown in advance. John Morley, who had gone to the House of Lords in 1908 in order to conserve his strength, announced that the king had promised to create a sufficient number of peers to carry the bill if it was not passed on this occasion. The Lords were not only sweltering in the heat, but they were also very anxious to get away for the "glorious twelfth of August" when the grouse season starts in Scotland.

Clearly, most of the Lords wished to abstain. The "ditchers" and the "die-hards," led by Lord Willoughby de Broke and Lord Halsbury, wanted to defeat the bill and go down with flags flying. The abstainers did not want to vote for a bill that would end their power. But there was a group of Unionists who felt it would be wrong if the bill did not pass, and a mass creation of peers had to take place. The question was how many Tory lords would be willing to be cut at the Carlton Club, the great Tory club, and vote in favor of the bill. Although many more lords were present, the vote was only 131 to 114 in favor of the bill. Victory for the Liberals had been assured by the thirty-seven Tory peers and thirteen prelates who supported eighty-one Liberal peers. The House of Commons had won.

Violence, Women's Suffrage, and Ireland

Change has often taken place in England because those in control have recognized that change was necessary to preserve their sort of society. But in the years before 1914 either the leaders were remarkably imperceptive or they felt that meeting popular demands would end rather than preserve that society.

The Women's Suffrage Movement followed a most curious course. During the nineteenth century women had been making slow and respectable progress. They were no longer in the eyes of the law chattels of their husbands, with no rights over their own property. They even had the right, if they had suitable property qualifications, to vote in certain local elections. Quite a few politicians, in the abstract, supported their claim to the vote. Some women preferred, and continued to prefer all through this period, the more indirect ways of influencing elections; there were wives who proclaimed that no woman was worthy of her sex if her husband did not vote exactly as she wished. But more and more women wanted direct access to the franchise, and they were not uninfluenced by the similar stirrings against Victorian rectitude that agitated the males. The Bloomsbury men at Cambridge *read* their Ibsen; but the women who lived outside of that rarefied atmosphere could not ignore the implications of *A Doll's House.* In these years, at an increasing rate, there was more and more literature of emancipation. In the serious journals there were many articles, mostly in the form of "A Daughter Objects," where the younger women turned against the restrictions placed upon their mothers. The only occupations for the middle-class girl in the nineteenth century had been wife or governess. But at the beginning of the twentieth century, these women gradually gained some, and demanded increasing opportunities in offices and shops. With these gains came an increasing desire for more political power.

Political agitation, on a serious scale, for women's rights was launched by a respectable widow, Mrs. Emmeline Pankhurst. Her husband had been a Manchester barrister, active in various radical causes, including women's rights, and also connected with the nascent Labour party. At first there was a strong connection between rights for workers and rights for women, and this double impetus was behind the formation, on October 10, 1903, of the Women's Social and Political Union. It began as yet another suffrage society, but eventually became the dominant and most active group, concerning itself only with problems pertaining to women and their right to vote. Soon there were elements of the sex war in the campaign, and it developed into a violent and at times macabre fight for attention. The women's activity certainly proved that rationality—for both men and women—was not enough for politics. It is difficult to find a direct source for the turns that the suffrage movement took. One possible source was the third great problem to plague prewar England: the oldest of them all— the Irish problem. There was the example of Parnell, the great Irish leader. He had rarely directly broken the law or flouted parliamentary custom, but he had caused so much trouble in Parliament that eventually the regulations had to be modified to restrict free discussion. Outside of Parliament he had frequently urged his followers to vote against the Liberals—although they were more favorable to the cause of Irish Home Rule than the Unionists—because they were not favorable enough. This activity might well have set the example for the women's insistence of opposing sympathetic Liberals because they would not do enough for their cause. But the more extreme course they took may have come from another Irish tradition, which had appeared in the later years of the nineteenth century and would have its final excessive and tragic fulfillment in the 1920s—the tradition of violence, arson, and that sin of sins, from the English point of view, the destruction of property. A transmitter of the tradition was the Irish Eva Gore-Booth, one of the two sisters celebrated by Yeats who revealed some of the more violent techniques to the Pankhursts—for Mrs. Pankhurst was not alone but had her two distinguished lieutenants, her daughters Christabel and Sylvia. Eva Gore-Booth also represented a new lack of fastidiousness about one's companions in the cause, and she formed the Manchester Barmaids Association. The purpose of the Barmaids Association—heavily subsidized by the brewers who hated the Liberals because of their desire to cut down the number of pubs—was to attack the candidacy of Winston Churchill in Manchester, and this fitted into the campaign of "getting the Liberals."

One would think that the Liberals would have favored female suffrage, and many of them did, in principle if not in practice. They were pledged to making the franchise more democratic, eliminating plural voting and those property qualifications that remained, and they were not averse to including votes for women under this head. But they were in no particular rush to do anything about it. They claimed, with some justification, that if they enfranchised women on the basis of property qualification they would be adding to the Conservative vote. But the women chose to see this as a delaying tactic, which in part it was. They wanted the direct issue of votes for women to be considered exclusively as such and not as part of an eventual, overall increase in democracy. In fact, the Liberal leadership itself was divided. The prime minister, Campbell-Bannerman, had been sympathetic to the struggle, but his successor Asquith was not, and the cabinet was divided. Therefore, they refused to introduce a female suffrage bill as a party measure, although they would not prevent such a bill's being introduced. So bills were introduced and passed their first reading—the first stage toward becoming law—but since the party hierarchy really did not care what happened and had considerations that they regarded as more important, the bills got no further.

The women became impatient. They began to play the game with new rules or forgot about the game completely. At first they merely extended the normal political rights of Englishmen: they campaigned in elections against those candidates who opposed women's suffrage. They presented petitions to politicians; they heckled them at meetings; they demonstrated in front of the House of Commons. A conciliation committee (ominous name) of M.P.s was formed to introduce a bill which again lost, the excuse being lack of time. The women wondered if they would not do better to step over the bonds of propriety which had held them in for so many years. The marching on the House of Commons became more violent, and the police reacted with more dispatch. Downing Street was besieged with more persistence, heckling was more raucous, arrests were more frequent, and the more respectable leaders of the suffrage movement became more worried. At the same time, for some the fight became more exciting! Great crowds began to collect, and great demonstrations were held, one of half a million in Hyde Park. But how many of these were the merely curious? How many were Edwardian toughs out for a good time? Very few people seemed to change their mind. The women were not getting their ideas across. In desperation, they resorted to more and more violent means. If men would not give the women the vote, then the women would not respect the men's rules or their world of property. Women chained themselves to the rails outside 10 Downing Street, to the rails in the ladies gallery in the House of Commons, and shouted "Votes for Women." They attacked cabinet ministers with horsewhips, screamed and yelled at their meetings; they burnt the words "Votes for Women" in acid on golf greens and attacked Buckingham Palace.

The years 1910 to 1914 marked a crescendo of activity, and more and more the Pankhursts were alone in leadership of the militants, and increasingly they saw it in terms of the sex war. Most significantly, Sylvia Pankhurst would leave her mother and sister to their campaign of militancy. That campaign was marked with an increase of authoritarianism on the part of Mrs. Pankhurst and Christabel, both of whom moved to the right. They had less and less use for the support given them from the left, from the Labour party, from the workers. Only Sylvia had genuine interest in the workers, and she, disowned by the rest of the family, remained in the East End, doing her best for the sweated women workers. It might be said that a deputation from them to Asquith eventually, just before the outbreak of war, did the most for a favorable resolution of the problem.

Violence continued. Unoccupied buildings were burned down; the contents of mailboxes were destroyed. One morning most of the shop-windows on Picadilly Circus, Regent Street, and Oxford Street were shattered. The Rokeby Venus of Velasquez in the National Gallery and a rather strange companion piece, Sargent's portrait of Henry James, were slashed. Emily Davison threw herself in front of the king's horse during the running of the derby at Epsom and was killed.

The destruction and death were bad enough—sufficient indication of an unwillingness to accept the conventions of society. But then, when the suffragettes were imprisoned they discovered the effectiveness of another weapon: refusing to eat. They went on hunger strikes and reduced the government to feeding them forcibly. The successive home secretaries, Churchill and Reginald McKenna, told the House of Commons that there was no danger in forced feeding; rumor was that Churchill had submitted to the experience for purposes of investigation. But the painfulness, the ugliness, of it shocked and horrified many. Was it English? And perhaps more important, was it humane? It seemed to occur to very few that perhaps the solution was to give women the vote. But Parliament was not to be bullied. After starvation and the inadequacies of forcible feeding, many women were visibly ill and had to be released from prison. Recovered, they would return to their cause. McKenna had Parliament pass the so-called Cat and Mouse Act, which enabled the police to release a woman who was ill and rearrest her, at pleasure, when she was well again, without using any further legal procedures. One hunger-striker was Lady Constance Lytton, daughter of a former viceroy of India and granddaughter of the novelist Bulwer Lytton. When she went on strike the police said she was not well enough to stand forcible feeding, but when she had herself arrested under a false common name they did feed her forcibly—and as a result she was left a permanent invalid.

It is frequently said that the good work the women did during the war earned them the vote, while their earlier militancy had only put its achievement further off. But perhaps the extremism was necessary to make those in control, both Tory and Liberal, realize that the women were serious. They did not get the vote sooner because those at the top, either admittedly or covertly, did not want them to have it. It was that attitude that forced the women to extremes.

But what of the working class? We have seen how they were less and less involved with the suffrage movement. And, in a sense, they were going

Emmeline Pankhurst, founder of the Women's Social and Political Union, arrested after having led a demonstration at Buckingham Palace on May 21, 1914. (Radio Times Hulton Picture Library.)

in an opposite direction. While the women were battling to be let into the state, some of the workers, with almost equal persistence, were battling to be let out. Their activities contradict the comfortable notion that the state as it stood was a pretty good thing and that dissident groups were merely trying to get into an operating concern. They were inspired by a vision of a much more egalitarian society than appealed to their so-called betters, or perhaps even to the women. It was a reaction to the feeling that things were the way they were, and were going to stay that way, and it was foolish to talk of change. And perhaps, most of all, they wanted an increase in wages —at a time when real wages were static. They were impatient with the world of class and discrimination, in both the good and bad senses of the latter word. They had a tough course, as Duff Cooper, the foreign office man who had followed Eden into the wilderness in 1938, wrote in 1953 about the period before the war:

> Class is a word that in this age stirs passions and provokes people to talk nonsense. There are even those who would, if they could, create a classless society. If such a society were possible it would be as useless as a rankless

91

army and as dull as a wine-list that gave neither the names of the vineyards nor the dates of the vintages. Class is an inevitable adjunct of human nature. The aim of the lawgiver should be to render the relations between classes happy and to facilitate the passage from one class to another. When class, which is natural, degenerates into caste, which is against nature, it becomes an evil.

Along with the general noncomprehending attitude signified by Duff Cooper, more specific events made Labour impatient. The Taff Vale decision of 1901, making unions liable to be sued for damages that occurred during a strike, had provided the main impetus for political activity by the unions and their success in the 1906 election. They were rewarded with the passing of the Trade Disputes Act. It seemed that Labour was coming within the pale of the constitution. But then, at the end of 1909, they were thrown right out again with the Osborne judgment. W. V. Osborne, an official of a union in Walthamstow, an area where the Liberals' hold on laborers had always been strong, objected to paying the political levy imposed by his union. The case wound its way up through the courts and finally Osborne won. The Osborne judgment meant that Labour was prevented from playing a full role in politics as unions could not use their funds for political purposes. The state, in effect, had put a sign up on its inner precincts: "No labourers need apply." Labour men remained in Parliament, somehow finding money enough for the next two years; then the Liberal government helped by passing, in 1911, a resolution which paid M.P.s £400 a year. But the judgment crippled the general political activities of the trade unions. It did not discourage them from activity, but since it hindered them from acting in the legitimate political area they turned as the women had turned to the semilegitimate, the questionable areas of behavior which were much more dangerous to the state than having every union member support a Labour party even if he was not in complete sympathy with it.

From 1910 to 1914 was the period of near-crippling strikes. Strikes were hardly new; but these were more serious, more prolonged, more violent than practically any that had been known before. There was a feeling, which perhaps had not been so intense since Peterloo nearly a hundred years before, that the class system was turning into the class war. If the workers were not to be admitted to the state, then perhaps they would form their own state, a state within a state—some of the unions argued that their members had to pay political levies on the analogy that the state did not tolerate the refusal of its citizens to pay taxes. The Osborne judgment forced the union leaders to be somewhat more sympathetic to syndicalist thought, which before they may have regarded as an uncongenial idea from the Continent. The workers now were not coming, cap in hand, to ask for rights. Instead, some were now demanding, violently, to be let alone and to have power apart from the state. True, within the state Lloyd George and, to a

lesser degree, Winston Churchill, with their important social legislation providing unemployment and old-age insurance, had stolen some of Labour's
thunder, and the Liberals were still quietly attempting to cooperate with
Labour. Most of the strikes ended in reasonable compromises, thanks to
the efforts of Lloyd George and the chief industrial commissioner, Sir
George Askwith, who spent most of these years scuttling around the country settling the great strikes. The three crucial areas of strikes were in the
railways, the mines, and the docks, and finally these three great work forces
combined in 1913 to form the Triple Industrial Alliance. What is particularly
noticeable about the strikes is their increased violence and lawlessness; and
the need that Winston Churchill, when home secretary, felt to call out the
troops to enforce order. The great strikes of the late nineteenth century—
with the exception of a few well-thrown stones at the windows of clubs to
give the well-to-do a slight thrill of danger—are marked by their orderliness, as if to show that the workers were worthy of a little more pay. But
now a request was being transformed into a right, and the more extreme
aspects of the great London dock strike of 1889 were being carried forward. But it is doubtful whether there ever was any serious danger of
revolution. Certainly, the working classes were more conscious of their aims
and of their potential strength than in the past, and some of their leaders
were thinking in terms of an eventual General Strike which would take them
into power. But behind the scenes there was a lot of quiet cooperation between Liberals and the unions which prevented the unions' total alienation
from the state. And although the strikes continued up to the war and were
often marked by violence, outside the actual strike areas life, somehow,
went placidly on.

But the most extraordinary example of violence came from the right on
the issue of Ulster. As an issue it was the most dangerous to English society,
for it split the powers-that-be dramatically. Both sides of the House of
Commons, in varying degrees, had been distressed by the suffragettes, but
they did not take them as seriously as perhaps they deserved. Again, in
degrees—with Liberals likely to be much more sympathetic—both sides of
the house regarded the workers with some trepidation. But the forty-odd
Labour members were not sufficient to make either side quake, and the
Liberals did what they could for Labour.

The eighty-odd Irish members were another matter. The elections of
1910, forced on the Liberals by their opponents, made the power of the
Irish greater and made it even more necessary for Asquith to do something
about Ireland. He took up, with some reluctance, the Gladstonian inheritance. But the Tories were not going to accept this—the fight over the
House of Lords had in part been inspired by this issue.

Ulster, the northern part of Ireland, is still in the United Kingdom and
is still dominated by Protestant Scotch-Irish, although with increasing lack
of assurance and tragic violence and counterviolence. During the Glad-

stonian period the Conservatives had been fighting against the break-up of the union, against allowing any part of Ireland to have any independence whatsoever. In a sense, the forces of Home Rule had won a partial victory, for now the Conservatives were fighting for the exclusion of Ulster from any Home Rule bill. They were no longer so concerned with the property some of their members might own in southern Ireland. Why were they so vehement in the cause of Ulster? The most obvious explanation is anti-Catholicism. Many were determined not to see the Protestant majority in the North subjected to the religious and economic power of a Catholic South. Also, Ulster provided a vehicle for the new leaders of the Conservative party.

As part of the backlash of the Lords issue, under the slogan "BMG" (Balfour must go), Bonar Law, a Glasgow iron merchant of Canadian Scotch-Irish background, had become head of the party, triumphing over the older business tradition of Austen Chamberlain and the landed-squire tradition of Walter Long. Law was a much tougher man than his aristocratic predecessor. The nature of high-level politics was changing, and the gentlemanly aspect of it was disappearing; one no longer insulted one's opponents with classical allusions and then chatted amiably with them at a party afterward. With Bonar Law and with Edward Carson, an Irish Protestant chiefly famous for his brilliant and brutal cross-examination of Oscar Wilde, the resistance over Home Rule took on a frightening and almost hysterical form. It was as if the Conservatives, once defeated by the normal processes of democracy, would take to the field of battle—claiming all the while that the people were—despite their votes—truly on their side.

The movement for the defense of Ulster by legitimate and illegitimate means began in earnest in 1912. Before this time the South, the Irish Nationalists, had provided what violence there was, and they had, when caught, been severely dealt with. But now Carson formed the Ulster Volunteers, a private army that claimed they would fight for king and country against the government as though the two were separate things. Of course, they did have the legitimate complaint that something they opposed might happen. But it was debatable whether in England, as of 1912, the forming of a private militia was the proper way of replying—whether you could foment rebellion while claiming that you were being ultrapatriotic.

What Carson did, and Bonar Law abetted, was just as anarchic and fantastic as what the women, and to a lesser extent the workers, were doing; and as they were much more powerful, they represented a far greater danger to the state. On Easter in 1912 Bonar Law took the salute at a marchpast in Ulster of 100,000; and in July of that year in England itself Bonar Law addressed a huge meeting at Blenheim (Churchill's birthplace). Perhaps a minor purpose of holding the meeting there was to suggest to Churchill, who would say "let us . . . put these grave matters to the proof," that he was on the wrong side. And there Bonar Law called for yet another General Election and announced that there were no lengths to which the men of Ulster could go that he would not support them. Churchill accused the Conservatives of being as rebellion-minded as the syndicalists, a very apt comparison. The situation became increasingly intense, and some backstairs effort was made to alleviate it. Asquith and Bonar Law met privately at the house of Max Aitken (later Lord Beaverbrook), a friend of Bonar Law's soon to be a powerful figure in English politics. But to no avail. There were riotous debates over the new Home Rule Bill in the house; a book was thrown at Churchill and struck him on the forehead. But the bill progressed through Parliament, and finally "King" Carson left for Ulster, much like a medieval lord retiring to his own territory to prepare for battle.

The possibility of civil war, unbelievable as it might have seemed, became more and more an actuality: the Ulster Volunteers would fight it would appear if the attempt was made to incorporate Ulster into any Home Rule scheme. The Liberals had a further problem in the army if they attempted to force Ulster to do something it did not wish to do. The officer class was a pillar of the Establishment and would detest enforcing a Liberal Home Rule Bill. Yet they had certain instincts of duty to king and country and respect for properly constituted authority. Would that be sufficient if the army in Ireland, or troops taken over to Ireland, were given orders to march against Ulster? Many of the leading officers were Ulstermen, and certainly almost all of the officers believed in the Protestant Ascendency. Yet many were aware—surprisingly so, for the officer class—that in the past few years they had been asking their troops to take action and, in a few cases, to fire against other members of their class, the workers.

As with the Lords issue, the Liberals let themselves in for trouble by being overscrupulous, by being more conservative, more concerned with preserving society and the state than their opponents were. In March 1914, when the Liberals were anxious to send some troops to protect arms deposits and thought that soon the troops might be used to intimidate the Ulstermen, they sent an unusual communiqué to the garrison at Dublin—a communiqué which was not a secret from the Tories. The Tories were well informed, as the director of military operations, Sir Henry Wilson (assassinated by the Irish in London in 1922), did not think it disloyal to reveal the plans of his Liberal chiefs to their Tory opponents. The Liberal secretary of state for war, Colonel Seely, rather than sending over orders to Dublin, was doubtful about the loyalty of his officers. He sent over a request that he hoped as many officers as possible would obey should such orders be issued—that is, orders against Ulster—but that he would understand if those whose homes were in Ulster would "disappear" and that they could reappear when the fight was over with no loss in rank. He also gave other officers the option to resign. The Liberals were trying to act like gentlemen and hoped that the officers would be gentlemen in return. Many of them were.

But at the Curragh, a military base south of Dublin, most of the officers indicated that they would rather resign than take any moves against Ulster. The army, which had not been a threat to the state since the seventeenth century, was deserting the government. If this attitude should spread, and if the Ulster Volunteers continued to grow, there might well be a civil war. There were hurried consultations between London and Dublin. The whole thing quieted down and was referred to as a misunderstanding. But the government had lost face. The incident became known as the Mutiny at the Curragh—a strange mutiny of the officers. The government was not deposed by a military junta, but the situation continued to deteriorate. A large supply of guns was run into Ulster, a small supply into southern Ireland. The government offered various compromises about Ulster, but none were good enough for Carson and his supporters. One somehow does not believe that the dispute would have ended in civil war. But there was no logical reason that it might not have, if the world war had not intervened, and both southern Ireland and Northern Ireland turned their attention to Germany.

With the coming of the war, the women subsided, and the more militant among them devoted themselves to handing out white feathers to the men who they felt were shirking their duty; the strike wave subsided; the Irish were quiet until 1916 when the English—Liberal and Tory alike—began to reap the whirlwind in southern Ireland. But why—and, of course, no completely satisfactory answer can be given—had all these episodes of violence in national life taken place? Why at the same time is one's picture of England before the war still of calm and peace, even when that was incontrovertibly not the case? Certainly each of these causes—women, workers, Irish—had roots deep in the nineteenth century, and it would be possible to say that each was following a natural development, that each group felt that not enough had been done for it and was determined to take things into its own hands. That would be a logical explanation for the have-nots, the women, and the workers. For the Ulstermen, it might be said that the Conservatives, denied the use of the House of Lords, were determined to keep as much power and as much initiative as possible in their own hands, even at the risk of civil war. Each movement can be explained by its own past. It has been suggested in George Dangerfield's *Strange Death of Liberal England* that these three manifestations represent the victory of instinct over reason, of the triumph of the irrational over fuddy-duddy reasonable Liberal England, and as a sign of life rather than of death.

And why shouldn't many segments of English society try to throw over the traces, join the flight into irrationality which characterized much thought and some action on the Continent? The English are victimized by their own stereotypes—which in any case are more stereotypes of the upper classes than of all of England. Among the upper classes, the rigors and disciplines and ideas of the Victorian era had created a stereotype which had some validity: the stiff upper lip, the refusal to show emotion, the love of compromise and rationality, and so forth. The achievement—if it is an achievement—of these qualities was at the price of repression of emotions and of feelings. England might be understood better if one started with the idea of the English as being passionate, excitable, irrational, temperamental, and hence needing powerful institutions to curb them.

CHAPTER FOUR

The English system, on the whole, was able to accommodate itself to violence. Although at times repressive, it appeared to be able to be so without brutalizing itself. The English upper classes, and their servants, could be cruel and arrogant, but there was usually some continuing respect for the "decencies" and for the rights of the "free-born" Englishman. The system tried to respond, for the most part, in an ameliorative rather than in a repressive way. Despite the solidity of English institutions and the sense they manage to convey of being eternal—even if they have only begun the previous day—they nevertheless have a considerable degree of "give." Ultimately, the women gained the vote. Ultimately, the unions achieved better working conditions, shorter hours, more pay. Ultimately, even the Irish question was temporarily resolved, and southern Ireland achieved political if not economic independence after the war although at the price of the northern counties remaining part of the United Kingdom. Backwoods peers shouting in the House of Lords and fulminating in their clubs; ladies slashing the Sargent portrait of Henry James; workers out on strike: all this is very different from a full-scale revolutionary uprising.

Modern England

The First World War

But just before the outbreak of war, violence in England was becoming worse and more frequent. It would be rash to suggest that this would have resulted ultimately in a cataclysm of violence. The aim of many of those who were using violence in England, was, on the whole, to win an accommodation within the system, not to overturn and destroy it. Indeed, the event of ultimate violence, war itself, came from another direction: the steadily worsening international situation that culminated in the outbreak of the First World War in August 1914. It was then, in the famous phrase of the English foreign minister, Sir Edward Grey, that "the lights went out all over Europe." It was not until the war was over that many members of the upper middle class realized that what they had considered a civilized way of life was no longer available, although the war helped to bring about a better society for the majority. When the "lights" went on again in November 1918, they illuminated a changed Europe.

In the struggle for international power, England was a "have" nation.

Winston Churchill pointed this out with surprising and engaging candor in a memorandum that he wrote shortly before the outbreak of war:

> We are not a young people with an innocent record and a scanty inheritance. We have engrossed to ourselves, in times when other powerful nations were paralysed by barbarism or internal war, an altogether disproportionate share of the wealth and traffic of the world. We have got all we want in territory, and our claim to be left in the unmolested enjoyment of vast and splendid possessions, mainly acquired by violence, largely maintained by force, often seems less reasonable to others than to us.

It was hardly surprising that other nations should be envious, and that Germany in particular should feel that the English belief in their own financial and naval power stood in the way of German plans for rising to greatness and dominance. Although England can be acquitted of actively helping to bring about the war, her very existence and the challenge that she represented to a nation such as Germany go far to explain why that nation should have been anxious for some act of violence to break the status quo. It was, however, Germany that took actions that England and France found threatening, such as the widening of the Kiel Canal to permit the movement of large battleships into the North Sea. Such actions were regarded by many in England as "illegitimate." There was a growing conviction among too many people in Europe that war was "bound" to come; when it did, there was a sense almost of relief. In the great capitals, the populace demonstrated joyfully in the streets on the outbreak of war. Despite many exceptions ranging from police actions to small wars, the peace of Europe had been preserved in a broad sense since 1815. It was now shattered, although many had the illusion that the war would be of short duration. But after a first successful German campaign, which brought them almost within reach of Paris, the war bogged down in the vast, immobile, and murderous trench warfare which would characterize the Western front until the war's end four years later.

In England Lord Kitchener, the popular general who became secretary of state for war, believed that the war would be long and planned accordingly. But apart from this insight he was slow-minded and too intent on doing everything himself. As a heroic figure he gave psychological comfort to the nation: his famous face looked out everywhere from posters and his finger pointed toward the young men who passed, "Your King & Country Need You." Whatever his initial value as a morale builder, he failed as an administrator; and he was too popular to be fired.

For many peace had become a bore: hence the dancing crowds in the streets in London as war began. On a more sophisticated level, the sense of excitement is reflected in the autobiography of the poet Robert Graves, *Goodbye to All That*, published in 1929. In 1914 Graves was about to "go up to"—that is, to enter—Oxford. He had attended one of the boarding schools to which the boys from the upper middle class were traditionally

Lord Kitchener, 1914.
Poster by Alfred Leete.
(Imperial War Museum.)

sent when they were eight and ready to begin a traditional English educa-
tion for that class; then he had gone to Charterhouse, a distinguished Public
School. Oxford represented the culmination of the traditional pattern, and
Graves was excited about the outbreak of war as a change in that pattern.

The cabinet had been hesitant about entering the war. By tradition, the
Liberals were the party of "Peace, Retrenchment, and Reform." John Morley, the last great proponent of the Gladstonian approach to the world,
resigned from the cabinet, as did John Burns. Both were holding firm to the
idea that England could do more to bring the war to an early end by remaining neutral and also thus best serve her own interests. Morley was unhappy,
too, at the prospect of England fighting alongside what he considered the
untrustworthy France and the brutal Russia. Racist feelings were strong at
the time, and many Englishmen felt that the Germans were "Anglo-Saxon
cousins" and the French were unreliable and more "foreign," although the
Entente Cordiale of 1904 and a similar understanding with Russia in 1907
were directed against the Central Powers. The trade unions, however, did
not loudly object to war, and the hoped-for solidarity of the working class
against a "capitalist war" evaporated. The workers were either silent in
favor of peace or loud in their cries for war. A few—most notably, the
leader of the Parliamentary Labour party, Ramsay MacDonald—objected to
the war; their number would grow slowly during the coming years. But in

the early months there was no popular outcry that needed to be taken seriously.

All through the nineteenth century, England had regarded herself as committed to peace. Yet when it came to the point, she went to war for traditional reasons, harking back to her treaty of 1839 that guaranteed Belgian neutrality. If Germany had changed her military plan—to march through Belgium on the way to France—England might well not have entered the war, but Germany had no other plan. Still, it was not so much England's anxiety to protect "gallant little Belgium" as it was a cornerstone of English foreign policy that the coast closest to her own should not be controlled by a great power, be it Germany or France. Further, by the development of the entente England felt obligated to protect the French coast and the Channel from hostile acts against the French, as they had undertaken similar obligations in the Mediterranean. These strategic concerns, as well as the naval and commercial competition of the prewar years, pushed England into war. The war became a mass war, the first since the French wars of a century before, and England slowly mobilized herself.

Because of concentration on the war effort and the obligation for politicians within the government to present a solid front to the nation and to their country's enemies, politics became more secretive and, in effect, more vicious and a matter of "back-stairs" intrigue. Issues could not come up as freely as they had before the war in the House of Commons and in the newspapers. Rivalries which might have turned on principles became more and more a matter of personalities, a tendency of English politics in any case. Never is the intensity of personal animosity and jockeying for power—all carried on beneath a bland and noncommittal face—more clearly revealed than when one political leader is replaced with another. And this was especially notable in December 1916 when Lloyd George replaced Asquith, the event that might be taken to mark the real extinction of the Liberal party. Paradoxically, it might have been the Tory party that went under in 1916, if Bonar Law had tied his fortunes to Asquith.

The Liberals had been battered by events since 1886. The interparty struggle in 1916 pitted on one side men such as Asquith and Sir Edward Grey, men trained at Balliol College, Oxford, by Benjamin Jowett. They were attacked by those who were on the outside—from the fringes, generally the Celtic fringes—men such as Lloyd George, Bonar Law, and Edward Carson. At the same time, there were those who were at the heart of the Establishment, such as Curzon, Balfour, and others, who assumed, generally with justification, that their power would continue no matter which side won. They tended simply to wait for the outcome of the political battles, or to put their weight on the side that looked as if it would win. The "outsiders" were less willing to accept the conventions of politics, or more willing to use politics for their own aims. The entrepreneur who was behind many of the intrigues at this time was Max Aitken, shortly to be

Lord Beaverbrook. He was a Canadian who had come over to England to speculate in stocks and had become increasingly involved in English life, particularly the newspaper world. When he and Bonar Law originally met, they did not get on: Bonar Law thought that Aitken was just an undependable speculator; Aitken, who believed in phrenology, did not like the look of Bonar Law's head. But after this initial mutual disapproval they became good friends, and by the middle of the war Aitken succeeded in persuading Bonar Law that he owed it to the country to help bring about the fall of Asquith. Asquith, after leaving Balliol, had done very well for himself in politics and had adopted a style that made it possible for him to be called "the last of the Romans." He was a superb chairman of committee and a masterful parliamentary politician in time of peace. But he had an irritating tendency to rise above everything. He had been able to work with a cabinet and achieve an operation by consensus. But he was not an ideal war leader. A politician's "image" was becoming increasingly important. A politician had to *seem* to be dedicating every minute to problems of state, particularly in time of war.

The spring of 1915 was marked by the tragic failure of the Gallipoli campaign, by which Churchill had hoped to defeat Turkey. It was an attractive idea for upper-class Englishmen, some of whom saw themselves as latter-day Greeks attacking Troy. Lord Fisher, creator of the modern English navy, had come back to the admiralty as the first sea lord, but Fisher and Winston Churchill, who was the head of the admiralty in the cabinet, disagreed profoundly about the campaign. Fisher felt it was a great mistake. Perhaps if the English had persisted, it would have succeeded, but the losses in men and material were considerable, and the English withdrew without coming close to taking Constantinople. The control of that city was another long-standing concern of English foreign policy, since whoever controlled it could threaten the Mediterranean and the route to India. The failure of the campaign brought Churchill down, and he was not to be a prominent figure again until after the war.

As we have seen the war had quite soon moved into a stalemate: the two sides stuck in trenches opposite each other, rarely changing positions. Then, in May 1915, the revelation of a serious shell shortage on the Western Front brought the first change in government: it was reconstructed as a coalition. Haldane was dropped as a concession to a considerable jingoistic popular opinion that he represented the German spirit—he had had the temerity to admit before the war that he regarded Hegel as an important philosopher and was not outraged by German culture. A number of Tories were brought into the government. Inevitably, Asquith's power lessened when he created his Government of National Unity. Unlike Churchill in the Second World War, Asquith simply was not powerful enough, ultimately, to overshadow the men from the other party or his own. But at the beginning, although the government was a coalition of both parties, it was

David Lloyd George and Winston Churchill in Whitehall, October 1915. At this time, Lloyd George was minister of munitions and Churchill was chancellor of the duchy of Lancaster. (British Information Services.)

still firmly controlled by Asquith and the Liberals. The war, nevertheless, continued to go badly; the country was forced to abandon its initial reaction of "business as usual" and to face the rigor of a more organized economy. Originally, it had been thought that there would be a sufficiently large army without conscription. Necessity, now, seemed to dictate that it be introduced, after various quasi-voluntary schemes had failed to produce enough men for the fighting forces. In May 1916, when conscription was introduced for the first time, many regarded it as a betrayal of the ideal of freedom for which, purportedly, the war was being fought. A considerable number became conscientious objectors. On the whole, they were treated badly by the tribunals before which they pled, and some suffered badly in prison.

The navy was England's pride and joy, so much so that the government appeared somewhat reluctant to use it. During the entire war there were a few small engagements but only one major battle: Jutland on May

31–June 1, 1916. There both Germany and England claimed victory; more English ships were sunk, but the German navy never ventured forth again. England did prevent Germany from using the navy which had been the product of so much competitive building before the war. That rivalry ended as a stalemate, although later Germany would pose a serious threat at sea through submarines.

The government now faced increasing difficulties. In Ireland, which had been fairly calm up until that time, there was a rising against the government in Dublin in Easter week, 1916. It was put down rapidly and bloodily, but it suggested a danger of rebellion and revolution within part of the United Kingdom. Morale was further lowered in 1916, when the *Hampshire*, carrying Kitchener, the secretary of state for war, on a secret mission to Russia, struck a mine on June 5 and sank. In fact, Kitchener had been a bottleneck in the war effort, but as a popular figurehead his loss was a serious blow to the government.

On the Western Front, the Germans had been finally stopped outside Paris in the battle of the Marne, and they and the English and French had dug in for trench warfare. Trusting to the experience of the Boer War, Haig, the commander in France, kept a large troop of cavalry horses ready for mobile battles such as had taken place in South Africa. That was exactly contrary to what happened in France. Eventually, the invention of the tank would provide a radically different and very limited mobility. The casualty and death lists began to grow, and brought with them a significant change in feeling. The course of the war from enthusiasm to disillusionment was paralleled in the poetry that was written about it by the generation of soldier-poets. The first and most famous was Rupert Brooke, who in a sort of exhilaration as the war began wrote, in his sequence *1914*: "Now, God be thanked Who has matched us with His hour/And caught our youth, and wakened us from sleeping. . . ." But in the second stage of the war, exhilaration gave way to disillusionment, caught in the bitterness and sarcasm of the poetry of Siegfried Sassoon, and even more movingly in the work of the greatest of the war poets, Wilfred Owen. Owen, who felt an overwhelming sense of pity for the pain and anguish suffered by the men fighting in the trenches, was himself killed in the last week of the war.

There was growing dissatisfaction with the generals who were conducting the war. General Sir John French was brought back to England in December 1915 and was replaced by a better, but far from perfect, general, Douglas Haig, of the whisky family and a crony of the king's. Haig would continue in charge of English troops until the end of the war, although eventually Lloyd George would get his way and place him, a general he did not trust, under the command of Marshall Foch, the French military leader. In domestic leadership, Asquith continued to convey a sense of indecision. The press, particularly in the person of Lord Northcliffe, who owned both *The Times* and the *Daily Mail*, played a significant role in agitation against Asquith and in favor of Lloyd George. The press could play politics more easily than it could before the war because of the suspension of ordinary politics. Northcliffe sent orders out to his newspapers to print the worst possible photograph of Asquith, putting under it a phrase associated with him before the outbreak of the war, "Wait and See"—a slogan not necessarily without virtue in peacetime but not inspiring in wartime. Northcliffe ordered that the best possible photograph of Lloyd George be published with the caption, "Do It Now!"

Max Aitken, as the middleman, did succeed in keeping Bonar Law, the leader of the Tories, loyal to Lloyd George. (He might have maintained his loyalty to Asquith, in whose coalition cabinet he was the leading Conservative.) Finally, Lloyd George sent an ultimatum to Asquith in which he wrote: "Unity without action is nothing but futile carnage; vigor and vision are the supreme need at this hour." Lloyd George was capable of providing "vigor" in huge quantity. He was now, although a leader of "outsiders," able to gain the support of central Establishment figures. Ironically enough, Max Aitken, the intriguer who, to a large extent, brought about the fall of Asquith, got nothing out of his accomplishment. He had hoped to be brought into the cabinet as president of the Board of Trade; an enemy of his, Albert Stanley, received the post. Stanley was not a member of Parliament, and Aitken was forced to resign his seat in Parliament so Stanley could have it. As a compensation he was made a peer, Lord Beaverbrook. George V was quite irritated at having to do this, as he felt that Aitken was unworthy of a peerage; Aitken himself did not wish to spend the rest of his life in the House of Lords. But from that base he was able to run a career as a public man, as owner of the very successful *Express* papers; he also continued his intriguer's role. Later, he became an important figure in the Second World War as minister of aircraft production, helping to produce the planes that won the Battle of Britain.

The intrigue finally culminated on December 4 and 5, 1916, and resulted in the overthrow of Asquith and his replacement by Lloyd George. Lloyd George was a Liberal prime minister, and officially there was still a Liberal government. In the new government that was now formed, the Tories were much more powerful than Asquith had allowed in his coalition of May 1915. There was a considerable and successful effort to avoid a General Election. Some historians feel that if there had been a General Election during wartime Asquith would have been defeated because of discontent with conduct of the war. But despite the fact that there was much unhappiness with Asquith he might well have won, as many would have wished to avoid a drastic change in the middle of the war.

At the end of 1916 Lloyd George formed a much more effective government. He created a small war cabinet which consisted of himself, Bonar Law, the Marquis of Curzon, Alfred Milner—a financial genius and a much more tough-minded Balliol man than his friend Asquith—and Arthur Hen-

GREAT BRITAIN

NORTH SEA

NETHERLANDS

GERMANY

London

ENGLISH CHANNEL

Calais

Bruges

Ghent

Antwerp

Cologne

Ypres

Lye

Scheide

Brussels

Liege

RHINELAND

Lille

Mons

BELGIUM

Namur

Frankfurt

Arras

Cambrai

Charleroi

Meuse

Somme

St-Quentin

ARDENNES

LUX.

Amiens

Noyon

CHEMIN DES
DAMES

Seden

Luxemburg

Moselle

Laon

Aisne

ARGONNE

Compiègne

Soissons

VIMY RIDGE

Reims

Verdun

SAAR

Paris

Marne

Château-Thierry

CHAMPAGNE

St-
Mihiel

Nancy

Toul

Rhine

Strasbourg

Seine

FRANCE

VOSGES

**FIRST WORLD WAR—
WESTERN FRONT**

Farthest German penetration

Winter 1914/1915

Summer 1918

Armistice line

German occupation

Allied occupation

SWITZERLAND

Map of the First World War—Western Front.

derson, representing the Labour party. Bonar Law was the one member of the war cabinet who dealt with the House of Commons. The others operated as a small group to plan general policy. Also, Lloyd George initiated formal minutes of cabinet meetings for the first time. He later set up a "garden suburb" behind 10 Downing Street, consisting of civil servants who would help the cabinet expedite its business.

Political intrigues gave place to the intrigues of Lloyd George against his generals. In terms of policy, he was not successful, and his imaginative hope for more action in the East came to very little. The war of attrition in the West continued, but finally he was able to place Haig, who was in France, and Robertson, the chief of the imperial general staff, in London under control. In fact, he finally managed to get rid of Robertson entirely; Robertson one day read of his resignation in the newspapers. The fighting in France continued with a horrible similarity as the same ground was fought over. There were heavy attacks; there were gains, often not held. The English and French losses in these battles were frequently greater than those of the Germans. Haig was willing to send troops off to their deaths, but he had little choice, as the men were there to be used in futile offensives.

After Jutland the navy did come back into prominence for convoy duty to protect ships against the submarines that were taking a considerable toll of·English shipping. The navy had been determined not to risk its ships in such duty. The admirals pointed out that there were 5,000 ships leaving English ports every week and that it would be impossible to protect that number. (This extraordinarily high figure came from counting ferries going back and forth across the Channel. It had been concocted to cheer the home front and mislead the enemy, but the admirals used it for their own purposes.) In fact, only 140 freighters left weekly. But Lloyd George forced the navy to protect ships, dramatically curtailing the effectiveness of German submarines.

The cost for Britain, in human terms, was appalling—almost one million killed and two million wounded. The dead included the "cream" of England, in a social sense. Public School products had volunteered, almost to a man, to go into the services, and these were the men who would have helped lead England in the years after the war. There might have been a loosening of the English class system if, because of these deaths, men from other classes had come into political prominence. It is often claimed that to a far greater extent than would otherwise have been true, older and more mediocre men, also from the ruling classes, ruled the country for much of the next twenty years. The Germans, French, and Russians lost even more men. The total number killed was thirteen million, far more than in the Second World War. Some had literally drowned in the mud of France. For instance, in July 1917 at the battle of Passchendaele, the third battle of Ypres, there were 500,000 casualties on both sides.

Three Englishmen were killed or wounded for each German. There was a four-mile advance, as well as the very dubious claim that German morale was hurt slightly more than English. The war, in fact, was reaching a stalemate of ever greater desperation. But, finally, America entered the war in spring of 1917, and toward the end of 1918 her contributions in men and material pushed the balance in favor of the Allies. It might almost be said, however, that the side won that collapsed last. On November 11, 1918, the war ended as it had begun, with fervor, relief, jubilation, and cheerfulness. Later, there was a sense that people had been tricked, but, with the exception of some pacifists, radicals, and a few others, the country remained fairly well united during the war. It was not until after the war's end that there were serious doubts about its wisdom.

The war brought much greater government control to English society and also loosened its conventions somewhat. (When a war has to be fought, domestic problems and attitudes are forced to take second place. Class barriers are challenged.) Money was spent much more freely, and a sense of living better—for tomorrow one might die—extended to all classes. Styles, standards, and principles of conduct changed dramatically.

Domestically, the first period of the war was marked by an attempt to maintain "business as usual," to pretend that the war was not really affecting the home front. But a belief that the war would be similar in its effects to the smaller military actions that had been fought since 1815 could be maintained only for eight months. The essential increase in state control would also occur during the Second World War. Both wars brought important social change, most notably in making English society more adaptable to state control and more prone to see such control essential, not only in ensuring a successful prosecution of the war but also in improving the quality of life in peacetime. During both wars the hierarchy of English society, and its class structure, was modified and relaxed, but certainly not destroyed. Except for a small minority during the First World War, as A. J. P. Taylor has pointed out, national loyalty transcended class consciousness. The state took upon itself, with little question, the right to tell people what to do, and the strong tradition of laissez-faire economics, only challenged sporadically before the war, was temporarily abandoned because of wartime necessity. (The attempt to return to prewar conditions after the war would have disastrous consequences.) During the First World War there was some rationing, and the government introduced, to a limited degree, a supervised economy. It exercised some control over prices, and it also took over temporarily some of the major industries, such as the railroads. The government also maintained greater supervision of individuals, most notably through "Dora"—the Defense of the Realm Act—which gave the government the right to curtail personal liberties if it deemed it necessary, interfering with the hitherto sacred rights of the free-born Englishman.

The Menin Road to Ypres: This land was first fought over in October 1914. (Imperial War Museum.)

Labor was treated with more care, as it became a valuable resource whether it provided soldiers or manned the factories. For the first two years of the war, there was a comparative industrial truce. But in its last two years shop stewards in many areas—that is, the foremen in the factories—became increasingly radical and, often contrary to their unions' wishes, led strikes of varying degrees of effectiveness. The unions did try to protect themselves against "dilution," as it was called: the use of unskilled workers, particularly women; they were concerned about the implications of such actions after the war. They also became increasingly distressed over wages which did go up to a certain extent, but clearly far less so than the profits of many of the owners of the means of production. Through the experience of the war workers came to feel both a sense of their own importance and of the extent to which they were held down by their society.

Liquor supply provides a good example of the effect of the war on the habits of Englishmen and their willingness, given the circumstances, to be told what to do and to relinquish their traditional individual rights. Lloyd George maintained that liquor was a more serious enemy than Germany— perhaps a pardonable exaggeration—and certainly it increased the problem of absenteeism. The hours that a bar was open were limited by law during the war, and the wishes of the Nonconformists of previous years were finally realized by the necessity of the war effort. The king made the gesture of "taking the pledge" and not touching drink for the duration. In order to control the consumption of spirits, prices were increased and potency reduced. The technique worked. In England and Wales in 1914 the convictions for drunkenness were 3,388; in 1918 they were 449. On the Clyde, the great industrial area outside of Glasgow in Scotland, the regulations did not have much effect, for the Scots would not give up their national drink; they were already accustomed to avoiding the rigors of Scottish sabbatarianism.

After the war capital assets of England were not quite as seriously consumed as some had feared, or said subsequently. The war had destroyed 40 percent of British shipping, but the merchant marine was rapidly rebuilt. Finances were seriously hurt. One quarter of British overseas investments had had to be called in and turned into cash, so to speak, to pay for the war. The war did accentuate and hurry changes which had started before. It provided an easy excuse, explanation, and accelerator for change.

The conventional attitude toward money taken by the United States caused England much difficulty. If all countries had reneged on their debts, the situation would have been much improved. England, in fact, was a creditor nation toward its other allies, but a debtor nation to the United States. England felt, to some extent, that it was bound to honor its debt to the United States if that country demanded it, even if those countries that owed debts to England, most notably, the formerly tsarist Russia, could not or would not pay them.

In sum, the war had weakened class lines but had not destroyed them. It had introduced some degree of wartime socialism which, although abandoned to a considerable extent after the war, was an experience that provided a model for the future as well as concepts, few of which were realized, for reconstruction after the war. The civil servants were full of interesting plans for the postwar world, but the politicians lost courage or never had much desire for such plans. They returned as quickly as they could to the status quo ante bellum. The new agencies that the government had created to take care of wartime needs were closed down before they could turn their attention to peacetime problems.

The Rush to "Normalcy"

After 1918 England appeared to be a more "small-minded" sort of country. To a certain extent, she had lost her innocence, as well as some of her zest. It had been grand to be an Englishman, and this vicarious sense of being "top dog" had extended down to the ordinary reader of the *Daily Mail*. But the inhabitant of the slums had not necessarily enjoyed the period when England was the most powerful country in the world. In fact, from 1918 on, despite the serious setback of the Great Depression, the lot of the "common man" steadily improved. There was, however, an increasing failure of imagination by government after 1918. Many who might have provided new ideas for peace were dead and were replaced, in Baldwin's phrase, by the "hard-faced men of business who had done well out of the war."

Lloyd George was anxious to maintain himself in power: there was a rush to a General Election in mid-December 1918, the so-called coupon election. The "coupon" election is too frequently viewed as an aberration of the "natural" two-party system in England; in fact, the two-party system had frequently been in abeyance in the past. Fights for leadership can reveal as much if not more of those disagreements that change the course of English political development than does a General Election. A General Election represents a vague if blanket approval for one leader or another.

The "coupon" election was arranged between Lloyd George and Bonar Law, the leaders of the coalition and, technically, the leaders of two rival parties. Lloyd George and Bonar Law issued letters of endorsement, which Asquith derisively labeled "coupons," to those M.P.s whom they wanted reelected. It had been presumed that these letters went to the M.P.s who had supported the government in May 1918 in the Maurice debate. General Maurice had accused the government of lying in its report of the number of men in France. It was a dubious accusation for a military man to make, but in the circumstances, and considering Lloyd George's own way of operating, it was not totally unjustified. Asquith, the leader of the Liberals out of office, seized upon the issue as one of confidence and organized one of the very few substantive debates to take place in the House of Commons during the war. The government was victorious: Lloyd George flatly denied the accusation. It has subsequently been maintained that Maurice was right, but Lloyd George may have been provided with the wrong figures.[1] Feelings were running high, since not only political survival but the actual survival of the country was at stake. Now that Lloyd George was the victor in war, it was thought that he would destroy those who had shown open opposition. In fact, Lloyd George used the coupon in an ultimately vain attempt to preserve, rather than destroy, the Liberal party. He realized that most electors, in the flush of victory, would probably vote for the candidates of the coalition. Of course, in most cases, these were the candidates to whom the "coupon" was issued, but it was also issued to a certain number of Liberal members who probably would have gone down to defeat without it.

Nevertheless, the atmosphere of the election was vindictive, not so much in internal terms but in a continuation of the worst aspects of the

---

[1] See A. J. P. Taylor, *English History 1914–1945* (Oxford, 1965), pp. 117–18.

home-front war spirit. Lloyd George had originally not been in favor of a severe peace. But being so much of an opportunist, he gave in to what he felt was the spirit of the times and was likely to gain more votes: Germany would have to be "squeezed until the pips squeak"—"Hang the Kaiser"—vindictive ideas which Lloyd George reluctantly supported.

Lloyd George felt that the soldiers would not be well-disposed toward those in power, thus he planned to have the election held so quickly that, in effect, most of the military were unable to vote. The election capitalized on the idea that one should support a victorious government. It was an overwhelming victory for the coalition, the Lloyd George-Bonar Law government. There were 707 M.P.s, and of those 335 were coalition Unionists, 133 coalition Liberals, and 10 coalition Labour. The election also marked a strong emergence of the Labour party as the official opposition, with 63 M.P.s in contrast to the Asquith Liberals with only 28 M.P.s. Such a step was important for the psychology of the Labour parliamentary group. The opposition, in effect, is a "shadow" establishment. "His Majesty's Opposition" is a characteristic English phrase, with its suggestion of official and loyal opposition. Their difference from those in power, it is implied, is not likely to be too considerable.

In the rush to return to "normalcy," as little attention as possible was paid to those who were profoundly discontented with English society. The spirit of discontent was not dead, however. It was caught by such men as the great economic historian R. H. Tawney, who had fought during the war and who became a source of intellectual and moral strength for the Labour party. He wrote about the Parliament election in 1918: "It is not for carrion crows like these that men have stiffened for three winters in the bloody salient round Ypres or flung themselves against machine guns on the solemn downs above the Somme." The English Establishment was rushing to patch itself up at the same time that others felt that this society which had survived the war did not deserve to survive the peace.

Perhaps one reason that there was not more discontent right after the war was that the government did attempt to make some changes, or at least to give the impression of doing so. There was a rational plan, at first, that no one should be released from the army unless he had a job available in civilian life. The soldiers would not accept this; there were riots and meetings at army bases. Eventually, soldiers were released on the basis of first in, first out. There were mutinies in the navy as well. The Russian Revolution of 1917 was exciting to the Labour movement as well as to others, most notably, groups in the armed services. It inspired a brief soviet movement of workers' committees, but such steps rapidly evaporated as England rushed toward peace. The exhilaration of the Russian Revolution was a continual inspiration to those on the far left, and it inspired the more moderate left to hope that they would be more powerful in postwar society than they had been before the war.

The most dramatic example of the influence of the revolution and postwar restlessness occurred in Glasgow in January 1919. The workers more or less took over the city and the Red flag flew from city hall. Glasgow had always been a radical center, and some of the leaders of this dramatic if brief development were elected to Parliament: the famous Clydesiders. But they became somewhat more conservative as the years progressed. There was no serious threat of revolution, in part because the economic situation was not too serious in the first three years after the war. A period of comparative boom, which lasted elsewhere until 1929, ended in England in 1921. That year brought a mild depression, which, of course, became much worse in 1929. But, ironically, although it is probable that during most of the years between the wars more people may have been out of work than before the First World War, the standard of living of those unemployed, as well as those employed, was probably higher, on the average, than it had been during the period of England's great power.

The most serious area of economic discontent and bad conditions was in the mines. The government tried, to a certain extent, to help the miners: there was some talk of nationalization of the mines. But the situation worsened, and the miners went out on strike on April 15, 1921, a day that became known among them as Black Friday because the other unions did not support them and the strike was a dismal failure. A contrasting day was the famous Red Friday in 1926, when the miners led the English unions out on a general strike. But even then, although the general strike lasted from May 3 to May 12, the miners were abandoned again to a long and ultimately unsuccessful seven-month strike. The mines came to represent the general state of malaise of English industrial society between the wars.

In the early 1920s bits and pieces of wartime socialism were still functioning but not as part of any consistent, coherent plan. There were some efforts by the coalition government to relieve worsening economic conditions. The Housing and Town Planning Act in 1919 led to the building of 213,000 houses. The Unemployment Insurance Act of 1920 affected, potentially, twelve million workers.

Ireland provided a continual problem for the government. The period between the Easter rebellion in 1916 and 1921, when a treaty was finally signed, saw the culminating deterioration of Anglo-Irish relations. Ireland was determined to have some sort of independence from England. The Royal Irish Constabulary was not sufficient to cope with the situation. The government sent over troops as well as officers who were unemployed after the war. There were the famous or infamous "Black and Tans," so named by the Irish after a pack of hounds and for the mixed uniform they wore. Their experiences in the war had brutalized these men; and they also moved to revenge the equally brutal attacks of the members of the Irish Republican Army. There were outrages on both sides in a ceaseless escalation. Groups of "Black and Tans" would enter a village and kill suspected Irish rebels; the I.R.A. would come back into the same village and victimize those whom they considered to be sympathetic to the English.

Lloyd George was anxious to solve the problem, and he was able to enlist the help of George V, who made what A. J. P. Taylor considers the greatest contribution a monarch has made in the twentieth century. The king had always been more compassionate than many of his subjects: for instance, he had resisted the excessive anti-Germanism that was rife in England during the First World War, although he was forced by public opinion to deprive enemy monarchs of their Knighthoods of the Garter. He also had objected to Haldane's being forced out of office because of his alleged sympathy for Germany. In his way, the king represented an older idea of the international aristocratic class, who might be fighting one another, yet believed that civilities could still be maintained between them. A comparable belief—essentially, in behaving civilly—moved him where the Irish were concerned. He objected particularly to the brutalities done in Ireland in the name of law and order. He persuaded the government to allow him to go to Belfast in Ulster—Northern Ireland—to address, in a conciliatory way to all sides, the opening of the first meeting of the Stormont, the Northern Irish Parliament. This speech was an important prelude to the peace negotiations between the English and the southern Irish. The Irish were in the middle of what was, in effect, a civil war, and so it was somewhat equivocal as to who represented whom, on the Irish side, in the negotiations. Lloyd George managed, through flattery and threats, to persuade the group who seemed to be in control in Ireland to agree to a treaty that promised peace and limited independence. In December 1921 a truce was achieved and a treaty signed which led eventually to the creation of the Irish Free State: Eire. Civil war continued in Ireland after this between the pro- and antitreaty forces, but it was a civil war from which England could remain aloof.

From the English point of view, the solution of the Irish problem was a great success and triumph for Lloyd George. But it decreased his power domestically. As a Liberal who was the leader of a largely Conservative government, he was weakened when he solved problems and hence made himself less necessary. The Tories questioned increasingly why they should not have a Tory leader. They found Lloyd George less and less congenial. He was aware of his dangerous position and was anxious to build up a party organization of his own, separate from the official Liberal party organization, which was still controlled by Asquith. Lloyd George acquired large sums of money for his own party organization through the virtual sale of honors: knighthoods, baronetcies, and peerages. In the past, of course, it had been necessary to have a great deal of money to maintain a peerage, but before it had almost generally been money that three generations of possession had made thoroughly respectable. Lloyd George bypassed such traditions and was willing to try to arrange to give the first generation—the man who had acquired the money—a knighthood or a peerage if enough money were paid to his political organization. One might say this showed a refreshing Welsh attitude toward the English Establishment. Lloyd George finally went too far in 1922, when various dubious businessmen, who had already advanced to the baronetage, were proposed as barons; the outcry over their questionable credentials reached such proportions that one had to be withdrawn, and Lloyd George, on the verge of losing his position in any case, withdrew from the "Honours Game." As Stanley Baldwin remarked of Lloyd George, he is "a great dynamic force which is a very terrible thing." Lloyd George represented the war and further frenetic activity. A. J. P. Taylor wrote of Lloyd George in his *English History 1914–1945*:

> He was the most inspired and creative British statesman of the twentieth century. But he had fatal flaws. He was devious and unscrupulous in his methods. He aroused every feeling except trust. In all his greatest acts, there was an element of self-seeking. Above all he lacked stability. He tied himself to no men, to no party, to no single cause. Baldwin was right to fear that Lloyd George would destroy the Conservative party, as he had destroyed the Liberal party. With his fall, the sheet-anchors of party came back.

Such figures as Lloyd George and Winston Churchill are feared by ordinary politicians who believe that party is all-important and conventional party conduct the ideal. The mavericks, such as Churchill and Lloyd George, believe that the party should be exploited both for personal advantage and for what they consider the greater good of their country. Such figures can either act with lack of concern and some stupidity or with great bravado and grandeur. With both Lloyd George and Churchill, it was a question, frequently, of timing. At the time of the First World War, for Lloyd George, and at the time of the Second World War, for Churchill, the man was matched with his hour. But, particularly between the wars, both these men seemed to flounder, unable to realize their full potentialities. They both made mistakes, and they both appeared to turn away from their commitment, no matter how tenuous it might have been, to the kind of social reforms they had championed before the First World War.

Lloyd George's fall from power in 1922 marks a reversion to a myth of an older England. Beaverbrook once more was the central intriguer in the plot to bring Lloyd George down. He had been involved in successful intrigue in 1911 under the slogan "BMG": Balfour Must Go. He had been deeply involved in the intrigue that led to the fall of Asquith in 1916. Now the situation was shaping up for a way to topple Lloyd George from the premiership. Bonar Law, the leader of the Tories who had replaced Balfour in 1911, was a new-style businessman; men like him were becoming increasingly important in the Tory party. Bonar Law had resigned because of ill health in March 1921. This would have appeared to mean that Lloyd George now was in a stronger position because his most serious rival had left the scene. Despite the fact that the series of international conferences that he was engaged in were less and less successful, his reputation abroad was still very high: he was regarded as the man who had won the war. At home, he was still very popular. Yet in many constituences he was losing by-elections. Also he was losing the support of many political figures who had been with him in the past. Churchill, for example, was becoming increasingly restless, and his activity in politics was more and more sporadic. He was not in a position to, nor did he choose to, give much help to Lloyd George. (Churchill was playing a less sympathetic role than he had before the First World War. The 1920s and 1930s were to be his years "out-of-joint": the twenties because he was overly aggressive, the thirties because he was ignored and sulking. He felt in the 1930s that England should be stronger, but he was in political exile because he disapproved of the conciliatory policy toward India.) Curzon, the foreign secretary, represented an important group which had given support before. Now he was becoming more and more distressed. He was a curious figure, rather supercilious and offensively aristocratic. He wrote to his wife at this time: "Girlie: I'm getting very tired of trying to work with that man. He wants a foreign secretary to be a valet, almost a drudge, and he has no regard for the conventions or civilities of official life." In this period of the so-called new, open diplomacy which Lloyd George carried on after Versailles, Curzon felt increasingly neglected.

Beaverbrook, the intriguer, thought there were plenty of issues to be used against Lloyd George: discontent in the cabinet, the state of the coal industry, continual and increasing unemployment, the still unsettled question of reparations. Many Tories were upset over the Irish settlement. In the spring of 1922 Lloyd George tried to reestablish himself through diplomacy and by continuing to make himself an essential figure. With such a hope, he went to the Genoa conference on postwar reconstruction, but the conference was not a success, and he failed to bolster his position.

As it had been in the past with military questions, it was now with diplomatic procedures: those in control tended to learn the wrong lessons from past errors. For instance, the Union of Democratic Control, an important left-wing group formed during the First World War, had preached that one very important reason the war had come about was the practice of secret diplomacy. This theory was dramatically supported by the revolutionary Russians, who published the treaties they had found in the imperial archives. It was now revealed that Constantinople was to have been given to Russia as one of the secret arrangements designed to spur nations to participate in war. In order to avoid war, according to this theory of the U.D.C., there should be, in Woodrow Wilson's phrase, "open covenants openly arrived at." But open diplomacy was practiced in the postwar period with disastrous results. The politicians played to the gallery and avoided the older "realistic" approaches. If they had remained more traditional, a softer attitude toward Germany might have emerged and prevented the rise of Hitler. In this very tentative and "iffy" sense the new open diplomacy was one of the causes of the Second World War. The Union of Democratic Control had a very good point that secret arrangements had helped bring about the First World War. But, frequently, a reaction to a fault in the past raises up a whole new set of problems.

In any case, in Genoa nothing was achieved from the point of view of Lloyd George and his policy. Germany and Russia conferred on their own up the coast at Rapallo and undercut the other powers. *The Times* said about Lloyd George's foreign policy that he

> made a treaty and departed from it . . . dallied with Bolshevism and supported campaigns against it . . . coquetted with Germany and played fast and loose with France, dragged from conference to conference the failure to face the reparations issue, [and finally came] to the verge of an armed conflict in the Near East, the course and outline of which no man could foretell. As a result of his inconsistencies, the word of England lost currency throughout a great part of the world as the word of an upright land.

In effect, *The Times* was accusing him of not being a gentleman, and what accusation could be more serious? Beaverbrook began to move. He now felt that it was possible to jettison Lloyd George as he was a man without a party. It was a moment when, as Beaverbrook himself wrote, "Old friendships were severed. Alliances were broken down, companionships were sundered, and relationships were strangely altered." And he remarked of Lloyd George that, desperate to keep power, he resorted to "Promises and promotions . . . honours were sprinkled from Downing Street on the green benches with a hose."

The final blow to Lloyd George's prestige was the incident at Chanak in the spring of 1922; this was the "armed conflict" referred to by *The Times*. It had its origin in 1920, when a monkey bit the hand of the King of Greece, Alexander I, fatally poisoning him. King Constantine, his father, who had abdicated in 1917, returned to the throne. He upset the policy of his son and was much more aggressive toward Turkey. Lloyd George took a stand on behalf of the Greeks, who had been England's allies in the Great War. As it turned out, Lloyd George's aggressiveness on behalf of Greece backfired, lowering English prestige. This was one reason the English were not to take a strong stand internationally again until 1939. The Greeks had started the altercation between the two countries through a threat to take Constantinople. Only the moderation of the English general on the scene at Chanak, a post on the Dardanelles held by the English, prevented England from going to war against Turkey. Although Lloyd George asked for their help, the dominions held back. They could now pick and choose when they would support the mother country; no longer would they automatically come to her aid, as on the whole they had in the past. The result of the Chanak incident was to make Lloyd George look foolish, and it weakened him greatly.

Bonar Law, lured out of retirement by Beaverbrook, wrote to *The Times* that the antics of Lloyd George simply would not do and that some changes were necessary. But he was very reluctant to take steps himself, and Beaverbrook had to use all his gifts of persuasion to make him move against Lloyd George. On October 19, 1922, the Conservative parliamentary party met and decided to withdraw its support of the coalition, to reassert traditional party activities . . . and to abandon Lloyd George.

After Lloyd George's fall, a General Election gave the Tories an overwhelming victory. Lloyd George would never again be in office. The Conservatives now had 345 M.P.s; Labour, with 142 M.P.s, was still the official opposition. The party system was still in flux, the Liberals continuing to decline, even though they were still important. The Asquith Liberals had 54 M.P.s in the new Parliament, while the coalition Liberals, led by Lloyd George, numbered 62 and were much richer. Traditional politics was trying to reassert itself: the Tories were thought to represent a greater degree of stability and "normalcy" than the other parties and were to dominate English politics for the rest of the interwar period.

"Normalcy" rather rapidly became translated into "complacency," and Stanley Baldwin became the leading exponent of this style, succeeding the ill Bonar Law as leader of the Tory party. But the most impressive figure in the Conservative government was Neville Chamberlain, the man who would come to stand for all that was weakest in English foreign policy. Neville, the younger son of Joseph Chamberlain, was not as attractive or as fashionable as his elder brother Austen. Yet it would be Neville alone, of the three Chamberlain politicians—Joseph, Austen, and Neville—who would eventually become prime minister. His foreign policy in the late 1930s has tended to obscure his high capabilities as a planner of domestic policies, most particularly in housing. Both Labour and Tory government made progress in the continuing problems of building "homes for heroes"; not enough were ever built, but more progress was made toward such a goal than in any other economic area.

Now that he was freed of the overlordship of Lloyd George, Curzon was able to achieve a more successful foreign policy. After the fiasco of Chanak, England could not hope to assert herself thoroughly, but she could reestablish herself in a limited way in attempting to adjust the "balance" in Europe. Curzon settled the border question with the Turks at a conference at Lausanne, and thus he solved the immediate Greco-Turkish rivalry which had led to the fall of Lloyd George. He managed to a certain extent to establish good relations with France, but the two victorious nations were not able to agree on their attitude toward Germany. France was primarily concerned with security and hence wished to limit Germany's power. England was more interested in achieving some degree of reconciliation. But although, in the 1920s, the issue was troublesome, it did not, despite the occupation of the Ruhr by French and Belgian forces in 1923, become as serious as it would after the accession of Hitler to power in 1933.

In May 1923 Bonar Law resigned, mortally ill from cancer of the throat. The political system again experienced a temporary crisis over the question of who should be prime minister. Curzon was convinced that he would be the man. But the king and powerful elements in the Conservative party, among them, some said, Bonar Law himself, who did not give any official advice, felt, particularly with the Labour party the opposition party, that the prime minister should be in the House of Commons and that the man should be Stanley Baldwin. Baldwin had been chancellor of the Exchequer in Bonar Law's cabinet; but he had not been in politics long and he hardly had the stature of the Marquis of Curzon. Curzon would not deign to have a telephone at his country house, and so a telegram was sent summoning him to London. He came up to town convinced that he was the next prime minister, only to be told by the king's secretary that it was to be Stanley Baldwin, the last blow in a career that had received its share of disappointments. Curzon referred to Baldwin as a man of "utmost insignificance" but consented to remain in his office of foreign secretary. The spirit of Baldwin was dominant for the next ten years. He adroitly provided what he believed the British public wished: a sense, indeed a myth, of "normalcy."

Labour in Power

Baldwin felt that the policy of protection—tariffs against foreign goods—would help England during her period of economic difficulty. At last, the solution that Joseph Chamberlain had advocated before the First World War became official Tory party policy. Large segments of the public, however, still regarded free trade as an article of faith not to be betrayed. A strong belief in this long-held Liberal principle was, ironically, the chief reason Labour came into power for the first time in its history. In the General Election of 1923, although the popular vote was barely different from the previous election, the Tories lost eighty-seven seats, as switches in votes were crucial in various constituencies. A very small percentage change of the votes—in this case, one-tenth of one percent—if distributed in an advantageous way, can mean a considerable change in the makeup of the House of Commons. The Tory party was still the largest single group, with 258 M.P.s. The Liberals, with Asquith and Lloyd George reunited in defense of free trade, had 159 M.P.s, and Labour had 191 members. The Liberals had to decide which party they would support. Since the issue of the election had been protection, and this was the very issue which had united the factions of the Liberal party, it was felt that they should support the Labour party. Asquith thought that since support by Liberal M.P.s would give Labour power, the Liberals would hence be able to control the course of events. The leaders of both older parties, in fact, felt that it would be "gracious" to give Labour a chance, so that the newest party would have the training and taming experience of being in power.

In January 1924 the Labour party assumed this power. The party's history since 1914 had paved the way. During the First World War Arthur Henderson, the leader of the parliamentary party, was a member of Lloyd George's small war cabinet. A few other Labour leaders also had the experience of being figures in the government. At the same time, and equally important, the party maintained its dissident role. Ramsay MacDonald had resigned as head of the parliamentary party, and some other leaders continued to oppose the war. Arthur Henderson and Lloyd George had a bitter parting of the ways over the Stockholm Conference—a conference called by the Russians for September 1917, where socialists might meet and perhaps consider ways in which the war could be brought to an end. Henderson's hope was that an English socialist delegation might be able to keep Russia in the war. But the cabinet regarded his going as too much a gesture of conciliation; and Henderson resigned over this issue in August 1917. In fact, his resignation was a fortunate event from the point of view of the Labour party. Doubts were reappearing about the war and its conduct. Labour had had the experience of being in government but was now no longer part of the coalition; a few leaders remained within it, but Henderson's departure signified a break and renewed independence.

There had been some union unrest during the war, increasing as the labor force became more restless and felt itself exploited. This feeling continued after the war, and many unions were particularly distressed at the miners' defeat on Black Friday in 1921. As a result, the unions rededicated themselves to political action. From the General Election of 1918 to that of 1923 Labour's percentage of votes increased from 22.2 percent to 29.5 percent; in 1910 it had been 7.2 percent. On the other hand, clearly a considerable part of the working-class population failed to identify with the party which was supposed to represent it.

The Union of Democratic Control had served as a recruiting ground, and means, for Liberals to move over to the Labour party. More and more Liberals felt that the old Liberal party was done for. This was particularly true of the more adventuresome of the upper-class intellectuals, who had provided much of the verve in the prewar Liberal party. They were profoundly distressed that, to their minds, the Liberal party had betrayed its tradition of peace and had led England into war. Great Liberal names moved into the Labour party, among them Russells, Wedgwoods, Ponsonbys, Trevelyans. Haldane became associated with the Labour party and so did even a few Tories, such as Lord Parmoor, Beatrice Webb's brother-in-law, and Stafford Cripps's father. Such figures made the Labour party more respectable. The new Labour party constitution made it possible to join the party directly and not necessarily as a member of a constituent group, most commonly a union. The Labour party was now more clearly open to workers by both "hand and brain."

Their upper- and upper middle-class backgrounds gave many of these new recruits a more conservative style. Assured of their social position, they had that sense of "belonging" so characteristic of the English upper classes. Yet, in general, they were willing to be more daring than many a more traditional Labour supporter from a poorer background. Such a man might be, as John Burns was, less willing to make changes in the system. Frequently, the richer recruits were more imaginative than those who had risen through hard work to positions of union leadership. On the other hand many who had risen in the Labour party had not lost their fire and determination to change the system, at least to some degree. Such men as Ernest Bevin, the founder and the secretary of the Transport and General Workers' Union, regarded the new, more intellectual recruits as flighty.

Ramsay MacDonald, the leader of the Labour party dissidents during the First World War, came back as leader of the party. Now, in retrospect, he was regarded as a hero because of his opposition to the war, although, in fact, where domestic policy was concerned he tended to be on the right of center, even in Liberal terms. MacDonald shared with Baldwin the ability to produce a fog of rhetoric, which the public seemed to desire in the 1920s. Here is part of the program he put forward in 1920:

> The offices in Whitehall would hum with the new industry. The administration of Labour would be as new as its legislation. Its influence, exerted in a thousand different ways, would be to advance liberty, to set people on their feet, to give Labour responsibility, to produce the citizen of robust mind and of faithful service, to curb the powers that do injustice in the State and that exploit and break men. . . .

Labour formed a ministry in January 1924. The Labour leaders were anxious to be respectable and responsible. A few middle-class Englishmen and women felt that the end had come and that Reds were loose in the land, thinking only of rape and robbery. *The English Review* commented:

> We stand now at a moment when the sun of England seems menaced with a final eclipse. For the first time in our history the party of revolution approach the hands to the helm of the state, not only as in the seventeenth century, for the purpose of overthrowing the crown, of altering the Constitution, but with the design of destroying the very bases of civilized life.

Nothing could have been further from the truth. The chief interest of Labour leaders was not how to destroy the state but, it might be said with only slight exaggeration, what clothes they should wear when they were presented to the king. Trivial as such concerns were, they reveal the power of English society, and its power to make trivia important. Court dress might show that a Labour leader was "selling out." On the other hand, it might appear silly to make such a fuss about something as unimportant as clothes. The majority, but not all, of the Labour ministers, when they were presented to the monarch, wore court dress. It was a symbol of a relationship to the state. Beatrice Webb worried about the problem of social life; she feared that Labour leaders, and perhaps even more their wives, might be seduced to the high life of London. Therefore, she very consciously and conscientiously went about establishing some sort of social circle for Labour so that they would not be taken up by those who might corrupt them. Haldane also relished the role of teacher to these new masters of the English state. He gave dinner parties at which, against his own inclination, he served orangeade and lemonade rather than wine.

Labour had a more serious choice to make. They could try to govern as calmly as they could and demonstrate that they were respectable. Or they could, aware that their power base within Parliament was likely to end soon, use the opportunity to set up a model "socialistic" program as an ideal for the future. Such a picture might capture the imagination of the electorate and eventually gain them votes. Although they chose the respectable course, their government only lasted nine months before the Liberals withdrew support.

MacDonald appointed a cabinet of twenty, eleven of whom were of proletarian origin. The other nine members came from the Union of Democratic Control and from the traditional classes who were generally in power. Still, the majority was from a new group. Working-class men, except for John Burns and Arthur Henderson, had virtually never served in a cabinet before. There was, however, a strong conservative streak in the eleven workers. Stephen Walsh, the secretary of state for war, assured his civil servants and generals that his first principle was loyalty to the king. J. H. Thomas at the colonial office told his civil servants that "I'm here to see that there is no mucking about with the British Empire." The most impressive and radical figure in the cabinet was John Wheatley, one of the Clydesiders. He had begun as a coal-miner but was now quite prosperous as owner of a firm which manufactured religious calendars; he was a devout Roman Catholic. Wheatley put through the House of Commons a very strong Housing Act, the best passed during the interwar years. It resulted in the building of a quarter of a million houses by 1927. He showed extraordinary tact and skill in putting through the bill; his future seemed promising, but he became increasingly eccentric after Labour fell; he died in 1930 at the age of sixty-one.

Labour was unable to do much about the more serious problem of the time: unemployment. From 1923 until 1929 the unemployment figure was at 11 percent; from 1929 on it rose considerably higher. England was, indeed, in a state of mild depression for most of the twenties; the coming of the major depression of 1929 intensified, rather than inaugurated, a downward economic plunge.

The great failure of Labour in power was in the ambiguous area of planning. Labour leaders were so involved in immediate problems that they either did not wish to or did not have a chance to worry about what a socialist government should do in a general way. MacDonald lost himself in work and in coping with immediate problems. In addition, Labour leaders may have taken responsibility too seriously. They did not have that rather arrogant and possessive attitude toward power frequently found on the right among those accustomed to be in ruling positions.

Labour's excessive caution was particularly noticeable in finance. Philip Snowden, the chancellor of the Exchequer, was a bitter and brilliant man who pulsated with moral indignation. He had been a powerful opponent of the capitalist system. At party conferences during the First World War he attacked those who wished to cooperate with the government. Now that he had authority and was chancellor of the Exchequer he turned out to be a perfect proponent of Gladstonian finance, whose chief aim was to spend as little and save as much as possible: a form of financial thinking out-of-date for the problems of the 1920s, although it was still financial orthodoxy. Snowden now reserved his considerable supply of moral indignation for those who wished to be adventuresome about money. He was a willing captive of his civil servants. He chose to forget that the socialist analysis of society—which in a reluctant way the Labour party had pledged itself to in its new constitution of 1918—called for a change of the economic arrangements. Snowden now felt that laissez-faire capitalism should be preserved, albeit with some modifications. Snowden's own civil servants in the treasury also mounted guard. The treasury men were the mandarins of the civil-servant system and were committed to caution; both they and Snowden believed that public works schemes must be self-supporting. The 1920s was a pre-Keynes era, but still a socialist government might well have risked a less conservative role. In fact, Keynes himself was deeply disappointed in the course the Labour government took. His old pupil at Cambridge, Hugh Dalton, now a minor figure in the government, felt, unlike Keynes, that debt redemption was much more important than public work.

Snowden recognized that eventually there should be some sort of tax on the landowner, but he also believed in being kind to the private investor and to the working businessman. He was not, in any sense, any longer a radical. The left of the Labour party, which might have been expected to be unhappy with Snowden, did not, on the whole, protest. Snowden's conservative budget was greeted with cheers by the right because it was so much less "dangerous" than expected; the left, other than the lonely Liberal voice of Keynes, did not make any objection. Snowden did want to increase consumer purchasing power, but he could not think of a way to do it. There was no mention in his budget, or elsewhere, of nationalization, to which the party had committed itself in 1918.

Labour even had trouble with strikes; they were somewhat victimized by their position of power. They felt that they could not be overindulgent to the unions because they had to prove that, although they were in large part a product of the union movement, when they were in power they were impartial.

The government operated very well in foreign policy. This was Mac-Donald's personal triumph. He was both prime minister and foreign secretary. He was among the most successful, if not the most successful, international politician of the between-the-wars period. In part, his actions were also a justification for his position during the First World War. To begin with, he got on very well with his civil servants, but without kowtowing to them as some other ministers did. The civil servants found his manner a pleasant change from Lloyd George's rambunctiousness and Curzon's superciliousness. He had a breezy style which paid off in foreign policy; he managed to retain the trust of the dissidents, who had been his colleagues during the war; he now acquired the trust of at least part of the establishment. He appeared sincere, unlike Lloyd George. Curzon had been overly conscious of protocol; MacDonald was willing to cut through it. In August 1924 the London Conference, one of the many international conferences about money and reparations held in these postwar years, took place. France applied continual pressure to get money from Germany, and at this conference the plan of the American banker Charles G. Dawes was accepted, proposing a scheme of reparations that Germany theoretically was to pay (but actually did not). MacDonald threw his support to the Dawes Plan and so was crucial in achieving a temporary settlement.

MacDonald was capable of spreading a great fog of language over his activities, giving many the impression that something good was happening. It is, perhaps, rather unfair to give a sample of his rhetoric, but here is one of his more baffling paragraphs from a speech in the House of Commons:

> A guarantee cannot be a guarantee of a separate pact with only one nation or two nations, but it must change its nature and become a guarantee of some cooperative organization of the wide scope and amplitude and moral authority of the League of Nations; that so soon as you aim at a guarantee by a body like the League of Nations you minimize and subordinate the military value of the pact and raise to a really effective standard the moral guarantees that flow from conciliation, arbitration, impartial and judicial judgment exercised by the body with which you are associated.

MacDonald and Baldwin, the two dominant politicians of the period, specialized in this sort of language. Both of them were great showmen. They knew what they were doing and that it was what the British public appeared to want. Ambiguity and lack of clarity are not necessarily vices for the running of a state. Crystal-clear concepts are much harder to implement. They commit politicians to positions they might not wish to hold for long. MacDonald and Baldwin worked effectively in a London fog and thereby maintained greater freedom of action. Their aim was wooliness and muddling through at the same time that they were tough politicians.

MacDonald was loyal to his membership of the Union of Democratic Control in his attempt to achieve international agreement in new ways, to steer a middle course between international anarchy and secret treaties. But as was true with every English leader in the interwar period, he too was unable to achieve a coherent policy of cooperation with France. He was unable to persuade France to abandon her intense concern with security and to be more conciliatory to Germany.

England had participated in the somewhat vindictive aspects of the Treaty of Versailles, but almost immediately thereafter she had changed her position into a softer one toward Germany. In good part this change in attitude was achieved through John Maynard Keynes's extremely influential book, *The Economic Consequences of the Peace* (1919). There he denounced the treaty, arguing that Europe was a community that must be treated as a whole. This was a good point, but it easily led to what might be regarded as excessive softness toward Germany and a sense of guilt. Keynes, in this sense, helped lay the groundwork for the thinking behind the appeasement of Germany in the 1930s.

There now tended to be a continuity in foreign policy no matter what party was in power in England. MacDonald, however, was more sympathetic to the French desire for security than Baldwin had been, and although he was vehemently against war he was willing to placate the French and to build more cruisers; he also felt this would help to create employment. But antiwar feeling in the country was too strong and he could not implement this policy. His greatest effort during his government was the Geneva Protocol, an attempt to achieve some degree of cooperation and international reconciliation, combined with forcible arbitration. But the Tory government later rejected the protocol, largely because the dominions were not interested in it and would not support it.

Labour's problems are summed up in its attitude and relationship to Russia. The Labour party had been enthusiastic about the Russian Revolution in 1917. At the same time they were adamant in keeping the Communists out of the Labour party organization. They were obviously friendlier to Russia than the Tories and wished to recognize the new government. They conducted negotiations with Russia on the governmental and also on the party level and achieved an agreement leading to recognition. In return, Russia acknowledged some of the tsarist government's debts to English creditors. (Baldwin undid these agreements when the Tories returned to power.) Despite these reasonable steps, Labour could not dissociate itself from the Reds. As one Tory candidate for Parliament said, "A vote for the Socialists is a vote for the Communists. They pretend to be separate but at every crisis we find them together, the same sinister power directs them both and they both march to the pipers of Moscow under the shadow of the red flag." A sufficient number believed such allegations to cause Labour a great deal of difficulty, particularly as many were prone to believe that the Communists were about to blow up the world. The Labour party had to try to be unusually severe toward any sign of sedition or treason, and, finally, it was over such an issue, the Campbell case, that the Liberals withdrew their support and the Labour government fell in November 1924. MacDonald had insisted that the Liberal motion for a committee of inquiry was a matter of confidence on whether the govern-

Left: Stanley Baldwin; *right:* Ramsay MacDonald. (*Left:* Bettmann Archive; *right:* Culver Pictures.)

ment had been justified, or unduly soft, in withdrawing its prosecution of J. R. Campbell, the editor of the *Workers' Weekly*, for urging soldiers not to fire upon fellow-workers.

A further "Red scare" decreased Labour's vote in the General Election: the publicity given to the so-called Zinoviev letter (a forgery) which urged English Communists to seditious activities. The letter was allegedly written by a leading Russian Communist, and, in effect, it suggested that Labour might be pro-Communist; its publication may have caused some voters to switch their vote. The incident—the timing of the letter's publication—was awkwardly handled by the civil servants, perhaps deliberately so, and did not give Labour time to discount effectively the letter's significance. In the General Election 419 Conservatives were elected, with 48.3 percent of the vote; Labour had 151 M.P.s, with 33 percent of the vote (actually 3 percent more than in 1923); the Liberals paid most heavily for their decision to end the Labour government: they went down 12 percent in the popular vote to 17.6 percent.

Despite all the red scares, Labour did not do half badly. But this election was yet another deathblow for the Liberals. They had three million votes, but between Lloyd George and the Asquith factions there were only forty M.P.s, a loss of 118 seats. There were approximately eight million votes for the Tories and approximately five and one-half million for Labour, a million more popular votes than the latter had had in 1923. The most important fact about the Labour government of 1924 was that, through ordeal and experience, Labour had become undoubtedly the alternate party in the state: His Majesty's Loyal Opposition. The government had achieved an important reparations agreement. Perhaps too great a sense of tactics rather than a sense of policy had marked the ministry. Yet they had proved themselves, had shown the strengths and weaknesses of being in power and the particular dangers for Labour of responsibility making politicians too respectable. As MacDonald himself said, in Glasgow, there had been

> this extraordinary phenomenon of a Labour government that did not fail: this extraordinary phenomenon of a Labour government that has met kings and rulers of the earth, that has sat by them and has conducted itself with distinction and with dignity, this Labour government that has met ambassadors, that has faced the rulers of Europe on terms of equality; this Labour government that has sent its representatives forth and its representatives have been held as statesmen.

But perhaps there had not been sufficient attention to social policy.

The Age of Baldwin

The second Baldwin ministry, from 1924 to 1929, was a singularly empty time for English government. As already noted, Baldwin reversed recognition of Russia and English involvement with the Geneva Protocol. In 1926 an important imperial conference recognized the quasi-independence of the dominions, to be ratified in the Statute of Westminster of 1931. The General Strike of 1926 marked an increase in class tensions. Baldwin seemed intent on a search for a myth of business-as-usual and tranquility. England gave the appearance of not coping with its problems, of almost pretending they weren't there in the hope that they might go away. The most imaginative thinking about English society took place neither in the Labour nor Tory party but among the Liberals. It could be said that the true shaper of twentieth-century England was the Liberal party, although after 1916 it ceased to be a power in the state. Asquith had retired to the House of Lords in 1925, having been defeated for election in his constituency. He died in 1928. (His irrepressible wife, Margot, Countess of Oxford and Asquith, desperately wanted to bury him in Westminster Abbey in order to spite Lloyd George. However, Asquith's wish to be buried in a country churchyard was honored.)

Lloyd George was now head of both factions of the Liberal party and was willing to use his Fund to finance studies on the state of England. From 1927 to 1929 he pumped £400,000 into the investigation of England's social problems. Under his aegis reports were issued in a series of books known by the color of their jackets: the Green book, on problems of rural land; the Brown book, on urban land; and, most important, the Yellow book, whose formal title was *Britain's Industrial Future*. In effect, these books charted the future policy of the Tory and Labour parties. John Maynard Keynes, the great economist, was deeply involved in their writing and felt that they represented "real" Liberalism. He differentiated this sort of Liberalism from the Asquithian "true" variety, the old-fashioned principles of the creed. To Keynes's way of thinking, real Liberalism remained true to Liberal purposes but tried to use new ways to achieve them: the state could be made to serve individualism.

The Liberals urged much more state ownership of land, with actual control to be vested in the tenants, who should have the maximum possible authority and independence. The state would take over ownership, set down very broad lines of policy, and then exercise a minimum of control, avoiding bureaucracy and encouraging individual initiative. These thoughts were the prelude to the ways Keynes would justify capitalism in his great work, *The General Theory of Employment, Interest and Money* (1936). Keynes, recognized that government was not, as Liberals had previously maintained, the individual writ large, but that it was a different order of being dedicated to doing the things that individuals could not do for themselves. Keynes's view of the powers of individualism was much less sweeping than that held by traditional laissez-faire Liberals. His ideas owe a great deal to his Bloomsbury background—his friendship with Leonard and Virginia Woolf, Lytton Strachey, and others. Their thought was that the state was

The General Strike, May 1926: A gas truck being escorted by mounted police along St. George's Road, Southwark, a working-class district in London. (Radio Times Hulton Picture Library.)

obliged to provide a framework within which all individuals would be able to fulfill themselves in their own ways, an idea most nineteenth-century Liberals would have rejected in theory. This idea was not only part of the Bloomsbury ethos but was shared by the Liberal study groups of the late 1920s.

Baldwin did worry, but in a limited way, about the state of England. The failure of the General Strike reassured the ordinary member of the middle class. The strike was considerable in its scale: approximately 2.5 million workers left their jobs, but they were defeated after only nine days, although the miners continued on strike, unsuccessfully, for another six months. It was easy to see the General Strike, despite its immensity, as in some respects a typical English lark, full of good sportsmanship, represented at its most characteristic in the famous soccer game between strikers and policemen in Plymouth. Nevertheless, the strike left a bitter legacy, not resolved, from the point of view of Labour, until 1945. The workers felt beleaguered and betrayed to an extent by their own leadership and to a degree victimized by the Tories.

At another General Election in 1929 Baldwin advocated "safety first," but the voters of England found this a little dull as a platform. Labour waited, not in vain, for the swing of the pendulum. The results were disastrous for the Liberal party, although that party had provided most of the liveliest points of discussion in the election: the ideas for the future. There were forty-three Liberal M.P.s when the General Election was called. Lloyd George financed 513 candidates for a House of Commons of 615. Only fifty-nine Liberals were returned. It hardly seemed worth all the effort and expense. In the new House of Commons there were 260 Tories with 38.2 percent of the popular vote and 288 Labour M.P.s with 37.1 percent of the popular vote. Although Labour had a smaller percentage of the popular vote, they had because of distribution more M.P.s, and there was no question but that they would form a government. The Liberals did increase their popular vote from 17.6 percent in the previous General Election to 23.4 percent. Yet the election clearly meant that the chances of the Liberal party's revival were practically nil.

Labour formed its second government, which lasted from 1929 to 1931. It was an ineffectual government, faced with events far beyond the control any government of the time felt it could exercise. Labour could not cope with the effects of worldwide depression; it almost did not appear to wish to do so. Labour's failure contributed to the sense of the ineffectiveness of traditional government that many were feeling in England, most particularly many intellectuals. For them, from Versailles on, there had been a growing disillusionment not only with the Victorian world of the past but with the present as well. Lytton Strachey's *Eminent Victorians*, published in 1918, was a study of four makers of the Victorian world: Florence Nightingale, Cardinal Manning, General Gordon, and Thomas Arnold. In it Strachey demonstrates what a tawdry public world the Victorians had created. In 1922 T. S. Eliot, an American who had become an expatriate, published *The Waste Land*, in so many ways the most important English poem of the twentieth century. At one of its many levels of meaning, it can be read as a depiction of the sterility and banality of postwar England. *A Passage to India*, by E. M. Forster, published in 1924, was the last novel of the man who had written four superb novels before the First World War. The obscure events in the Marabar caves in that novel convey a sense of negation, a sense that the world was no longer rational. Perhaps the most characteristic writing of the twenties which put forth this new attitude was the work of Aldous Huxley, in his *Antic Hay* (1923), and Evelyn Waugh, most specifically in his first two novels, *Decline and Fall*, published in 1928, and *Vile Bodies*, published in 1930.

CHAPTER FIVE

The writers of the twenties rejected the world about them in ways ranging from benign negativism to aggressive nihilism. But in the twenties many people did not care how the country was run. It was in the hands of politicians who, although not very inspiring, at least made some gestures toward being serious and professional. Until 1929 England seemed to get along—not particularly well and somewhat more depressed than the rest of the West—yet she survived. And by 1929 the rest of the world joined England in a deepening slump.

In the 1920s the right was generally in power, but in 1924 and again in 1929 Labour had a taste of power and some training in responsibility. In 1929, having won the General Election with twenty-eight more M.P.s than the Tories, Labour was the ruling party. Again dependence on the Liberals acted as a curb to any sweeping experiments. Some slight progress was made in international relations by the prime minister and his foreign secretary, Arthur Henderson, through the League of Nations and by naval agreements with the United States and Japan.

The government refused to adopt the more radical plans offered as a way of dealing with the economic situation, and its leaders, most notably Ramsay MacDonald, the prime minister, and Philip Snowden, the chancellor of the Exchequer, were reluctant to take any drastic steps. In 1931, as an emergency measure, MacDonald requested the resignations of the members

Their Finest Hour

of his cabinet, and they expected that this would be followed by the resignation of MacDonald himself. He, in fact, came back as prime minister with a charge from George V to form a National Government. The Labour government had been deeply divided over the recommendations of the May Committee, which had suggested considerable cuts in government expenditure. The May report had followed traditional economic wisdom, and it also led to stipulations by bankers of cuts in expenditure so that French and American banks would support the pound. The National Government was willing to follow such a policy, and MacDonald served as its prime minister until 1935. This coalition government achieved 554 M.P.s out of a house of 615 in the General Election of 1931, the so-called Doctor's Mandate. The "National Government" was, in fact, a Tory government supported by a National Labour party and a National Liberal party. It did attempt to cope with the depression in a limited way.

Criticisms of English Society

The events of 1929–31 left two major impressions on many, particularly on the intellectuals of the period, but obviously not on the majority of the voters. More alert observers of the political scene now felt that the economic situation was so serious that the 1920s' attitude of pursuing one's own pleasures and interests and not worrying about the actions of the government was no longer tolerable. On the other hand, the possibility of accomplishing anything through traditional politics seemed far less likely than it had been before. Ordinary politics appeared bankrupt, and the reaction of the Labour party to the worldwide depression had been inadequate. But at least between 1929 and 1931 there had been an illusion that the two-party system was functioning. After 1931 it seemed to have collapsed; the "they" who were running the country did so not only for their own benefit but also inefficiently. With the formation of the National Government, some of those who might have involved themselves with the running of the state came to feel that politics as practiced in England and probably elsewhere in the world was "a cheat, a ramp, a plot to keep the old boys in." This sense of a betrayal in 1931 and the subsequent discrediting of the parliamentary system set the mood of the 1930s. From 1931 on through most of the decade, some of the more significant political thinkers of the time came to believe that traditional parliamentary democracy should be abandoned.

During the depression unemployment increased approximately from one to two million, and this figure did not sink below 1.5 million until the Second World War. The grim quality of life was captured in George Orwell's *The Road to Wigan Pier* (1937), a picture of the industrial life of Wigan as affected by the depression, accompanied by an idiosyncratic declaration of socialist faith. Orwell's sense of individualism, a common English characteristic, triumphed over every obstacle, and he created his own private sort of socialism dedicated to preserving what he considered the sense of decency of the ordinary Englishman. Even in the 1930s the poor may well have been better off than they had been in the nineteenth century, but it was not the sort of world that English society felt it had been promised after the First World War. Life on the "dole"—meager government support—was desperate; income was far short of adequate.

The Liberals had concerned themselves with the worsening economic situation before 1929, but they had failed to receive any backing from the electorate. The Labour party too had worried about conditions from 1929 to 1931. There had been some planning in both the 1924 and 1929 Labour governments. The 1931 National Government moved away from any overall commitment, no matter how slight. In 1925 a book concerned with planning for the future had been published within the Labour ranks: *Revolution by Reason, an account of the financial proposals submitted to the Labour movement by Mr. Oswald Mosley, written by John Strachey*. The book advocated socialism, in a mild way; it suggested ways of increasing the spending power of the working class and so making England a better place for them to live. Until 1931 there seemed some faint possibility that this sort of overall, if vague, plan would be put through by the Labour party. After 1931 neither the Tories, nor Labour, nor even the Liberals were interested in such a plan; and quite a few of the adventuresome young turned away from the ordinary processes of Parliament.

The two men who published *Revolution by Reason*, Oswald Mosley and John Strachey, best represent the two more extreme alternatives presented: Fascism and Communism. Fascism had taken over the government of Italy, and Nazism was becoming more powerful in Germany. In those countries the movements were led by members of the lower middle class, Mussolini and Hitler, respectively; men who corresponded to those to whom the movements most appealed. In England it was not surprising to discover that the leader of the Fascist movement was a member of the upper classes, as were some of the leading Communists. Oswald Mosley came from a family that had become wealthy in the approved English fashion: in trade from cloth in the sixteenth century, advancing into the gentry. In 1596 the family had wisely bought the manorial rights of Manchester for £3,500; it sold them in 1846 for £200,000. Oswald Mosley was born in 1894 and had an unhappy childhood. (Numbers of well-off sensitive Englishmen tend to have quite unhappy childhoods as they are sent away to boarding school at the age of eight.) After prep school Mosley went on to Winchester, perhaps the most intellectual of the great Public Schools—a school that also trained Edward Grey and Hugh Gaitskell, the leader of the Labour party in the 1950s. Mosley was an officer in the First World War, in which he was injured and acquired a permanent limp. The war was the shaping experience of his life. His reaction to it was similar to that of the war poets, such as Sassoon, Graves, and Owen: anger at the older generation who had sent the cream of England off to the wars. In 1918 he ran successfully for Parliament for Harrow, a suburb of London, as a Conservative coalition candidate. He was Conservative more by family tradition than by inclination. In 1920 he married his first wife, Lady Cynthia Curzon, the daughter of the Marquis of Curzon. He was at the heart of the Establishment. Shortly after, he became more discontented. He disapproved of the use of the "Black and Tans" in Ireland. He began to meet advanced politicians of all parties, and being a distinguished member of the upper class by birth he was greeted well. He achieved the accolade of being praised in the diary of Beatrice Webb, the great Fabian. Mrs. Webb thought Mosley's mind and ideas were extremely impressive but that he seemed so perfect that, she felt, there was bound to be some rottenness somewhere in him. In 1924 he moved from the Conservatives to the Labour party, where he was extremely popular, and in 1925 he published his proposal for the future state. In 1927 he was elected to the national executive of the party. He had had a very easy career; his origins had, it is clear, helped him in the Labour party, where members of the upper class tended to be infrequent. In 1929, in the Labour government, he was given the post of the senior minister outside of the cabinet, with special concern for unemployment. In 1930 he put forward to the cabinet a memorandum, which in moderate terms demanded that something more be done to cope with the depression, that the government take steps in banking, industry, agriculture, and tariffs. The memorandum represented an effort to do something about an extremely serious situation, and should have been carefully considered. But Snowden, the chancellor of the Exchequer, dismissed the proposals completely.

In May 1930 Mosley resigned his position as minister and arranged a meeting of the Parliamentary Labour party in order to discuss the situation. Arthur Henderson—whose peaceable role was indicated by his nickname of "Uncle"—ran the meeting. He attempted to please everybody, suggesting to Mosley that after full discussion he should withdraw the memorandum and not put it to a vote. But Mosley insisted and the memorandum was defeated 202 to 29. He again demanded that the memorandum be discussed at the annual conference of the party. There it was much more narrowly defeated, but even if it had passed it would not necessarily have been binding on the leadership. After the defeat Mosley issued a manifesto against the old politics. He acquired a greater sense of mission, and his activities became more characteristic of a megalomaniac. Seventeen M.P.s signed the manifesto and temporarily became the nucleus of the new party, of which John Strachey was a member, as was, at least temporarily, the later, very important left-wing Labour leader, Aneurin Bevan. Mosley now committed himself to going it alone; as a result, he was expelled from the Labour party. (Strachey left Mosley in 1931 over the question of trade with Russia, which he favored and Mosley opposed.) Until 1931 Mosley had been an important and imaginative figure: after 1931 his career as a Fascist became the dominant note in his life. Mosley's original idea was that his party would be a "ginger group," that it would put forward an imaginative plan that might be adopted by one of the traditional parties. After 1931 he thought in terms of a new political party that would attempt to take over power and changed its name in 1932 to the British Union of Fascists. To be a Fascist was not quite as unusual in England as it would be after Hitler came to power in 1933. Mosley spent about £100,000 a year on his movement, and many thought that a good part of this money came from Mussolini. Mosley became increasingly prone to use strong-arm methods against his opponents.

Mosley did have the appeal of his generation, as caught in the peroration of a speech he made in 1934:

> This is the generation which faced 1914, which in four years made an effort which staggered the world with the display of manhood, of courage, and of sacrifice, that mankind had not previously witnessed. The story of our generation is an epic of the human race that has gone on from victory to victory, from triumph to triumph. In the laboratories of science it has conjured up the wonders that are transforming the modern world; in the field and in the upper spheres it challenges the very dominion of nature with the triumphant mind of man. *This is our generation not theirs.* We have fought and conquered while they muddled and destroyed. This Movement of our

generation, of New Britain, of the New World, raises itself to challenge, to sweep away, to destroy, and *then to build again!*

By the time he made this speech in 1934, the power of the movement was already beginning to weaken. Mosley was regarded increasingly as a crank. There was more brutality at meetings; stewards would beat up hecklers. Mosley deliberately sought confrontations, marching through the East End, the Jewish area of London, at a time when German anti-Semitism was virulent. Mosley himself was becoming increasingly overtly anti-Semitic. This sense of violence put off many to whom Fascism might have appealed. There were elements in the upper class in favor of Italian and, to a lesser degree, German Fascism, but Mosley was becoming too "continental" in style to win influential followers.

There was no official membership figure for the Union of Fascists but probably it was never over 10,000, although quite a few more might have passed through the party. Despite its small membership, however, Fascism was a significant movement, even in England. Because of the failure of government to solve its economic and social problems, many were looking

Peace march by students in Cambridge, Armistice Day, November 11, 1933. (Mrs. Christopher Morris.)

for alternatives to parliamentary democracy. A belief in respectability some-times has its advantages; certainly it helped defeat Mosley.

The Communist movement also challenged the premises and the practices of parliamentary democracy. Communism was associated with a wider range of people than was Fascism, and it did more to set the tone of the decade. As G. M. Young, the historian of Victorian England, suggests, one can tell most about a period if one can sense what its conversation is likely to have been about. The chances were that a "contemporary" con-versation among intellectuals of the period would be about Karl Marx, even if few actually had read him, or about the new poets and how they were influenced by Marxism. The left-wing movement was new and dis-tinctive, as were the new poets. They did not sell in large numbers, but they were well known: W. H. Auden, Stephen Spender, C. Day Lewis, Louis MacNeice, Rex Warner; and they were very sympathetic to the left.

The Communist party in 1938 had about 15,000 members. But it probably had many more sympathizers than the Fascists. It was a more respectable movement at the time, with a more distinguished intellectual pedigree. Marx had spent a great deal of his life at the British Museum, doing his research and writing. Engels had been a manufacturer in Man-chester. Also Marxism's economic theory and conception of scientific method owe much to English intellectual traditions. In some senses, Marx-ism was appropriate for England in terms of its concept of the class struc-ture, although the country failed to live up to Marxist expectations of class war. The English have a proclivity, easily exaggerated, to be peaceful. Although Marxist theory made important contributions to the Labour movement, Methodist and Evangelical traditions frequently submerged and smothered it. The Social Democratic Federation, led by H. M. Hynd-man, regarded itself as a Marxist movement, and there were considerable elements of Marxist thought in many of the movements on the left. The Russian Revolution of 1917 had inspired many and had transformed Rus-sia from an ally regarded with suspicion to a comrade. Shortly thereafter, however, Russia left the war. The Communist party was founded in Eng-land in 1919–20. Lenin arranged that the Socialist Labour party should merge with the British Socialist party. By the end of the 1920s a small Communist party was well-organized and subservient to Russia, controlled by Harry Pollitt and R. Palme Dutt—one the general secretary of prole-tarian background, and the other an Anglo-Indian intellectual. It might have continued a small Marxist-Leninist party, continually unable to make up its mind about how much it wanted to cooperate with the Labour party. The latter, however, was always going through periods of soul searching about whether it was willing to accept any cooperation with the Communists; eventually it always refused to do so.

But the depression gave a sense to many that drastic action was neces-sary to save England. Russia tended to be viewed with a starry enthusiasm throughout the first half of the 1930s, and Communism appeared a sensible way to handle the problems of English society. It is questionable, however, whether the conversion of some small groups in the upper and middle classes in England to Communism genuinely meant an increase in power for the Communist cause. As one commentator wrote:

> Many of the sons of governing families following the best English tradition have prepared for the leadership of the next revolution by joining the Communist party. When England goes communist, no doubt the party in power will call itself the conservative cooperative party, and as usual, half the government will be old Etonians.

John Strachey, an old Etonian, is a good example of Communism and the upper classes. (The party had a base in the working class, and there one would locate a "typical" party member, but in terms of how change takes place in England, it is revealing to study the actions of a dissident member of the "ruling class.") Strachey's background was far less wealthy than Mosley's, but more distinguished intellectually. The Stracheys were civil servants and army officers associated with India. John Strachey's father was an important member of the intellectual Establishment. He owned and edited *The Spectator*, an important opinion-making weekly. He had absolute political views: a Liberal who had become a Liberal Unionist over Home Rule. He believed in free trade and the British empire. John Strachey was born in 1901; his godfather was Lord Cromer, the great proconsul in Egypt. He went through the ordinary education for the upper classes and was at Eton during the First World War. He was too young to participate in the war, but it had a strong effect upon him, and his most vivid memory of school was going to weekly chapel and hearing the list of names read out of the old Etonians killed in the war. At Oxford, he reacted against his father by becoming a high Tory. But by 1924 he was moving toward the left and thereby lost his inheritance, in the sense that his father felt he was not "sound" enough to run *The Spectator*. He was associated with Mosley and left the Labour party, but in 1931, as we have seen, he broke with Mosley over Russia. For the rest of the 1930s, he became the leading Communist propagandist. In 1932 he published *The Coming Struggle for Power*, the single most important book in convincing many that the Marxist analysis of society was correct.

The book was a brilliant exposition of the Marxist interpretation of the world situation of the 1930s; it was once very popular but is now quite dated, as are many books that were extremely influential in their own time. Strachey held that capitalism was bankrupt, that the Labour party, as demonstrated so vividly in 1931, was nothing but a stooge for capitalism, particularly Wall Street, and that the world had no choice but to move toward Communism. It is possible that the book may have led some into the Communist party itself, but, perhaps more important, it influenced a great many in England to regard Communism (and Russia) much more sympathetically than they had in the past. The book was published in

1932; the accession of Hitler to power in Germany in January 1933 seemed to fulfill its prophecies and justify its analyses. The threat of Fascism abroad (and perhaps even in England), the depression, the political inadequacy of the older parties and politics set many in the intellectual vanguard, that minority that determines the spirit of an age, on the road to the left.

Strachey called himself Communist although he was never a member of the party. In an essay he contributed to a book with a symptomatic title for the decade, *In Letters of Red*, he wrote:

> I have a stock answer to dear old ladies who ask me, and why Mr. Strachey did you become a Communist? From chagrin, madam, I reply, from chagrin at not getting into the Eton cricket Eleven. I do not want this answer to be taken quite literally, except by the old ladies. All the same, there is in it more truth—if one takes getting into the Eton cricket Eleven as a symbol for making an adjustment to one's environment as a whole—than I altogether enjoy admitting.

Strachey is pointing out that even if personal and class reasons led one to Communism, that does not invalidate the theory itself. But he did not underestimate the transition of attitudes between the 1920s and 1930s. As he wrote:

> [In the '20s] we were chiefly interested in defending the bold descriptions of sex in the novels of Mr. D. H. Lawrence or Mr. Aldous Huxley; or if we thought of public affairs at all, in the question of birth control. Thus unevenly, irregularly, and out of step as it were does a great historical process, such as the breaking up of the British capitalist-imperialist system, come to consciousness in the minds of the various social groups which are affected by it.

Until 1931 Strachey himself was nothing more than a "bourgeois" intellectual Labourite. But then his eyes were opened, he writes, by the events of 1931:

> It was necessary for me to see with my own eyes and at close range the mingled impotence and treachery of social democracy in action; to put my fingers upon the stigmata of the poltroonery of Henderson, Lansbury and Greenwood [Labour party leaders], and my hand into the gaping spear wound of the turpitude of MacDonald, Thomas and Snowden, in order to know that this corpse would never rise again. Not until this indisputable evidence had been thrust upon me was I willing to admit that British Social Democracy was not the friend, but the deadliest enemy of the interests of the British workers.

Despite this passionate conviction, Strachey, in fact, was one of the first to change his mind and return from a "god that failed"—to use the title of a book of memoirs by ex-Communists. No man of the right, he did move somewhat rightward into the left of the Labour party.

Communism never became as discredited as Fascism, although its appcal to the intellectual young of the middle and upper classes eventually declined during the 1930s, in part because their entry into the party was not well regarded by the rather unimaginative leadership. The poet Stephen Spender, for example, was a member of the party very briefly during the Spanish Civil War and, according to his interpretation (which has been questioned by the party hierarchy), he was told to go and be killed in Spain, as Byron had in Greece, in order to provide a martyr for the cause.

The depression was at its worst in 1931. After that year there was an excruciatingly slow improvement and a decrease in the highest total of three million unemployed. The psychological response to the situation lagged behind the actual improvement in society. It was not until mid-decade that it began to appear to some on the left that perhaps, for better or worse, capitalism was not bankrupt and could adapt to changed conditions, as it was clearly doing in the United States through Roosevelt's New Deal. Keynesian economics, emerging as the salvation of capitalism, was demonstrating ways in which the capitalist system could work if it co-operated with the state, socialized itself, to a certain extent, and showed itself more responsive to the needs of greater numbers of the population. Shortly after Keynes published his *General Theory of Employment, Interest and Money* in 1936, John Strachey came to the conclusion that capitalism might survive. On a more immediate level, the power and popularity of the Communist party in the late 1930s suffered because of the purges in Russia and eventually because of the Nazi-Soviet pact. Communism, like Fascism, was too obviously and closely associated with groups and interests outside of England. Yet parliamentary democracy had not been able to find a solution to the depression. England, like other countries, was finally pulled out of the depression by the industrial demand created by the threat of war, and eventually by war itself.

A few of the outcasts of society turned to Fascism, which was more important as a symptom of the troubled decade in England and as a reflection of the sense of a need for a radical solution than as a powerful force in and of itself. Communism was much more significant in England because many people saw it as an humanitarian and romantic movement and believed that joining it would show their commitment to changing the great inequities of their society.

Moving Toward War

In the 1930s there was a sense of withdrawal in both domestic and foreign policy: an attempt to come to terms with England's having become a far weaker power than she had been before the First World War. A pattern of withdrawal from commitments was combined with a realistic and at times imaginative facing up to the changed situation. In 1931 the Statute of Westminster established the terms on which England's relation to the commonwealth was set. The statute marked the abandonment of most supervisory rights England had over the dominion part of her empire; the tie was now essentially sentimental. In other ways, too, there was now an undoing of the past. In 1932 the protective tariffs that Stanley Baldwin had advocated earlier were introduced, and the period of free trade was officially over. The Ottawa Imperial Conference the same year established a form of imperial preference.

In 1935, Ramsay MacDonald, who had become almost a figurehead, resigned as prime minister and was succeeded by Baldwin. Baldwin did little: he is now chiefly remembered for not having done enough to prepare England for war with Germany. The most influential unofficial group about Baldwin was made up of those who had been known as Milner's kindergarten. As young men, mostly from Oxford, they had been protégés of Alfred Milner, when he was high commissioner in South Africa at the time of the Boer War; they included such men as Geoffrey Dawson, the editor of *The Times* of London. These now prominent figures were concerned about the empire and tended to be uninformed about Europe. Dawson conveyed a message to his correspondents that they should soft-pedal stories discreditable to Germany, for he believed these would hurt the cause of peace in Europe. Baldwin laid the groundwork for the appeasement of Hitler, a policy that his successor, Neville Chamberlain, pursued more vigorously. Perhaps the policy gave England more time to prepare for war, but it also gave her enemies more time. In any case, that policy reflected the feelings of the greater part of the electorate, and in this sense there was an element of self-punishment or self-deception in the vehemence and hatred with which some of the appeasers were regarded once the war began.

The Labour party was committed on principle to not preparing for war. The then dominant Tories—because they felt England was weak, because they were more concerned with the empire than with Europe, because they were not deeply upset by Hitler and Mussolini—agreed not to take a strong international position. But the Labour party began to change its attitudes in the later 1930s. George Lansbury, who replaced MacDonald as head of the party after the latter's defection, was a deeply revered and popular man. But he was a devout pacifist, and the change of mood in the party forced him to resign. Clement Attlee replaced him as leader of the parliamentary party, the most important post in the Labour party organization. Attlee was much tougher-minded than Lansbury, a dedicated socialist of the middle classes who would gradually move the Labour party away from its commitment to disarmament. But the prevailing mood was more nearly expressed by such activities as the Peace Pledge Union, and for most of the period only Winston Churchill and a few others were calling for rearmament. And Churchill was regarded as a discontented maverick who was attacking his own party because of its comparatively enlightened attitude toward India.

Mussolini's invasion of Ethiopia in 1935 presented a further problem. The League of Nations had been somewhat discredited three years earlier by its failure to act effectively when the Japanese had invaded Manchuria, but England still felt committed to trying to use the League and to trying to persuade France that the League was capable of providing some sort of international security. Also, she had some hope of disengaging Italy from Germany, and because she was very concerned about her position in the Mediterranean she wished to take a mild position toward Italy. Yet there was a limit to how much appeasement the public would tolerate. This had become evident at the time of the Hoare-Laval Pact. Sir Samuel Hoare, the foreign secretary in Baldwin's government, had come to an agreement with Pierre Laval, the French premier, that Italy should be unhampered in her attack on Ethiopia. The English public, considerable segments of which were committed to the League of Nations, and the Cabinet found this repugnant. Hoare resigned and Anthony Eden replaced him. Eden was willing to use the League's power of sanctions against Italy, but the sanctions imposed were not effective, and Italy succeeded in conquering Ethiopia. After Chamberlain became prime minister, Eden's own course grew increasingly difficult; he finally resigned in February 1938, because he disapproved of the extent of Chamberlain's attempt to appease Hitler and his desire to ignore the United States and President Roosevelt in making his plans. The Earl of Halifax, more amenable to Chamberlain's directing of foreign policy, became foreign secretary after Eden.

In December 1936 there was fascinating light relief from the problems, in the poet W. H. Auden's phrase, of the "low, dishonest decade" in the first voluntary abdication by a monarch in England's history. George V had died in January 1936 and had been succeeded by Edward VIII, who had been very popular as the Prince of Wales, particularly for touring the "distressed" areas in Wales during the depression. Edward had also been identified somewhat with the "bright young things," suggesting the possibility of a monarchy with a little more swing. But he fell in love with a woman not thought "suitable" and abdicated, after a famous speech in which he said that he would rather give up the throne than "the woman I love." The woman, Mrs. Wallis Simpson, had the disadvantage of being an American and of having been twice divorced. Edward did have considerable popular support once the public knew of the intriguing scandal, but the support was not profound, and the Establishment was almost completely against him. The story provides an extraordinary example of how cooperative the English press could be with the governing powers, even on an ultimately trivial matter. It was not until issues of the American magazine *Time* managed to get through customs with the details of the story that the English public—beyond those "in the know"—learned about Mrs. Simpson and their king. Winston Churchill, who was friendly with Edward, tried to lead a campaign in his favor. Baldwin spent a great deal of time worrying and weeping over the issue: on one occasion Edward and his prime minister wept together, but Baldwin was adamant that Edward had to chose between the throne and Mrs. Simpson. Edward finally chose Mrs. Simpson and went on to enjoy a life of semi-exile as the Duke of Windsor. His brother the Duke of York, trained in the navy, had a firm sense of duty, and came to the throne as George VI. He and his daughter, Elizabeth II, raised the English monarchy to new levels of popularity.

Baldwin retired; in May 1937 Neville Chamberlain, the younger son of Joseph Chamberlain, became prime minister. His considerable accomplishments in domestic policy have been overshadowed by his role as the man with the umbrella who was the main force behind the policy of appeasement. He saw himself as a knight in shining armor, who would bring peace "in our time," his phrase on his return to England, after treating with, or rather, being outfoxed by, Hitler at Munich in September 1938. The Munich crisis turned on Hitler's ultimatum to Czechoslovakia and the basic question of whether England and France would defend that country. There had been earlier meetings in September between Chamberlain and Hitler at Berchtesgaden and Godesberg, and Chamberlain, as well as Daladier of France, put pressure on the Czechs to accept the German demands for some of their territory. (Hitler claimed the area on the basis of the alleged German nationality of the Sudetens.) Hitler increased his demands which initially both Chamberlain and Daladier found unacceptable, but at Munich at the end of September they met with Hitler and Mussolini and yielded. Thereafter, England and France applied pressure to Czechoslovakia to accede to German demands. What was left of Czechoslovakia was fully occupied by Germany in March of 1939. Chamberlain realized that he had made a crucial mistake in believing that Hitler would stop his aggressive plans and maintain the peace. England and France then committed themselves to the defense of Poland, if she were attacked. In August German forces crossed into Poland, and on September 3, 1939, England and France declared war on Germany.

Churchill and the Second World War

During the Second World War Churchill, eventually and finally, came into his own, was "matched with his hour," in a Rupert Brookian sense. What Churchill stood for is well captured in a letter from an observer at the time of Churchill's state funeral in 1965:

> I went to the lying in state, and like the 300,000 or so other people waited in the queue for about two hours of some of the coldest weather we have had to see the catafalque and the guards with bowed heads. The procession was all that it could have been, making the Englishmen proud of their Churchill and their finest hours and their . . . blitz, and I even heard people

say that if the British could not send one of their men to the moon, they could at least put on one hell of a State Funeral. . . . I was astounded at how strongly people still felt about him and about what he represented about the British past. Little mention comparatively about the decline of British power, and rather more of the glory of the battle of Britain. Nostalgia not so much for lost strength as for a sort of lost nobility. It is curious . . . how much people saw the Blitz as a kind of national *Testing*—a kind of ritual purification by fire—only without the disillusionment of the first world war, since in this there was none of the we-they division. All shared in the great effort and, at least for a moment, Churchill seemed the embodiment of it all.

For all his flaws and mistakes in strategy, Churchill was a great and appropriate war leader. He appears as a *deus ex machina*, emerging from his comparative state of exile in the 1930s with a moral fervor that Chamberlain so conspicuously lacked. Churchill had not had an easy time with the right or left of the political spectrum in England during his career. Most politicians are profoundly suspicious of those who rise above party rather than submit to the party yoke. Churchill had disassociated himself from the Tory party because it was too "soft" in its attitude toward the possibility of Indian independence. Yet it was Churchill's element of old-fashioned imperialism that helped him to suggest the right mood for a country at war. And it might also have been some vestigial memory of his interest in social legislation before the First World War that enabled him to empathize with the great majority of the people. His policies during the First World War had been imaginative, but they had failed—notably, at Gallipoli. In the 1920s he had been discredited, although he was a prominent figure in the government, through his tendency to call in the troops at almost any provocation and his having been thought to favor—though he actually had resisted—the government's mistaken policy of returning England to the gold standard. By temperament he had a good spirit for waging war, although earlier, when he wanted to use troops in Ireland and at the time of the General Strike, such moves had smacked more of class war than of defense of the nation. Until this moment, he had been an important politician whose career, in spite of some successes, ultimately had been a failure.

His personal qualities—courage, stubbornness, grandiloquence—were indispensable at the time of war. Even his appearance, oddly similar to that of an English bulldog, helped him to become a national symbol. He was a clever politician and statesman. He had an intense sense of strategy of how best to defend England's interests. His speeches set exactly the right tone of resolute defiance. He had an oratorical genius and was able to summon up the right spirit for the war, in phrases that were memorable in their evocation of heroism and grandeur. He was also capable of making the same sort of universal appeal his father had made in the spirit of Tory democracy, a generous rhetoric which harkened back to the nineteenth century. He was not afraid of sentiment, nor of tears. He was a clear contrast to the narrower traditions of the Chamberlains and to small-mindedness of policy in all aspects: economic, political, international. (The danger was that he might, at times, think in too grandiose terms.) Especially in the early years of the war, he struck the note that would appeal to the English mood of muted heroism and determination, forcing the country to be heroic in spite of herself, with her back to the wall, and her belief that although she might lose battles she would never lose a war.

Even with Churchill to lead them, however, the populace lacked the sort of enthusiasm that had stirred them at the outbreak of the First World War. They had learned a lesson and, disillusioned, applied it inappropriately to a later experience. The lesson drawn from the First World War was that wars were not fought for good causes but as a result of secret deals by armament manufacturers and diplomats. In the period of debunking in the 1920s, it had been proved that many atrocity stories of the First World War—such as that of the Germans raping Belgian nuns—had been fabrications. As a result, many felt that the stories about concentration camps in Nazi Germany in the 1930s were similarly untrue.

The two great threats of the 1930s had been Fascism and war. Those who were vehement against Fascism were also those who were against the idea of the country ever going to war again. But the realities of the Fascist threat gradually were recognized, and war was seen as the lesser evil. The sense of excitement had long ago been expended. The disillusionment that followed the First World War had given way, for the left, to the enthusiasm and passion of the Spanish Civil War—"the last great cause," in the famous phrase of Albert Camus—and became for its enthusiasts a tragedy which left all emotions spent. The Munich settlements in September 1938 brought a short-lived burst of enthusiasm. When war itself came in September 1939, there were a series of anticlimaxes. After the tension of Munich, there had been the period of "phoney peace"; then England went to war over Poland, for most Englishmen not an inspiring cause. At the outset of the war, Chamberlain was a broken man who felt he had been betrayed by Hitler. Although he was the "man of Munich" whose policy had failed, he remained prime minister until May 1940, through the period of the so-called phoney war. During that time the air-raids that had been anticipated did not materialize; Hitler did not move against England as swiftly as expected. The task of fighting the war got under way ponderously.

It was after the failure of the English campaign to save Norway from the Germans that feeling against Chamberlain reached its highest pitch. On May 2, 1940, the House of Commons began a two-day debate on the question of the Norwegian failure. The Labour party, the official opposition, was determined to force a vote of censure. Lloyd George joined the attack: "I say solemnly that the Prime Minister should give an example of sacrifice, because there is nothing which could contribute more to victory in this war, and he should sacrifice the seals of office." But the most devastating attack against the Conservative prime minister came from the Tory side of the House, when Leo Amery drew on the words that Cromwell had used when dismissing a Parliament: "You have sat too long here for any good you have been doing. Depart, I say, and let us have done with you, in the name of God, go."

Churchill, who was first lord of the admiralty, did his best to defend the government, not only out of loyalty but also because it was largely his policy that was being criticized. Although the division of votes was technically a victory for Chamberlain—281 to 200—some thirty Tory M.P.s voted against their chief and more than sixty Tory M.P.s abstained. Chamberlain was well aware that he was in trouble. There was a move to make the Earl of Halifax prime minister. He had been a supporter of appeasement and now was foreign secretary. His claim to the post was strengthened, in a negative way, by the fact that Labour still did not have full confidence in Churchill, the more logical figure to head a national government than Halifax. Churchill himself was, at first, the most upset at the idea of Halifax becoming prime minister. While he said that he would serve under anyone, in fact, when he was consulted on the question, he simply did not react: his best policy was silence. As he wrote, "I became aware that I might well be called upon to take the lead. The prospect neither excited nor alarmed me. I thought it would be by far the best plan." The move to marshal support for Halifax came to nothing, and the king asked Churchill to be prime minister. When he formed his government, he kept both Chamberlain and Halifax in the cabinet. It was essentially a diplomatic gesture. Chamberlain retired shortly after it was made and died soon afterward. Halifax left the cabinet to be a successful ambassador to the United States. Churchill's aim was to have a government expressing national unity. Crossing party lines, he included in the inner cabinet two leaders from the Labour party: Clement Attlee and Ernest Bevin. Perhaps Churchill's most memorable paragraph about the war effort was in his speech on taking office on May 13, 1940:

> I have nothing to offer but blood, toil, tears and sweat. . . . You ask, What is our policy? I will say: It is to wage war, by sea, land and air, with all our might and with all the strength that God can give us. . . . You ask, What is our aim? I could answer in one word: Victory—victory at all costs, victory in spite of all terror, victory however long and hard the road may be.

Then he recorded in his diary that night:

> As I went to bed at about 3 A.M., I was conscious of a profound sense of relief. At last I had the authority to give directions over the whole scene. I felt as if I were walking with destiny, and that all my past life had been but a preparation for this hour and for this trial.

Among the intellectuals, there was to be no outpouring of enthusiasm, no Rupert Brooke to write passionately of the cause. In a poem by C. Day

Winston Churchill surveying the ruins of the Houses of Parliament, May 1941. (Topix, Thompson Newspapers, Ltd.)

Lewis, these lines summed up the attitude of his generation: ". . . Where are the war poets? the fools inquire./ Spain was a death to us. Munich a mourning." Only the intellectuals of the old guard, including some who had been active in the First World War, responded promptly to the need for men of letters to say something about the war. The novelists Hugh Walpole, J. B. Priestley, and H. G. Wells all wrote pamphlets on behalf of the war effort. But this was not regarded as sufficient activity from a group who in England is thought of as very much a part of the middle class and who themselves have less a sense of alienation than of security within their society. Letters began to appear in *The Times* demanding inspiring words from the nation's intellectuals. Here, too, C. Day Lewis (who would become poet laureate of England in the 1960s) had the right response: "It is the logic of our times/ No subject for immortal verse/ That we who live by honest dreams/ Defend the bad against the worse."

Bloomsbury's ambassador to the outside world, John Maynard Keynes, threw himself into the war effort and was a central figure in arranging

England's financial future in relation to the United States. E. M. Forster, the famous novelist, reflected the mild yet firm tone adopted by so many of England's intellectuals at the time of war. In broadcasts and pamphlets Forster sounded a note of optimism about the English system—a subdued note, captured in a few sentences in his essay "What I Believe":

> So Two cheers for Democracy: one because it admits variety and two because it permits criticism. Two cheers are quite enough; there is no occasion to give three. Only Love the Beloved Republic deserves that. . . . I believe in aristocracy, though—if that is the right word, and if a democrat may use it. Not an aristocracy of power, based upon rank and influence, but an aristocracy of the sensitive, the considerate and the plucky.

In an impressive and unexpected way, however, the pressure of war created a feeling of unity, purpose, and dedication and some sense of a coming together of the classes. This was the spirit that Churchill summoned forth and augmented, lessening for a time that feeling of "we" and "they" so characteristic of English society. Fire-watching and the Home Guard allowed those on the home front to participate. The division between home and the front lines which had been so clear and disconcerting during the First World War largely evaporated, mostly, of course, because of the Blitz, the heavy bombings that London and other centers suffered. There was a great growth of popular interest in culture, a conviction that this was one of the aspects of English civilization for which the war was being fought. The conditions of the second war did not inspire a poetry as furious or as anguished as Wilfred Owen's in the earlier struggle. Poets, many of them in uniform, accepted the necessity of the war, but a tone of resignation rather than exhilaration emerges from their verse. Even Churchill in his most magnificent speeches never denied that what was at stake was not England's glory but England's survival. The sense of everybody's being "in it" made a difference; and the dominant note in the poetry of the Second World War is neither the anger of a Sassoon nor the pitiful compassion of an Owen, but instead a kind of rueful irony.

The war subjected English society to considerable strain. Politically, a Labour opposition still functioned at the same time that its leaders were in the cabinet. In fact, England had to become much more egalitarian in order to wage war, yet its society was not basically changed, the hierarchy preserved itself through its flexibility. The government controlled a vast area of life. It committed some errors and injustices which were not forgivable, for example, the illogical decision to send German Jews to Canada because they were enemy aliens! But by imposing sweeping regulations, the government accustomed its people to accept similar actions in peacetime. Many felt that England could not return to her prewar society, a conviction that was emphasized by the great popularity of the Beveridge Report issued in November 1942. The report, one of the very few official government papers to become a best seller, argued that the state was fully obligated to

Narvik

FINLAND

SWEDEN

NORWAY

Oslo

U.S.S.R.

APRIL 1940

BALTIC SEA

NORTH SEA

DENMARK

Copenhagen

GREAT BRITAIN

1940-1942

Hamburg

POLAND

Berlin

Rotterdam

GERMANY

Coventry

RUHR

NETH.

Dresden

1941-1945

Cologne

SPRING 1945

London

BELG.

CZECHOSLOVAKIA

Dunkirk

LUX.

WINTER 1944/45

JULY 1944

Stuttgart

SUMMER 1944

Paris

AUSTRIA

HUNGARY

Brest

SWITZ.

SPRING 1945

ATLANTIC OCEAN

FRANCE

Milano

YUGOSLAVIA

ITALY

WINTER 1944/45

Bologna

ADRIATIC SEA

FALL 1944

Florence

FALL 1944

Marseille

Nice

SUMMER 1944

ALBANIA

Rome

WINTER 1943/44

PORTUGAL

Madrid

Anzio

Naples

SPAIN

FALL 1943

Palermo

SUMMER 1943

MEDITERRANEAN SEA

MALTA

Map of the Second World War—Western Front.

take care of its people, as the popular phrase had it, "from the cradle to the grave." Beveridge himself was not a socialist, but a Liberal with strong Fabian aspects who nevertheless believed in individualism combined with state activity and direction from above. He attempted to serve the traditional individualistic aims of Liberalism through socialist means. Churchill was not particularly pleased by the report, but he recognized to a degree the necessity for this sort of planning for the future. He appointed Lord Woolton as minister of reconstruction. But social change in any extensive way beyond wartime necessities did not take place during the war. The report was one of the most important preconditions of change.

By 1945 the war itself had been gradually won. Hitler, having conquered much of Europe, was not strong enough to invade England. Russia and the United States entered the war in alliance with England, but it had taken aggressive actions by Germany and Japan for the alliance to come into full, fighting existence. Through lend-lease America had supported England before entering the war on her side, in December 1941.

Winston Churchill dominated England during the war and perhaps the entire Allied side as well. He gave the roar of the lion and devoted himself to pressing matters of strategy, cooperating with Roosevelt and Stalin to conquer Germany. Gradually, in Africa, in Italy, finally in France and Germany itself, Hitler was defeated. England had saved herself but in the process had confirmed her position as a secondary power, a fate that had threatened her since the conclusion of the First World War.

Churchill's chief virtue was to inspire; his military genius should not be exaggerated. Despite his complaints that England was not sufficiently armed during the 1930s, it was he who had been instrumental in cutting down English armaments in the 1920s. He made mistakes: the Norwegian campaign which had brought him to power and destroyed Chamberlain was his idea and may have precipitated Hitler's invasion of Norway; he was mistaken about the results of heavy bombing, which probably cost more in lives and materiel than it accomplished; he was wrong in sending troops to Greece, although his decision to send troops to Africa was wise. But every leader makes mistakes, and perhaps he made fewer than others; he was certainly geared to war, and he delivered victory to his people.

Adulated as a victor, Churchill was not trusted to build the new society after the war. In a way, the distrust of the Tories associated with the Munich settlement, put aside in 1940, reappeared. Much to his distress, Churchill was voted out of office. The army vote was especially effective against him. Some left-wing intellectuals had served in the education corps during the war and convinced numbers of their fellow soldiers that their best interests would not be served by being working-class Tories. Self-interest (and the inevitable postwar reaction) played a part. For mechanical reasons, the soldier vote in the First World War had come in too late and had not been counted; this time it was counted, and it proved very favorable to Labour.

Victory had preserved England's intellectual and social values, yet she emerged from five years of total war a broken and secondary power, still forced to contend in the years to come with her position in the world, with the empire (now the commonwealth and a decreasing number of colonies), and with a vast number of sociopolitical problems at home. The basic structure of English society still bore a rudimentary resemblance to what it had been before the Second World War, indeed, even some resemblance to its state before the First World War: a top-to-bottom stratification. In wealth, power, and privilege, the top was still extremely strong. But there was a popular determination that there should be great change, that society should care far more for its members. Basic values, however, remained very similar. There was an attempt to expand social services but to preserve individualism. In 1944 a government report projected the concept of free medical care for all; its realization became one of the great achievements of the postwar Labour government. Before the war was over, a few accomplishments took place under the Churchill government: most notably, the Education Act of 1944, which raised the school-leaving age to fifteen.

Labour Comes into Its Own

The Labour party won the greatest victory of its history in the General Election of 1945. For the first time, they were a majority party in power. In the House of Commons there were 393 Labour M.P.s and 213 Conservatives. There were also twenty-three Liberals and twenty-two various Independents, which conveys the suggestion that there were other solutions in the air for the problems of England's postwar world. But it was the Labour party's great triumph and opportunity: it had come into full power after less than a fifty-year history of political development as a party. The inheritance might not have been what Keir Hardie had expected, for the Labour party to a great degree had been taken over by the meritocracy. Of the 393 M.P.s, only half had begun life as manual workers and approximately a third were representatives of trade union interests. The rest were professional men, lawyers, teachers; the sort who might earlier have been Liberals. While few of the Labour M.P.s had gone to Oxford or Cambridge, the new M.P.s were not working class. Hugh Dalton, for example, a Labour leader and chancellor of the Exchequer, was the son of a Canon of Windsor and tutor to Edward VII. In a paraphrase of Baldwin's famous description of the M.P.s after the First World War, Dalton said that the new M.P.s were "a lot of smooth faced young men, who looked as if they meant to do well out of the peace."

Labour's sense of exhilaration at being in power sustained it during its first three years in office. As one leading Labourite, Hartley Shawcross, remarked, "We are the masters now." Earlier, beginning with Arthur Henderson's participation in the cabinet during the First World War and even with the government of 1924 and 1929–31, Labour had felt itself to be in power by the courtesy of others. The change was so abrupt that Attlee took over from Churchill in the middle of the Potsdam Conference of the Great Powers. In July of 1945 he formed a strong Labour government with himself as prime minister and minister of defense; Hugh Dalton as chancellor of the Exchequer, the first Etonian to be so since 1902; Ernest Bevin, the great leader of the Transport and General Workers' Union, as, rather surprisingly, foreign secretary; and Aneurin Bevan as minister of health. The Labour party began its rule in a lively manner in the House of Commons. When Herbert Morrison, the old-time Labour leader, lord president of the council in the government and acting leader in Attlee's absence, came into the House of Commons at its first meeting, he was applauded, a violation of parliamentary procedure. Tories, in retaliation, sang "For He's a Jolly Good Fellow" when Churchill walked into the House. Then Labour members, in order to assert themselves as the masters of the situation, sang "The Red Flag." In fact, the only real business of this first meeting was to elect a speaker, and as frequently happens the House consented to be guided by a Tory. The speaker-elect remarked that he did not know if he was going to be elected speaker of the house or director of a musical show.

Labour succeeded in putting through a sweeping program of change in its first years in office. The program implemented the Beveridge plan to a large degree, so that social services and social security became available to far more Englishmen than had enjoyed such benefits before. In itself, the Beveridge plan seemed more technocratic than inspirational. As a Liberal document, it lacked that peculiar fervor or idealism characteristic of some in the Labour movement; their object was "to build Jerusalem in England's green and pleasant land." The most representative figure of this strain in the Labour government was Aneurin Bevan, a passionate Welshman, who was the architect of the National Health Service. He was a brilliant orator who seemed to have a real sense of socialism and of the need for egalitarianism. In many ways, however, the Labour party was a middle-class one which owed as many debts to Liberal as to socialist thinking, except for its commitment to some degree of nationalization. The party was less doctrinaire than it had been before it was in power. Still, in its first three years, the Labour government did nationalize approximately 20 percent of the economy, most particularly, coal. There had been talk about the need to nationalize coal ever since the time of the First World War, when it had been done temporarily under the pressure of the war effort. Nationalization had been urged at the time of the General Strike of 1926. Now it finally came about under a Labour government. Railroads also were nationalized, and so for a time was the trucking industry. Nationalization meant the creation of vast public corporations. The state as employer is not necessarily more benign and far-seeing than private industry, but it is obligated to think in terms of public welfare rather than in terms of private profit. The welfare state—some nationalization and such services as the National Health Service; more education, including university education, available to more members of the community—has, on the whole, been very successful. The Tories, with their genius for adaptation, have accepted most of the welfare state, but maintain that they are more capable of administering it than the Labour party, who brought it into being. A party on the left, once it has achieved its set of reforms, has great difficulty in maintaining the spirit of innovation and no longer is it so evident to as many voters that it should be in power. As it continued in power, the Labour party was not able to keep alight the sense of mission that had impelled it to make its great steps of new legislation immediately after the war. A Trades Disputes Act was put through which finally, from the Labour point of view, righted the balance upset after the General Strike by what Labour considered a vindictive Trades Disputes Act. India, under Labour direction, became a member of the commonwealth and acquired self-government, although there was much bloodshed in India and Pakistan in the limited civil war at the time of their partition.

Hugh Dalton was forced to resign as chancellor of the Exchequer in 1947, after having inadvertently revealed part of the budget to a journalist just before giving the actual speech. Stafford Cripps replaced him, and this fortuitous change was appropriate. Dalton had helped lead the moments of great change; now the changes had to be solidified. Also, the international economic situation was becoming so severe that an austere chancellor was needed: Cripps could play that role to perfection. For the next three to four years, England experienced an austerity that was more intense than that suffered during the war itself: for instance, bread was rationed, which had not happened before. In many ways, existence in the immediate postwar years was tougher, although not as dangerous. England was paying the enormous price for having won the war. Lend-lease from the United States stopped as soon as the war was over; eventually it was replaced by Marshall Plan aid. But it was, in fact, very difficult for England to get back on her feet.

Not surprisingly, the necessary austerity programs caused considerable discontent. The English people were upset at being made to suffer deprivations as the result of winning the war. Nor was the United States as generous as she might have been with economic aid immediately after the war. Keynes was able to negotiate a loan at 2 percent interest, although he had hoped to persuade the Americans to make a loan to her ally on an interest-free basis. England tried to help herself through exports: "export or expire." She relied much more on the sterling and commonwealth area than she had before the Second World War.

Enthusiasm for Labour began to wane in the late 1940s. A new utopia had not arisen; although Labour had accomplished almost as much of its program as it could at the time, yet the drabness and dreariness of the war economy continued. There were serious splits within the Labour party over foreign policy, chiefly over the "special" relationship with the United States. Bevin was a tough-minded foreign secretary, but he pursued what some Labourites considered policies too close to the traditional concerns of English foreign policy. For instance, he took a tough attitude toward Jewish immigration into Palestine. There was considerable uproar among Jews in the United States over the issue. Bevin honestly and tactlessly pointed out that the American emigration laws kept the same Jews out of the United States. But the repressive military tactics necessary to maintain English power in Palestine were not congenial to quite a few Labourites. Also, the apparent dependence of England on the United States dismayed those on both left and right who wished to see England play a more independent role than her economic position allowed her.

In the General Election of 1950 Labour's majority went down to seventeen. In the next General Election, held in 1951 because of Labour's weakness, the Tories returned to power, with a majority of twenty-six; in fact, they did this with only 48 percent of the vote. Labour maintained a plurality with 48.8 percent of the vote, but its distribution in the constituencies accounted for the Tory victory. The Tories remained the ruling power for the next fourteen years. The principles of the welfare state had already been firmly entrenched, however, and the Tories had no choice but to maintain them. Labour had achieved great economic changes and made the ordinary individual much more secure than he had been in any other time in English history. For instance, Seebohm Rowntree had made a survey of York in 1899, in which he discovered that 30 percent of the population lived below the poverty line. In 1950 his survey of the same area revealed approximately 1.5 percent of the population below the poverty line.

There had been change in the fabric of society, although it is striking to what a degree social snobbism and a sense of hierarchy in society have survived the welfare state. One reason the upper classes survived well into the 1960s was England's lack of a capital gains tax. A family that over a long period of time had accumulated a lot of money and goods could live extremely well. The head of the family could sell a valuable painting, say, and maintain the high standard of living for some time longer. Now (1973) there is a 30 percent capital gains tax as well as extremely high death duties. Even so, the rich are frequently able to create trusts and manipulate the laws so that less money than the state expects comes into the treasury. But the possibility of preserving a family fortune through generations is considerably less likely than it has ever been before in English history. By contrast, there is among the populace at large a greater sense of egalitarianism and security.

CHAPTER SIX

Tory Rule

The primary concern of the Labour government in its years of power (1945–51) had been with England itself: to restore the state after the ravages of war, to reshape and reform it, to make it more egalitarian. Foreign affairs had been subordinate, tending to center on existing commitments and obligations—the most notable example was, perhaps, the commitment to self-government for India; that was finally realized in 1947, when the subcontinent was divided into the two independent nations of India and Pakistan. But by the time the Tories came to power in 1951, the degree of recovery and stability at home was sufficient to justify a renewed attention to international questions by the new government and an attempt to reestablish England's position as a major power on the world stage. The achievement fell far short of the aspiration: events were to prove that England was no longer able to claim or sustain even the lessened influence and position which had been hers in the years between the two world wars.

The leader of the Tory government from 1951 until his retirement in April 1955 was Winston Churchill, and his premiership was undoubtedly a personal triumph. But it might have been better, from the point of view

Coming to Terms

of England's position and future expectations—from a realistic assessment of what they might be in a changed postwar world—if he had not felt the necessity to return to office. But his electoral defeat in 1945 had been a bitter blow, and despite the continued adulation which was his as the architect of victory of the Second World War Churchill was determined to demonstrate that he was still capable of leading his nation in peacetime. In fact, he was fighting ill health—he was seventy-seven years old when he became prime minister again—and on June 23, 1953, he suffered a serious stroke which was kept hidden from the public. The situation at that moment was particularly difficult because his obvious heir, Anthony Eden, was ill and being operated on in Boston. But Churchill, seemingly as invincible as he believed himself to be, after a month of complete rest proved able to serve for another two years.

Churchill conceived of himself—rather as General de Gaulle was later to do—as a mediating force between his wartime allies, the United States of America and the Soviet Union, both of whom, unlike victorious but exhausted England, had emerged from the war as indisputable superpowers. England's close ties with the United States, by now traditional (and essential), were firmly maintained by the Churchill government. However, the idea of a rapprochement with the Russians was a remarkable late development for Churchill, given his deep-seated dislike of the Bolsheviks, dating back to the First World War. But whatever his hopes, England's interventions, more theoretical than practical, had little productive effect in ameliorating the cold war that was so much a part of the international situation of the 1950s, and to which Churchill, ironically enough, had made a small, memorable contribution of his own with his invention of the phrase "iron curtain" in a speech at Fulton, Missouri, in 1946—and a not-so-small contribution in his anti-Russian strategies during the final year of the war, and in his influence on President Truman.

Domestically, Churchill's government was less imaginative than its predecessor, but more successful in its endeavors. The period was notable for a recovery, finally, from the costs of the war and the austerities they had imposed. The welfare state and the expense of running it were now accepted in most part by both political parties, although the Tories had committed themselves to some denationalization, particularly of steel; the latter was to be a political football for years. But, in general, the policy imposed upon the state by the existing economic situation was similar for both political parties, so much so that the policy was popularly called "Butskellism," fusing the names of the two successive chancellors of the Exchequer: Hugh Gaitskell of the Labour party and R. A. B. Butler of the Tories.

The first of Butler's budgets, which he put forth in 1952, continued the early pattern of postwar austerity, but finally, in 1953, England apparently had "paid" for the successful war which had ended eight years before; rationing was ended at last, and prosperity was thought to have arrived. By 1954 there was full employment, which continued virtually until the economic recession of the mid-1960s. But in other respects there was considerable instability. Internally, a pattern developed—the so-called stop-go syndrome—in which successive chancellors of the Exchequer would, through their budgets and other means, alternately speed up and slow down the economy. John Maynard Keynes had taught that, contrary to the beliefs of the classical economists of the nineteenth century, the economy could be controlled; once this power over the economy was assumed, endless dispute emerged as to the correct decisions to be made. The most direct way of manipulation was through the bank rate, the rate of interest charged by the Bank of England which served either to impede or encourage investment in the economy. (But no matter to what extent the government has arranged to manipulate the economy, it has never been able adequately to control wage and price increases.) At the same time that Keynesianism had been accepted in the domestic sphere, England found herself increasingly at the mercy of the manipulations of a world economy no longer in her hands but dominated by money decisions made in Washington, New York, or elsewhere. England attempted a difficult balancing act: to maintain her traditional ties with the United States, the commonwealth, the major European powers, and those of other European countries still in the sterling area.

In the early fifties a further domestic economic pattern emerged, shared with other societies: a growing spiral of inflation, marked by severe labor troubles. The endless cycle of rising wages and prices was punctuated by bitter industrial strikes. This was not unique to the period of a Conservative government. When Labour returned to power, there was some confusion among the Unions. They were to discover that a Labour government would not automatically give in to all their wishes, and at times might be even more severe than a Tory administration. Also, the more radical members of the Labour party were to rediscover that, if anything, experience of power reinforced the conservative tendencies of union leaders. The idealism which had, at least to a degree, characterized the Labour movement in its earliest days tended to become less and less apparent, and some critics saw an increase of selfishness, among trade union members, summed up in the phrase of the period, "I'm all right, Jack, I've got mine."

In 1951, having been defeated, the Labour party had both the time and necessity to reassess its position and to sort out its balances between left and right. There were pressures in both directions—on the one hand, to "modernize" the party in the direction of efficiency and away from ideology, a program associated with Hugh Gaitskell, and on the other hand, to maintain a strong distinct ideological position, a program associated with the colorful Aneurin Bevan. Bevan had resented the modifications Labour itself had made in his National Health Act, a crucial aspect of the welfare state, generally in the direction of small fees for some services, and had resigned from the government in April 1951. And in foreign policy Bevan was in direct conflict with the official position of his own party.

It was a dispute which would go on for most of the 1950s within the Labour party. A tradition had grown up in the late nineteenth century, after the bitter foreign policy differences between Gladstone and Disraeli had subsided, that there should be a "continuity" in this area, whichever political party was in power. That tradition had persisted in the years after the Second World War, when Ernest Bevin, as a forceful foreign minister in the Labour government, had followed long-established English interests, particularly in his resistance to the creation of an independent Israel and in his willingness to cooperate with American policy.

When the Labour party was out of power, Aneurin Bevan chose to ignore the tradition of "continuity" and led an attack against Tory foreign policy, selecting for his issue Labour party support of the Tories' policy for the rearmament of Germany. Involved in the immediate issue was the larger problem of rearmament in general, which later in the decade of the 1950s would lead to the emergence of the Campaign for Nuclear Disarmament (C.N.D.), although Bevan himself, who died in 1960, disowned that movement. Nor did he take the strong stand expected by his followers against England's development of the hydrogen bomb, first exploded in May 1957. The issue was an important one, not only for the Labour party. Should England attempt to keep up with the superpowers, or should she take a moral stand against nuclear weapons and decide to disarm unilaterally? The C.N.D. called on the energies of many intellectuals and students. Its famous marches, between 1958 and the early 1960s, starting at the nuclear research station at Aldermaston and ending at Trafalgar Square in London, brought dramatically to public attention the considerable popular objection to nuclear arms for England. But it was a financial rather than a moral choice which ultimately led England to restrict its build-up of such enormously costly as well as deadly weapons.

The immediate story of Bevan at odds with his party took the traditional form of such disputes: in 1954 he resigned from the "front bench," that is, the parliamentary leadership of the Labour party. Thereafter, there was increasing acrimony between the Bevanites and the supporters of the official party line. Harold Wilson, who had been the youngest man to serve in a Labour cabinet, replaced Bevan in the shadow cabinet, and since he was thought to hold an attitude roughly similar to Bevan's, this could be counted as a victory of sorts. But Bevan lost his fight within the party: first in 1954 he lost the treasurership of the party to Hugh Gaitskell, then in March 1955, by a vote within the parliamentary Labour party of 141 to 112, he was deprived of the whip—that is, he would not be considered an ordinary member of the party. Yet he did not resign and was back in the fold by the time of the General Election later that year. When Attlee resigned his leadership at the end of 1955, Bevan, hoping to succeed him, lost again to Gaitskell, decisively, with the old party stalwart, Herbert Morrison, running a poor third. Gaitskell not only was willing to take a cooperative attitude toward the Tories on rearmament, but he also wished to remold the party itself, most notably calling into question Clause 4 in the party constitution, adopted in 1918, which advocated the nationalization of the means of production. Gaitskell and his supporters—for instance, Anthony Crosland, whose study, *The Future of Socialism* (1956), expresses their point of view—felt that nationalization was no longer the best way to achieve the party's aims and that equality could be brought about more significantly by means of the tax structure. Gaitskell lost votes at the annual party conferences, particularly because the secretary of the Transport and General Workers' Union, Frank Cousins, controlled the greatest number of trade union votes, and Cousins was to the left of the party rather than in the traditional union position on the right. Nevertheless, Gaitskell's revisionism tended to dominate the party's thinking, the more so since from 1956 on he and Bevan were able to cooperate. When this occurred, the discontented in the left wing of the party were deprived of their most effective leader. Dissension in the party, however smoothed over, contributed significantly to keeping Labour out of power.

Of course, there are positive reasons, as opposed to the negative contributions of Labour, that help explain why the Conservative government continued in office for thirteen years. At the very beginning of Churchill's premiership, the mood of England began to improve. The first visible expression of this renewed confidence and optimism was the Festival of Britain in 1951, celebrating the centenary of the Crystal Palace Exhibition of 1851, that triumph of the Victorian age. Although England had not entirely recovered from the effects of the war, the opening of the new Royal Festival Hall on the south bank of the Thames, almost opposite the Houses of Parliament, in a still growing complex of concert halls, theaters, and galleries, seemed to mark a recovery. The Festival Pleasure Grounds further up the river at Battersea symbolized the determination of Londoners in particular and Englishmen in general to lead a more pleasant life than had been possible in the gray years of postwar restrictions.

After the festival came the "new Elizabethan age." George VI died in February 1952. He had played his role well, a shy man who had done his duty when his elder brother, Edward VIII, had abdicated in order to marry the American divorcée he loved. George and his queen, Elizabeth, had remained in London all through the Blitz; they had won the affection of their subjects; they were representative of the spirit of the war years at its best and most "English." Their elder child, the young and attractive Elizabeth, equipped with the young and dashing Prince Philip as her husband, seemed to embody a new spirit. Her accession to the throne was made the occasion for an exhilaration that had little actual basis in fact. But at the moment, encouraged by Churchillian rhetoric, the press was prepared to declare a new Elizabethan age. This sentiment reached its height in the spring of 1953 when, on Coronation Day itself, the news was received of the conquest of Mt. Everest by a team of empire climbers. Perhaps England was about to reassert her position in the world. But such hopes, if they were ever seriously entertained, would not last past 1956.

Suez

Churchill finally retired in April 1955. It seemed that he had justified his return to power, and now could safely hand over the government to a younger man. The ten years of his retirement before his death were marked by the personal sadness of old age and senility, but, now that he had retired from partisan politics, he could once again be granted heroic stature by all his countrymen. At the time of his death in January 1965 he had become an almost mythic figure. The viewing of his coffin, as it lay in state, by the thousands who waited hours to do so brought back patriotic memories of the battle of Britain, and the funeral itself conveyed the greatest sense of past glory since the funeral of the Duke of Wellington in 1852.

For years, Sir Anthony Eden had been the designated heir to Churchill's position. A handsome figure of a man, a member of a prominent family of country squires, an adept foreign secretary, he had first become famous for his opposition to appeasement and his subsequent resignation from Neville Chamberlain's government. In 1955 he represented to the country a continuation of happy Tory rule.

The strength of the party and the popularity of Eden were demonstrated in the General Election that May, when the Tories greatly increased their numbers in the House of Commons. There were now 344 Tory M.P.s in the house, as contrasted to 277 for Labour. As it so frequently seems in England, the impression was that the party in power was going to remain so practically forever.

Yet under Eden's premiership England would suffer her most serious debacle of the postwar years, the Suez campaign—an event which dramatically marked England's decline to a secondary power. The situation in Egypt had been troubled for years; England's old domination of that nation had been weakened profoundly, and her influence was limited to the ability to apply pressure on Egypt's King Farouk. The revolution of 1951 had led to the flight of King Farouk, the abandonment of the monarchy, and the emergence first of Colonel Naguib and then of Colonel Nasser as the country's leaders. It was a time when the decolonization of the English empire was already well advanced. But the situation was particularly sensitive in Egypt because the Suez Canal was thought to be of crucial importance for England's trade and her position in the world. The Anglo-Egyptian treaty in 1954 had stipulated that England would remove her troops from Egypt in 1956 but would continue to control the canal. Relations with Egypt were badly managed and reached a crisis in July 1956. Nasser, anxious to build the Aswan Dam, had negotiated loans from the United States and England for that purpose. But both countries, feeling that Egypt was being too sympathetic to Russia, withdrew their willingness to support the project financially, the United States on July 19th and England on the 20th. John Foster Dulles, the American secretary of state, complicated English and French policy through his failure to make his intentions clear during these months. Six days later, on July 26th, ostensibly in order to secure the necessary revenues to build the dam, Nasser seized control of the canal and declared it nationalized. (The disapproving English attitude toward Nasser was indicated in a traditional way: in the pages of *The Times* he was no longer referred to as Colonel or President Nasser, but simply as Nasser.) Eden was now to demonstrate the danger of learning lessons from history; he had convinced himself that Nasser was a latter-day Hitler. Certainly, Nasser did share something of Hitler's attitudes toward Jews, largely because of the presence of Israel in the Middle East. But Eden felt that a strong stand must be taken: Nasser could not be allowed to seize the canal or in other ways infringe upon English rights in so high-handed and arbitrary a fashion. Although it was denied at the time that there had been collusion among three of the concerned powers—England, France, and Israel—in fact their actions were carefully worked out. The plan was that Israel should launch an attack on Egypt, in response to the threat to their shipping, represented by Egyptian control of the canal; then England and France would move in to protect the canal, and thus not appear to be attacking Egypt.

The Suez operation took place in the fall. On October 29, 1956, Israel moved against Egypt; on November 3 English troops, supported by French planes, made their move; on November 6 there was a cease-fire. The immediate object had been to save the canal, but that was frustrated when the Egyptians sank ships in the canal to block passage. The canal was not open to shipping again until the following April, and the question of who could use the canal and on what terms was not resolved for years.

A long-term object of the attack on Egypt was to assert England's position in the world, but in that she failed lamentably. Nasser was still in power; if anything, his position had been strengthened in the world's eyes for having been the target of an attack by leading European powers. In December the English, having failed in their objectives, withdrew, leaving control of the canal to the Egyptians. Her international reputation had been considerably tarnished. The United States, most particularly the secretary of state, John Foster Dulles, had not supported the operation. England had attempted an imperial gesture reminiscent of some of her actions in the nineteenth century, which had been so flamboyantly successful in various parts of the world, Egypt among them. Now, in the emptiness and unsuccess of the gesture, she had demonstrated to the world her limitations. The degree to which the Second World War had sapped England's strength was fully evident: she had no choice but to limit her commitments. Thereafter, she moved, or was moved, to a fuller cooperation with the rest of Europe. On the world stage her importance diminished.

Not only at the level of politics, but at emotional, psychological, and intellectual levels the events of 1956 were highly significant in their impact. They were reflected in the literature of the period, in which cynicism was allied to a kind of brusque idealism, a wish to turn the reassessment of England's changing position to good account. Actually, the change in literary styles had begun before Suez, but the new spirit it represented seemed to be vindicated by the later events. In May 1956 John Osborne's play *Look Back in Anger* had opened in London and was immediately recognized as one of the most important literary statements of the 1950s. In this play, as in Osborne's successor to it, *The Entertainer* (1957), in which the events of Suez directly figured, there was a sense of despair, a conviction that the Labour party, from which so much had been expected, and the Tories, from whom little in the way of idealism had been expected, had both failed to create any sort of new society. Yet this attitude of despair—often stated in comic terms—had produced a new literary movement, in Osborne's plays and in the novels of Kingsley Amis and Angus Wilson. Most of these works conveyed an ironic and somewhat bitter isolation and a disillusionment with the postwar world. Jimmy Porter, the antihero of *Look Back in Anger*, is searching, without much success, for a way to come to terms with life in contemporary England, to liberate himself so that the freedoms which appeared to be promised by the Labour government might be realized. In fact, he spends most of his time railing at the upper classes, in the person of his wife. The writings of the period reflected the problems of cutting loose from the past, from the no longer valid or feasible conceptions of empire. They were, on a literary level, a first step toward an English popular cultural explosion, of which the songs of the Beatles in the 1960s would be the most notable expression.

The immediate political result of Suez was the fall of Eden: the failure of the enterprise affected him both physically and mentally, and he recognized that he was in no state to continue as head of the government. With few exceptions the Tory party had remained loyal to him; and the Suez enterprise was not, on the whole, unpopular with the public, for it appealed to the patriotic sentiments of many Englishmen. Here, at last, the country was taking a stand in the old grand manner—and if it had succeeded, Eden would have emerged as a hero. Those Tory M.P.s who opposed the government's policy had to justify themselves to their constituency organizations; most of them disappeared as active Tories. Tories in the cabinet were put in an awkward position. For them the proper approach was to convey, as Churchill had managed to do in 1940, both a sense of strong loyalty to the party leader and an awareness that the situation might have been better handled. But whatever might have been thought about the wisdom or propriety of England's taking a stand over the seizure of the Suez Canal, there was no question that the operation had failed, and it came as no surprise when the man responsible for it resigned on January 9, 1957. Eden had been waiting to be prime minister ever since Churchill had taken over the post in 1940. His tenure, when the opportunity was at last his, was far briefer than anyone might have expected. Suez concluded his career.

The Age of Super-Mac

The Tories felt there was no need to follow Eden's resignation with another General Election. Party organization and loyalty were such that their parliamentary majority was still secure. All that was necessary was to choose a new leader.

For the next to last time a party leader would emerge in the old-fashioned way. Soundings were taken among the Tory leadership, the back benchers, prominent Tories in the country. Ultimately, the queen would consult with the Marquess of Salisbury, a traditionally grand figure in the party, as well as with Churchill himself. Many expected that Butler, who had been associated with the modernization of the party, would be chosen, but it was rumored that he had opposed Eden's Suez policy, and it was Harold Macmillan who was asked to form a government.

Macmillan had been an M.P. for many years and a Tory of the left in the 1930s. Like Eden but unlike Butler, he was known as an anti-appeaser at the time of Munich. He had held important posts during the war and had been foreign secretary and chancellor of the Exchequer under Eden. Not only was he a very capable politician, but he also had the right social background. His grandfather had been a Scottish crofter who had gone on to found the famous publishing firm of Macmillan. He himself, educated at Eton and Balliol College, Oxford, had married a daughter of the Duke of Devonshire. He was a figure who emanated confidence: he would reassure the country and the party after the Suez misadventure. At the same time, he was able to continue the party's acceptance of the new social world of the welfare state. He was a colorful figure, suggestive of Disraeli's Tory democracy, in contrast to Hugh Gaitskell's duller appeal of Gladstonian probity.

Macmillan became prime minister and leader of the party. He led the Tories to an amazing recovery. Contrary to all predictions and expectations, they won an even greater victory in the General Election of 1959 than in that of 1955, gaining 365 seats to Labour's 258.

During the Second World War Macmillan had gotten on very well with England's allies, and he now attempted, with some success, to revive his wartime cooperation with the American president, Dwight Eisenhower. Later, he was able to continue such friendly meetings when John F. Kennedy went to the White House. At the same time, Macmillan maintained comparatively cordial relations with the Russians. His hope—rarely realized, however, in a significant way—was that England could be the broker in preserving peace between the two superpowers. England's role tended to fade at crucial times, as when American-Russian relations worsened over the U-2 incident (the American spy plane shot down over Russia) and with the serious threat of war at the time of the Cuban crisis in 1962, when Russia was persuaded to withdraw its missiles from Castro's Cuba. But in July 1963 the treaty banning nuclear tests, of which Macmillan had been an enthusiastic proponent, was signed—an important step toward ending the cold war. In this significant instance, at least, Macmillan's policy of summitry had yielded some success. At the same time, England's own military situation became increasingly shaky. Her first hydrogen bomb was exploded in May 1957, but the principal immediate consequence appeared to be the first march from the nuclear research station in Aldermaston in Berkshire to Trafalgar Square in London at Easter 1958 and the Campaign for Nuclear Disarmament. The campaign became increasingly vehement, most particularly in the form of the Committe of 100 (Bertrand Russell was among the members) which participated in several sit-down protests. The campaign eventually faded away, but at the same time England's attempt to keep up militarily weakened; her part in various cooperative schemes with the United States involving nuclear weapons became less and less important.

Macmillan was unusually successful in his domestic policy. At long last, the sense of living in the aftermath of the war was over. England was, continued to be, and, indeed, still is (1973) in profound economic difficulties. It seems impossible to stabilize her currency, her economic situation is insecure, she does not export enough, inflation is a continual problem, the unions call frequent strikes. Yet during Macmillan's prime ministership the mood of the country changed and improved. Many thought—whether accurately or not—that life was better, and London increasingly became the center of a new "swinging" spirit. In large part, this was a figment of public relations, yet a determination to enjoy life, and enjoy its good things, became much more noticeable in English society. Much as the post-Suez period saw an abandonment of some international commitments, although there were still a few English outposts about the world, so now there was a sense of enjoying at home the easing of responsibilities. Purchasing on credit became much easier, and the bank rate was lowered. Rents were further decontrolled, making greater profits possible.

Housing became a continuing problem, however. Rent decontrol led to a discontent which boiled over when profiteer landlords jammed as many people as possible into deteriorating buildings. Landlords particularly exploited immigrants, most notably those from India, Pakistan, and the West Indies. The English, who had thought that such things were an American and not an English phenomenon, were shocked to discover that they too could have race riots, as they did in 1958 in Nottingham and in the Notting Hill district of London. Such outbreaks were rare and were severely dealt with, but they brought about a growing questioning of whether England should grant admission to those citizens of the commonwealth who were not assured of a job in England. Since 1958 there has been a policy of sharply restricted immigration, as in the Commonwealth Immigrants Act of 1963, and also an attempt to stamp out racial discrimination through a Race Relations Board. Yet the antagonism in England toward nonwhites has persisted.

Macmillan presided gracefully, even as his predecessors had been forced to do since the end of the Second World War, over the dissolution of the empire. Royal personages frequently went as England's representatives at the proclamation of a newly independent country. The prime minister, making a tour of such countries in Africa in 1960, felt it would be insulting not to go to the Union of South Africa. While there, he managed not to offend the Boer leaders yet to make a speech in which he talked of the necessity to accept the "winds of change" which were blowing across Africa. Whatever position England might take in relation to African events, it was clear that she would make less and less difference to what would happen on the continent where she once had played so important a role.

As the tie with former colonies and the commonwealth became less significant—although the sentimental tie is still very strong—the prospect of cooperation with European countries increased. In 1959 England associated herself with the European Free Trade Association, consisting of herself, Austria, Portugal, Switzerland, Denmark, Sweden, and Norway. In part, of course, it was a rival organization to the European Economic Community, known as the Common Market, which had been formed in 1958 and consisted of France, West Germany, Italy, and the Benelux countries. Whether England should attempt to join this group instead became an issue of deepening concern in English politics. The right wing within the Tory party was anxious to maintain England's independence from Europe; the left of the Labour party tended to regard the Common Market as excessively favoring business interests in the various countries. It was also opposed by agricultural interests and by those who wished to maintain and strengthen economic and trading ties with the commonwealth. Hugh Gaitskell had established his control of the Labour party, but he had a very difficult time with this issue. Although he was identified with those on the right of his party who tended to favor "going into Europe," on behalf of party unity he finally came out against England seeking membership in the Common Market.

Macmillan had followed an opposite course. In July 1961 he decided that the time had come for England to apply for membership, and the elaborate negotiations began, primarily under guidance of a comparatively new figure in the party, Edward Heath. Almost two years later negotiations were still in progress; in January 1963, Charles de Gaulle, President of France, vetoed England's application for membership, and the discussions in Brussels came to a halt. Having, after a great deal of hesitation, decided to apply for membership, England now found herself rebuffed; it was a serious blow to her prestige.

The "Age of Super-Mac" was coming to an end. Macmillan had managed to revive the fortunes of his party with extraordinary skill, winning a third election for the Tories in 1959, an almost unprecedented series of triumphs. But by 1963 his government was running out of steam, and the prospects for the opposition brightened. The Labour party had suffered a grievous blow in January of that year in the unexpected and early death of Hugh Gaitskell, and Harold Wilson was elected the new leader of the party. A brilliant economist, born of a poor family in York-shire, a former don at Oxford, Wilson was identified with the left wing of his party. Nevertheless, he kept the Gaitskellites and others who were more or less on the right in his shadow cabinet, and by doing so he managed rapidly to unify the party. (The smell of coming power was also a unifying force.)

That same year, 1963, the Tory party was seriously compromised by the Profumo scandal. John Profumo was the minister for war, not an office of cabinet rank. Gossip linked his name with that of Christine Keeler, a call girl also connected with Captain Ivanov of the Russian embassy. The central issue was one of security—had Profumo made indiscreet revelations to Keeler, who had passed them on to Ivanov?—but for the public the fascination of the case was in "naughty doings in high places." Profumo made a statement in the House of Commons in March 1963 that there had been no impropriety in his relations with Miss Keeler, but in June he had to admit that he had lied—that is, that he had enjoyed her favors but had not betrayed any secrets to her—and resigned his position. The scandal, coming after earlier security problems, did the government no good: there were suggestions of laxness, a feeling that Macmillan was losing his grip. An election seemed likely to take place soon.

But illness intervened. Macmillan became severely ill just at the time of the annual Conservative party conference in October 1963. It appeared that at long last "Rab" Butler would head the Tories, but he still did not have the confidence of any influential segment of the party. Lord Hailsham, taking advantage of a bill just passed on behalf of a Labour leader which allowed peers to renounce their titles, announced his intention to become plain Quentin Hogg and, he hoped, prime minister. But a surprising new candidate emerged, the Earl of Home, who had been described when an Etonian school boy as an appropriate prime minister for the eighteenth century. He had been a quite undistinguished foreign secretary in Macmillan's government; even then there had been objections to the appointment of a lord to the post. But now the powers within the party decided that Home, after having renounced his title to become simple Sir Alec Douglas-Home, should be prime minister. It was he whom Macmillan advised the queen to send for when she visited him in the hospital. Home was sufficiently unsure of himself that he told the queen that he would attempt, but could not promise, to head a government. But the considerable revolt against him within the party largely collapsed when Tory leaders were offered posts in the new government, and in due course he became prime minister.

Under his uninspiring leadership, the Tories remained in power for one more year. Macmillan, during his seven years as prime minister, had managed to restore a sense of confidence, however unwarranted, to English life. He had even managed to carry off with a certain Edwardian elegance

Harold Macmillan, April 1963. (Popperfoto, London.)

such crass appeals to the public as the electioneering slogans "You never had it so good" and "Life is twice as good under the Conservatives." But in 1964 the slogans proved less appealing than before—perhaps because Home could not carry them off as effectively as Macmillan—and in October, after a closely fought election which gave them a parliamentary majority of four, Labour returned to power for the first time in thirteen years.

Labour's Return to Power

Labour's second period of power after the Second World War was similar in some respects to Gladstone's second ministry of 1880–85. Harold Wilson was a far less impressive man than William Gladstone, but like Gladstone he had gained domination of his party, in his case rather rapidly. As party leader he dominated the 1964 election; through television appearances, news conferences in London, and his ability to handle hecklers, he practiced what some referred to disapprovingly as "presidential politics." Wilson did not do as well as might have been expected considering the weak state of the Tories, but he did achieve a net gain of 56 seats, with 44.1 percent of the vote. The Tories won 303 seats, with 43.4 percent of the vote, and the Liberals 9 seats with 11.2 percent of the vote, giving Labour a slender working majority of 4. Armed with his inevitable pipe, Wilson attempted to project two images—the friendly "ordinary chap" and the brilliant Oxford economist—a "technocrat" who understood the modern world. He presented a powerful contrast to Macmillan's suggestion of an older and more comfortable England. Wilson managed the House of Commons well, and for the first two years, despite his minute majority, he passed sixty-five bills. He attempted to make England more egalitarian—particularly for the "young marrieds," who he thought were likely to support a Labour government. For them, and others, he helped to secure progress in housing

169

and education. Wilson also improved social security benefits for the old and the sick, those who had been neglected in the increase of affluence and consumer goods which characterized Tory prosperity in the late 1950s. He tried to modernize England's economic procedures, with the assistance of two distinguished economists, Thomas Balogh from Oxford and Nicholas Kaldor from Cambridge.

One reason Macmillan's popularity had waned was that his contention of continuing prosperity was clearly false. Wilson promised to face the situation. Like Gladstone, he found himself caught in the dilemmas of the period—but this time they were not imperial commitments. Wilson took the sensible action of reducing military burdens, both of maintaining troops abroad, particularly "east of Suez," and of trying to compete as a producer of nuclear weapons. But the pattern of short bursts of prosperity, alternating with long periods of economic difficulty, did not appreciably improve under a Labour government. Wilson had to cope with the fluctuating situation as best he could. The balance-of-payments problem continued; exports rarely exceeded imports. The introduction of a capital gains tax helped to an extent. During Wilson's first two years as prime minister productivity increased 1.5 percent, but wages went up 5.5 percent. Workers went on strike as often under Labour as under the Tories—the main difference being that as the trade union leadership was more sympathetic to the government, more of the strikes were "wildcat" rather than ordered by the unions. Even so, Wilson's first two years in office were marked by a comparative boom.

In 1965 there was a sense of change, in a dramatic sense, with the death of Winston Churchill on January 24, at the age of ninety-one. Churchill was given the first state funeral for a private subject since those of Wellington and Gladstone. In the words of one commentator, while Churchill was dying, "The world waited for the news, perhaps the last time it would wait with such respect on news from London." As the giant passed from the scene, so too party leadership changed. Sir Alec Douglas-Home updated the procedures for leadership selection, replacing the inchoate system of consultation which in the past had brought about the "emergence" of the new leader. Sir Alec introduced a system of election by the Tory M.P.s, and some months later he precipitated its first operation by resigning the leadership. Home had not been as bad a leader as most people had expected, nor had he been as good as a few had hoped; he has continued as a prominent member of his party, and at present (1973) is foreign secretary. Edward Heath, who had handled the unsuccessful negotiations for England's entry into the Common Market, was elected leader. Heath was an appropriate parallel to Wilson. He was the first Tory leader who was not from a country or successful business background; his father had been a builder in the South of England, and Heath had managed to win a scholarship to Balliol College, Oxford. He represented a change for the Tories; he brought a greater emphasis on efficiency.

There was some feeling that the two party leaders were much alike, and Heath took longer than expected to assert his control of his party.

In foreign policy Wilson was caught by the consequences of England's secondary position. Despite the protests from the left of the Labour party, he felt he had no choice but to support America's policy in Viet-Nam— no matter how much he might deplore it—in order to preserve the "special relationship" with the United States. He resisted American pressure to send troops to fight there, and he attempted, unsuccessfully, to act as a peace negotiator. And throughout his premiership he would be unable, largely because of his country's weakness, to enforce her policy in areas of English sovereignty. Starting in 1965 there was a continuing problem with Rhodesia, whose government wished to pursue a policy of white supremacy. Wilson attempted to keep Rhodesia in line through the use of sanctions, conferences, and pressure from the United Nations, but he did not wish, nor did he feel strong enough, to use force as advocated by the black African nations. The situation in Ireland—the unresolved problem of how Catholics and Protestants could live peacefully together in Northern Ireland—flared again, and in 1969, England felt it necessary to send troops. Neither Labour nor now the Tory party has so far (1973) been able to work out a solution.

No problem facing contemporary England is easily solved, and some —particularly economic problems—appear to be insoluble. Yet the condition of life in England has improved. The material gains are obvious: many people have cars, refrigerators, television sets, compared with the very few who had such "luxuries" before the Second World War. In a more indefinite sense, the "quality" of life has also improved, in part, perhaps, because the strain of playing the role of a great power has gone. Probably, in these days of England's decline, more people than ever before are leading a better life.

Wilson took advantage of a temporary burst of prosperity in 1966 to call a General Election on March 31, in which he did very well: he had demonstrated that after a long period out of office, Labour could still rule. He emerged with a majority of 97, having won 363 seats, while the Tories secured 253, and the Liberals increased their strength to 12. There were mutters that perhaps the Tories should find a leader to replace Heath. Wilson had clearly dominated the election. In the next two years Labour devoted much energy to advocacy of the Common Market as a way to improve England's economic situation. There was considerable doubt both on the left and the right of the political spectrum, and in the populace, as to the wisdom of joining the European community. Critics were worried as to how the Common Market might affect English agriculture, labor, and relationships with the commonwealth. Wilson had not been too enthusiastic about the Common Market in the past, but he did push it through the House of Commons in May 1967 by a vote of 488 to 62, although the dissenters included 34 Labour M.P.s and some members of the party had

THE GENERAL ELECTION, 1970

Conservative and Unionist

Labour

Liberal

Scottish Nationalist

Protestant Unionist

Independent

Map of the General Election, 1970. (*The Times Guide to the House of Commons, 1970.*)

abstained. However, President de Gaulle again said no, and in November France vetoed England's request for entry. Shortly thereafter, England was forced yet again to devaluate the pound, from $2.80 to $2.40.

The improvement in the "quality of life" was purchased at a growing price: no government was able to prevent strikes with their inconveniences or to stop inflation. Wilson had no choice but to retrench, through further withdrawals from military obligations; and he continued to turn England toward Europe. England's application to the Common Market was officially still pending. De Gaulle ceased ruling France in 1968 after his government had managed to survive the extensive student disturbances of that year. England was still the "in" place for students to travel, but, undoubtedly to her relief, England did not participate in the serious student protests and violence that took place in other parts of the Western world, suffering little more than a blocking of the entrance way to the London School of Economics, over the question of the suitability of the new director, and some disturbances at art schools.

Although trade improved in 1968, the government, now four years in office, was growing increasingly unpopular. Yet Heath and his followers had failed to capture the public imagination; it was hard to imagine how the Tories might do better with the problems which continued to plague England: economic instability, the Rhodesian situation, Ulster, and immigration, particularly immigration from Africa where Asians, who claimed the protection of the Crown, were being persecuted by the native majority who believed they were avenging years of economic exploitation.

Wilson was convinced by the pollsters that the comparative prosperity of 1970 would assure him a renewed electoral victory. He called a General Election for June 18, 1970, conducting his campaign with extraordinary self-assurance—in retrospect, arrogance—and in a "presidential" manner, as if the only choice to be made was between himself and Heath, and that clearly he had much more to offer than the pallid organ-playing Tory leader. At the last moment the polls began to switch as a reaction to another trade deficit announced three days before the election. Only 72 percent of the electorate voted, and 25 percent of the newly enfranchised eighteen-year-olds failed to register. Wilson was defeated, and the Tories came into power, winning 330 seats to Labour's 287.

Going into Europe

Edward Heath has completed the turning toward Europe, and the move away from most of England's international obligations. He became increasingly committed to joining the Common Market, despite considerable popular opinion against such a move. The Labour party split over the question. Clearly, to oppose the move was a way of harassing the Tories, but Wilson, who had, after all, committed himself to the Common Market earlier, was curiously indecisive. His usual ability to impose his opinions on the party failed, the more so as those opinions wavered. He finally came out against joining, while not explaining satisfactorily why he had advocated joining when he was in office. His excuse was that the terms were no longer right. He lost the support of the "Europeanists" in his own party, most notably Roy Jenkins, who had been chancellor of the Exchequer and was the most impressive figure in the party leadership other than Wilson himself. Heath pressed forward in his campaign: in May 1971 he had friendly and successful conversations with Pompidou, the President of France; the French veto would not be exercised this time. Heath felt that joining the Common Market was the most important event for England since the end of the Second World War: it would increase the markets for England's trade and manufacturing, would make English industry more efficient, and would enlarge her market in agriculture. Critics assert the opposite: that in these areas England will lose out to continental competition and that she will become a marketplace for European goods at inflated prices. The decisive vote in Parliament on October 28, 1971, was 356 to 244 in favor of the Common Market, with 39 Tories voting against the party whip ordering support for the Market and 69 Labour M.P.s voting in favor of the Market (20 abstained), contrary to their leader's directions.

England officially became a member of the European Economic Community on January 1, 1973. It is too early to tell which predictions are correct: as usual, probably both will be both right and wrong, and some results, good or bad, will not have been anticipated. Undoubtedly, there will be great benefits in the envisioned economic and monetary unity; but it has yet to be demonstrated whether these will benefit the ordinary Englishmen and women or simply the business community—and even then how many of those businessmen will be English. Certainly some segments of English industry will profit: chemicals, airplane manufacture, textiles, shoes, and possibly automobiles. And English farmers are technologically able to compete. Joining the Market inaugurates a return for England to a position, with its great emphasis upon relations to Europe, she has not held since the earlier years of the eighteenth century.

In other areas, while accepting most of the obligations of the welfare state and its concept of social service, Heath has attempted to reintroduce a greater degree of private enterprise into the English system, as indicated in such small ways as the government divesting itself of the control of the great travel agency of Thomas Cook. Home, as foreign secretary, made peace with Rhodesia. Relations with unions deteriorated. The Industrial Relations Act of August 1971 was designed to impede the vast number of strikes. So far the act seems to have irritated the unions, but it has not prevented them from strike action and labor unrest has increased. The English economy is still unable to resist inflation. In the fall of 1972 Heath imposed a three-month freeze on prices and wages.

It remains to be seen what effect joining the Common Market will have upon England. The Common Market serves national interests in that it allows each nation a large market for its goods, but it also represents the sacrifice of some degree of sovereignty.

Despite all her difficulties, England has been able to achieve and maintain a rich civilization for almost all of her inhabitants. There are still those who are ill-housed, ill-fed, ill-educated, and who fail to achieve anything approaching a full life. But they are far fewer than they were at any previous time in England's history. London has its share of the overwhelming problems of all large cities, but it is still thought of by many as the most civilized city in the world. It has not ceased to be a hub of empire even when the empire itself has largely ceased to exist; the actualities of art and culture, and still a certain degree of economic power, make it an exciting place. It has not lost a sense of being a series of various towns, with more green and more houses "scaled to the human" than most great urban complexes. The countryside itself and other urban centers, with their cathedrals, country houses, and museums suggesting past glories, not totally vanished now, continue to exercise the fascination of an extraordinary past and an intriguing, if more limited, present.

England still projects a powerful appeal to, and at times a cultural dominance over, the English-speaking world. An American list of best-selling books is as likely to include the novels of John Fowles, Anthony Burgess, C. P. Snow, or Muriel Spark as those of American authors. George Orwell (not to mention Charles Dickens) may well be the novelist most familiar to American high school students through their reading of *Animal Farm* and *1984*. One English rock group, the Beatles, has been replaced as the most popular in the world by another, the Rolling Stones (1973). Perhaps England, with all her difficulties, has managed to come to better terms than most other societies with the implications of the modern world and has adopted a more skeptical attitude toward the great shibboleth of economic growth.

England has managed to modernize herself, to improve the lot of most of her inhabitants, and yet, in so many ways, for both better and worse, has changed far less than one would have imagined possible over the years of her history. Despite a tax structure meant to secure most earned and unearned income to the state, half of the wealth is still owned by 2 percent of the population. There exists what is still in many ways a hierarchical society, but one that has been combined with a welfare state. One should be chary of discerning too much of the present situation in England in its earlier history. Even so, looking back to the very beginning

The Beatles during a television recording session, 1966. (Keystone Press.)

it seems possible to trace certain continuities, which would appear to be more pronounced in England than in other countries: perhaps a slightly higher respect for law and custom; a more thought-out balance between the powers of the central authority and local power; a strong sense of the land, of the individual, of his own obligations and the obligations of the local and central authorities to him. England can claim to be as democratic in her institutions as any other country, and yet she has preserved many if not most of her class distinctions. There has been an extraordinary and special interplay of permanence and flexibility which has made England alternatively irritatingly stodgy and romantically old-fashioned, even as she has gone about adapting to the demands of contemporary society.

Select Bibliography

Chapter One

As a general introduction to the late nineteenth century, R. C. K. Ensor, *England 1870–1914* (1936), despite its age, is an excellent dense survey, and G. M. Young, *Victorian England: Portrait of an Age* (2nd ed., 1953) discusses in a long insightful essay the entire nineteenth century. Josef L. Altholz, *Victorian England 1837–1901* (1970) is a superb working bibliography and can be supplemented by the bibliographies published annually in the June issue of *Victorian Studies*. And, of course, articles on special topics appear in that journal as well as in *American Historical Review, Economic History Review, English Historical Review, Historical Journal, Journal of British Studies, Journal of Modern History, Past and Present*, among others.

On the particular topics covered in this section, readers might be interested in some of the vast literature on Gladstone. The most recent standard biography is by Philip Magnus, *Gladstone* (1954), although Magnus tends to undervalue his central figure. A very useful short survey is M. R. D. Foot and J. L. Hammond, *Gladstone and Liberalism* (1952). (Foot is in the process of editing Gladstone's voluminous diaries.) For Gladstone's background, S. G. Checkland, *The Gladstones: A Family Biography 1764–1851* (1971) is invaluable. A. R. Vidler, *The Orb and the Cross* (1945) is an interesting study of Gladstone's religious ideas. Vidler has also written a handy study of religion, *The Church in an Age of Revolution: 1789 to the Present Day* (1962),

while Owen Chadwick has finished a two-volume study of the Church, *The Victorian Church* (1966, 1970). Another useful study is K. S. Inglis, *Churches and the Working Classes in Victorian England* (1963).

For the Reform Act of 1867, the best study is F. B. Smith, *The Making of the Second Reform Bill* (1966); Maurice Cowling, *1867: Disraeli, Gladstone and Revolution* (1967) is useful. An important collection of commentary and documents comparing the three reform acts of 1832, 1867, and 1884 is James B. Conacher, ed., *The Emergence of British Parliamentary Democracy in the Nineteenth Century* (1971). Another interesting study, with a greater social emphasis, is Royden Harrison, *Before the Socialist: Studies in Labour and Politics, 1861 to 1881* (1965). A contrary view is taken, among other essays, in Gertrude Himmelfarb, *Victorian Minds: A Study of Intellectuals in Crisis and Ideologies in Transition* (1968).

The modern biography of Disraeli is by Robert Blake (1966); a very interesting study of his later political career is Paul Smith, *Disraelian Conservatism and Social Reform* (1967). The old multivolume biography by W. F. Monypenny and G. E. Buckle, *Disraeli* (1910–20), has much useful information, as does John Morley, *Life of Gladstone*, 2 vols. (1906). The most perceptive study of land policy is F. M. L. Thompson, *English Landed Society in the Nineteenth Century* (1963), which is, in effect, a social history of the century and beyond.

Chapter Two

In order to study further the nature of the working of political parties in nineteenth-century England, Harold J. Hanham, *Elections and Party Management: Politics in the Time of Disraeli and Gladstone* (1959) should be consulted as well as Hanham's collection of documents with commentary, *The Nineteenth Century Constitution* (1969). For a slightly earlier period, John Vincent, *The Formation of the Liberal Party 1857–1868* (1966), as well as Vincent's introduction to *Pollbooks: How Victorians Voted* (1966), is well worth consulting. Quite old studies can still be useful, such as M. I. Ostrogorskii, *Democracy and the Organization of Political Parties*, 2 vols. (1902), and A. Lawrence Lowell, *The Government of England*, 2 vols. (new ed., 1912). A much more recent study, with some sense of historical roots but primarily written from a contemporary point of view, is R. T. McKenzie, *British Political Parties: The Distribution of Power Within the Conservative and Labour Parties* (2nd ed., 1963).

On Ireland, a few studies which are particularly recommended are Conor Cruise O'Brien, *Parnell and His Party 1880–1890* (2nd ed., 1964); F. S. L. Lyons, *The Irish Parliamentary Party* (1951); L. P. Curtis, Jr., *Anglo-Saxon and Celt* (1968); and J. L. Hammond, *Gladstone and the Irish Nation* (2nd ed., 1964). Other political studies which might be mentioned are R. T. Shannon, *Gladstone and the Bulgarian Agitation 1876* (1963); E. J. Feuchtwanger, *Disraeli, Democracy and the Tory Party*

(1968); Walter L. Arnstein, *The Bradlaugh Case* (1965), as well as biographies of any important figure. Older biographies tend to be weak on interpretation, but still may provide material for the student to draw his own conclusions. Elizabeth Longford, *Victoria R. I.* (1964) and Frank Hardie, *The Political Influence of Queen Victoria 1861–1901* (1935) are useful for considering the role of the monarch, as are the selections from her letters, the first three edited by Arthur C. Benson and Reginald Brett (1907) and the next six by G. E. Buckle (1926–32). Biographies that might be mentioned, as they deal with figures mentioned prominently in the text, are James L. Garvin and Julian Amery, *Life of Joseph Chamberlain*, 6 vols. (1932–69); Roy Jenkins, *Sir Charles Dilke* (1958); Sir Winston Churchill, *Lord Randolph Churchill* (rev. ed., 1952), as well as a more modern version in Robert Rhodes James, *Lord Randolph Churchill* (1959). On the empire, a useful, if somewhat old-fashioned, account is C. E. Carrington, *The British Overseas* (1950) and Ronald Robinson and John Gallagher with Alice Denny, *Africa and the Victorians: The Official Mind of Imperialism* (1961). It should be emphasized that this is a somewhat arbitrary selection. The number of sources, collections of documents, textbooks, monographs, biographies, and so forth, not to mention articles in periodicals, are legion, and in order to investigate a topic it is necessary to attempt to combine thoroughness and selectivity!

Chapter Three

As usual, biographies of leading figures are extremely important in coming to an understanding of a period, although they may tend to overemphasize the personal approach. There is a good biography of Edward VII by

Philip Magnus (1964) and there are good biographies of most of the political leaders: Roy Jenkins, *Asquith* (1964); J. A. Spender, *The Life of the Right Hon. Sir Henry Campbell-Bannerman*, 2 vols. (1923); Robert Rhodes

James, *Rosebery* (1963); Lady Gwendolyn Cecil, *Life of Robert, Marquess of Salisbury,* 4 vols. (1921–32). There is not as yet a fully satisfactory life of Lloyd George, but Thomas Jones, *Lloyd George* (1951) is useful. Stephen E. Koss, *Lord Haldane: Scapegoat for Liberalism* (1969) is a valuable study. Peter Stansky, *Ambitions and Strategies: The Struggle for the Leadership of the Liberal Party in the 1890s* (1964) provides a picture of political infighting. And it is in this period that the extensive writings by and about Winston Churchill begin to add to the story —perhaps one need only mention here the ongoing mammoth biography undertaken by his son, Randolph Churchill, who before his death published the first two volumes (1966, 1967). The third volume, taking the story up to 1916, is by Martin Gilbert (1971), and further volumes are in progress.

On more specialized topics, a few books should be mentioned: Lord Ernle, *English Farming, Past and Present* (6th ed., 1961); in the economic sphere, David S. Landes, *The Unbound Prometheus: Technological Change and Industrial Development in Western Europe from 1750 to the Present* (1969), and Peter Mathias, *The First Industrial Nation: An Economic History of Britain 1700–1914* (1969). For social history, I would single out Bentley B. Gilbert, *The Evolution of National In-* surance in Great Britain: The Origins of the Welfare State* (1966) and the successor volume by Gilbert, *British Social Policy 1914–1939* (1970). For an account of the Liberal government, Peter Rowland, *The Last Liberal Governments* (1968) is useful; and on specialized topics: Roger Fulford, *Votes for Women* (1957); a very exciting discussion, George Dangerfield, *The Strange Death of Liberal England* (1961); and Roy Jenkins, *Mr. Balfour's Poodle: An Account of the Struggle between the House of Lords and the Government of Mr. Asquith* (1954).

On questions of labor and industry, E. H. Phelps Brown, *The Growth of British Industrial Relations* (1959) should be mentioned, as well as Hugh Clegg, Alan Fox, and A. F. Thompson, *A History of British Trade Unions Since 1889* (1964). For the history of the origins of the Labour party, the two best accounts are Philip Poirier, *The Advent of the British Labour Party* (1958) and Henry Pelling, *The Origins of the Labour Party 1880–1900* (2nd ed., 1965). London history can be tasted in Paul Thompson, *Socialists, Liberals and Labour: The Struggle for London* (1967). The three concluding volumes of Elie Halévy's classic History of the English People are well worth reading: *Imperialism and the Rise of Labour* (1951) and *The Rule of Democracy,* 2 vols. (1952).

Chapter Four

There are excellent surveys of England in the twentieth century, most notably, Alfred Havighurst, *Twentieth Century Britain* (2nd ed., 1966) and Charles L. Mowat, *Britain Between the Wars* (1956), as well as a discussion of historical material by Mowat in *Great Britain Since 1914* (1970); A. J. P. Taylor, *English History 1914–1945* (1970) and with a slightly greater emphasis on foreign policy, W. H. Medlicott, *Contemporary England 1914–1964* (1967). A useful compendium is David Butler and Jennie Freeman, *British Political Facts 1900–1960* (1963).

For military affairs, there are the great accomplishments of Arthur J. Marder, starting with his *The Anatomy of British Sea Power: A History of British Naval Policy in the Pre-Dreadnought Era 1880–1905* (1940) and followed by his subsequent studies of the later period. Robin Higham, ed., *A Guide to the Sources of British Military*

History (1971) covers all periods. For the war itself, one should look at C. R. M. F. Cruttwell, *A History of the Great War* (1936) and Paul Guinn, *British Strategy and Politics 1914–1918* (1965), and about the home front, Arthur Marwick, *The Deluge* (1965), while Marwick has written a more general study in his *Britain in the Century of Total War* (1968). Another valuable general political study is Samuel H. Beer, *British Politics in the Collectivist Age* (1965). For the First World War itself, from a participant's point of view, Robert Graves, *Goodbye to All That* (1957) is particularly recommended, as well as his study, with Alan Hodge, of the postwar period, *The Long Weekend* (1950), which tells more about the lighter side of events. Of course, many biographies could be mentioned, but for purposes of intellectual life and economics one should cite R. F. Harrod, *The Life of John Maynard Keynes* (1952), and among Keynes's many works, his *Essays in Biography* (1951). Other studies that would shed light on the period are John Raymond, ed., *The Age of Baldwin* (1960), as well as the monumental but not sufficiently discriminatory Keith Middlemas and John Barnes, *Baldwin* (1970). The works of Lord Beaverbrook, *Politicians and the War*, 2 vols. (1928–32), and the third volume, *Men and Power* (1956), as well as his study, *The Decline and Fall of Lloyd George* (1963), are worth reading for their extraordinary flavor of the times. There is a valuable biography of Bonar Law by Robert Blake, *Unrepentent Tory* (1956); and a general picture of the political world from a somewhat sociological point of view is presented in W. L. Guttsman, *The British Political Elite* (1963). There is an excellent account of Labour in Richard W. Lyman, *The First Labour Government* (1957), while the Liberals are treated by Trevor Wilson, *The Downfall of the Liberal Party 1914–1935* (1966). Harold Nicolson has written a model biography of a king: *King George the Fifth* (1952).

Chapter Five

There have not been many serious studies of the 1930s, although the sections on the period, as well as the bibliographies, in the general accounts mentioned in the previous bibliography would be very helpful. Colin Cross, *The Fascists in Britain* (1961) is a good brief account, and Oswald Mosley, *My Life* (1972) is of interest, although extremely self-serving. An excellent discussion of the Mosley Memorandum and the fall of the Labour government in 1931 can be found in Robert Skidelsky, *Politicians and the Slump* (1967). A clever if thin account of the period is Julian Symons, *The Thirties* (1960). Hugh Thomas, *The Spanish Civil War* (1961) is a good general survey. For English intellectual involvement as well as a picture of some aspects of cultural life of the time, Peter Stansky and William Abrahams, *Journey to the Frontier: Two Roads to the Spanish Civil War* (1966) can be consulted. Probably still the best account of appeasement is John W. Wheeler-Bennett, *Munich—Prelude to Tragedy* (2nd ed., 1963), and there are also biographies of most of the appeasers: Neville Chamberlain, Lord Halifax, Lord Templewood, Geoffrey Dawson, editor of *The Times*, and others. The Nicolson diaries, Harold Nicolson, *The Diaries and Letters 1930–1962*, ed. Nigel Nicolson, 3 vols. (1966–68), provide color and drama.

Of the vast literature on more recent English history, one could mention the one of the few government reports that was a best seller: Sir William Beveridge, *Social Insurance and Allied Services* (1942). Ronald Blythe, ed.,

Components of the Scene: An Anthology of the Prose and Poetry of the Second World War (1966) recreates the time of the Second World War, while Angus Calder, *The People's War*
(1969) tells of the home front. Of course, Winston S. Churchill, *The Second World War*, 6 vols. (1948–54), is glorious reading.

Chapter Six

The period since 1951 is too recent to have received much attention from historians; as usual biographies and autobiographies can provide vivid glimpses of political life, as those of Anthony Eden, *Memoirs* (1960–65), particularly *Full Circle* (1960), which deals with the time of Suez. (Hugh Thomas, *Suez* [1969] gives a more general account that is less favorable to Eden.)

Other important autobiographies, among others, are those of Harold Wilson, *A Personal Record: The Labour Government 1964–1970* (1971); Harold Macmillan, *Tides of Fortune 1945–55* (1969), *Riding the Storm 1956–59* (1971), and *Pointing the Way 1959–1961* (1972); and Clement Attlee, *As It Happened* (1956).

Other books that would be useful for recent English history are A. J. Youngson, *The British Economy 1920–1957* (1960); Richard Titmuss, *Income Distribution and Social Change* (1962); Almont Lindsey, *Socialized Medicine in England and Wales: The National Health Service 1945–1961* (1962).

Suggestive essays are found in Vernon Bogdanor and Robert Skidelsky, eds., *The Age of Affluence 1951–1964* (New York, 1970). Samuel H. Beer, *British Politics in the Collectivist Age* (1966) is a good overview. Successive editions of Anthony Sampson, *Anatomy of Britain* (1962, 1965, 1972) provide a picture of contemporary England. The forthcoming volume by Alfred Havighurst on twentieth-century Britain in the Conference on British Studies bibliographical series (Cambridge University Press) will be very useful.

Kings and Queens of England

Important Kings Before the Norman Conquest

Bretwealdas
c.	477–491	Aelle, King of the West Saxons
c.	560–584	Caelwin, King of the West Saxons
	584–616	Aethelbert, King of Kent
c.	600–616	Raedwald, King of East Anglia
	616–632	Edwin, King of Northumbria
	633–641	Oswald, King of Northumbria
	654–670	Oswiu, King of Northumbria

King of Mercia
758–796	Offa

Kings of the West Saxons
802–839	Egbert
866–871	Aethelraed
871–899	Alfred
899–925	Edward the Elder

(Beginning in Egbert's time the West Saxon kings exercised authority over most of southern England, and Edward the Elder and his successors exercised a varying amount of control over the Scandinavian kingdoms in the north. In 954 this control became permanent and from then onward the kings of the West Saxons ruled all England.)

Rulers of England
959–975	Edgar the Peaceable
979–1016	Aethelraed the Redeless
1016–1035	Cnut
1042–1066	Edward the Confessor
1066	Harold Godwinson

Normans
1066–1087	William I
1087–1100	William II
1100–1135	Henry I
1135–1154	Stephen

Angevins-Plantagenets
1154–1189	Henry II

1189–1199	Richard I
1199–1216	John
1216–1272	Henry III
1272–1307	Edward I
1307–1327	Edward II
1327–1377	Edward III
1377–1399	Richard II

Lancastrians

1399–1413	Henry IV
1413–1422	Henry V
1422–1461	Henry VI

Yorkists

1461–1483	Edward IV
1483	Edward V
1483–1485	Richard III

Tudors

1485–1509	Henry VII
1509–1547	Henry VIII
1547–1553	Edward VI
1553–1558	Mary (I)
1558–1603	Elizabeth I

Stuarts

1603–1625	James I
1625–1649	Charles I
1649–1660	Commonwealth and Protectorate
1660–1685	Charles II
1685–1688	James II
1688–1702	William III and Mary (II)
1702–1714	Anne

Hanoverians

1714–1727	George I
1727–1760	George II
1760–1820	George III
1820–1830	George IV
1830–1837	William IV
1837–1901	Victoria
1901–1910	Edward VII
1910–1936	George V
1936	Edward VIII
1936–1952	George VI
1952–	Elizabeth II

Prime Ministers of England

1866	Earl of Derby
1868	Benjamin Disraeli
1868	William Gladstone
1874	Benjamin Disraeli
1880	William Gladstone
1885	Marquess of Salisbury
1886	William Gladstone
1886	Marquess of Salisbury
1892	William Gladstone
1894	Earl of Rosebery
1895	Marquess of Salisbury
1902	Arthur James Balfour
1905	Henry Campbell-Bannerman
1908	Herbert Henry Asquith
1916	David Lloyd George
1922	Andrew Bonar Law
1923	Stanley Baldwin
1924	Ramsay MacDonald
1924	Stanley Baldwin
1929	Ramsay MacDonald (Labour)
1931	Ramsay MacDonald (National)
1935	Stanley Baldwin
1937	Neville Chamberlain
1940	Winston Churchill
1945	Clement Attlee
1951	Winston Churchill
1955	Sir Anthony Eden
1957	Harold Macmillan
1963	Sir Alec Douglas-Home
1964	Harold Wilson
1970	Edward Heath

Index

A 3
B 4
C 5
D 6
E 7
F 8
G 9
H 0
I 1
J